UNIT 30

INTRODUCTORY ACCOUNTING
AAT Certificate in Accounting

STUDY TEXT

British Library Cataloguing-in-Publication Data

A catalogue record for this book is available from the British Library.

Published by
Kaplan Publishing UK
Unit 2, The Business Centre
Molly Millars Lane
Wokingham
Berkshire
RG41 2QZ

ISBN 978-1-84710-822-7

KAPLAN PUBLISHING

CONTENTS

KAPLAN PUBLISHING

KAPLAN PUBLISHING

CONTENTS

KAPLAN PUBLISHING

CONTENTS

KAPLAN PUBLISHING

PREFACE

STUDY TEXT

The study text has been specifically written for the Diploma Pathway, Unit 30 (Introductory Accounting). The study text is written in a practical and interactive style:

- key terms and concepts are clearly defined
- all topics are illustrated with practical examples with clearly worked solutions
- frequent practice activities throughout the chapters ensure that what you have learnt is regularly reinforced
- test your knowledge section at the end of each chapter helps you to check that you have really understood the topics covered.

KAPLAN PUBLISHING

KAPLAN PUBLISHING

STANDARDS OF COMPETENCE – DIPLOMA PATHWAY

Unit 30 Introductory Accounting

Unit commentary

This unit relates to the role of processing accounting documents and leads to the production of an initial trial balance.

The first element involves producing sales invoices and credit notes, recording receipts, producing statements of accounts and making relevant accounting entries.

The second element requires the student to check purchase invoices and credit notes, record payments, including to employees, and make the relevant accounting entries.

The third element involves the control of the petty cash process, making adjustments and reconciling control accounts, reconciling the bank statement and producing an initial trial balance.

Elements contained within this unit are:
Element: 30.1
Process sales and receipts
Element: 30.2
Process purchases and payments
Element: 30.3
Process petty cash, reconcile accounts and prepare an initial trial balance

Knowledge and Understanding

To perform this unit effectively you will need to know and understand:

		Chapter
1	Business transactions and documents involved (Elements 1,2 and 3)	1, 2, 10, 15, 16, 19
2	Basic law relating to contract law and Sale of Goods Act (Elements 1 and 1)	24
3	General principles of VAT (Element 1, 2 and 3)	4, 10
4	Types of discounts (Element 1 and 2)	4, 10
5	Cheques, including crossings and endorsements (Element 1 and 2)	11, 12, 17
6	The function, form and use of banking documentation (Element 1, 2 and 3)	11, 13, 21
7	Automated receipts and payments (Element 1 and 2)	11, 17
8	Credit limits (Element 1)	10, 16
9	Double entry bookkeeping, including balancing accounts (Elements 1, 2 and 3)	1–9, 15, 19, 22, 23
10	Operation of manual accounting systems (Elements 1, 2 and 3)	1–9, 23, 10, 19
11	Methods of coding data (Element 1, 2 ans 3)	10, 19
12	Relationship between the accounting system and the ledger (Elements 1, 2 and 3)	1 – 9, 14, 19, 22, 23
13	Accounting for receipts from credit customers and customers without credit accounts (Element 1)	4, 6, 15
14	Credit card procedures (Elements 1 and 2)	11, 12
15	Documents for payments (Element 2)	16, 17
16	Accounting for payments to credit suppliers, and to suppliers where a credit account is not available (Element 2)	7, 9, 19
17	Different ordering systems: internet, verbal and written (Element 2)	16
18	Discrepancies arising from supplier invoices (Element 3)	16, 17
19	Capital revenue expenditure (Elements 2 and 3)	17
20	Batch control (Element 2)	22
21	Payroll accounting procedures: accounting for gross pay and statutory and non-statutory deductions through the wage and salaries control account; payments to external agencies; security and control; simple gross pay to net calculations but excluding the use of tax and NI tables (Element 2)	18
22	Methods of handling and storing money including the security aspects (Element 2)	13, 20
23	Organisational procedure for filing source documents (Elements 1, 2 and 3)	Through out

KAPLAN PUBLISHING

	Chapter
24 Understanding that the accounting system and administration systems and procedures will be affected by the nature of the organisation's business transactions (Elements 1, 2 and 3)	Through out
25 Petty cash procedures (Element 3)	20
26 The use of the petty cash book and cash book as part of the double entry system or as books of prime entry (Element 3)	6, 9, 15, 20
27 General bank services and operation of the bank clearing system (Element 3)	11
28 Importance of reconciling bank statements, control accounts and petty cash records (Element 3)	20, 21, 22
29 Use of the journal (Element 3)	22, 23
30 Function and form of the trial balance (Element 3)	23

Element 30.1 Process sales and receipts

Performance criteria

In order to perform this element successfully you need to:

		Chapter
A	Prepare sales invoices from source documents	10
B	Prepare sales credit notes from correspondence or other relevant source documents and ensure authorisation	10
C	Code sales invoices and credit notes	10
D	Enter sales invoices and credit notes into sales day book and sales returns day book	4, 5, 15
E	Post sales invoices and credit notes into the subsidiary (sales) ledger and main (general) ledger	4, 5, 15
F	Check receipts against records	12
G	Deal with discrepancies	12
H	Enter receipts into the cash book, subsidiary ledger and main ledger	6, 14, 15
I	Prepare paying in documents	13
J	Produce statements of accounts for debtors	14
K	Write to customers in an appropriate style to request payment of an overdue account	14

Range statement:

· Quotations
· Price lists
· Customer orders
· Delivery notes
· Discount policy

Code:

· Customer account codes
· Producr codes
· Main (general) ledger codes

Receipts:
- Automated receipts
- Cheques
- Credit cards
- Debit cards

Discrepancies:
- Wrongly completed cheques
- Out-of-date cheques
- Incorrect amounts

Element 30.2 Process purchases and payments

Performance criteria

In order to perform this element successfully you need to:

A	Check suppliers' invoices for accuracy and against source documents	16
B	Check calculations, including discounts, on suppliers' invoices and credit notes	16
C	Check suppliers' credit notes against correspondence or other relevant source documents	16
D	Code purchase invoices and credit notes	10, 19
E	Enter purchase invoices and credit notes into the purchases day book and purchases returns day book	8, 19
F	Post invoices and credit notes into the subsidiary (purchases) ledger and main (general) ledger	7–9, 19
G	Calculate supplier payments from source documents	17, 20
H	Schedule payments, and types of payment, as per company policy	17, 20
I	Enter payments in cash book and ledgers	7, 9, 18, 19, 20
J	Write to suppliers to resolve discrepancies in invoices	16, 17
K	Make payments to employees and record those payments	18

Range statement

Performance in this element relates to the following contexts:

Source documents:
- Purchase orders
- Delivery notes
- Goods received notes

Discounts:
- Bulk
- Trade
- Settlement

Code:
- Supplier account codes
- Main (general) ledger codes

KAPLAN PUBLISHING

Source documents:
· Ledgers
· Suppliers statements
· Payslips
· Cheque requisitions

Types of payment:
· Cheques
· Automated payments

Records:
· Cash book
· Main (general) ledger

Discrepancies:
· No evidence of delivery
· Incorrect goods
· Incorrect calculations
· Incorrect discounts

Element 30.3 Process petty cash, reconcile accounts and prepare an initial trial balance

Performance criteria

In order to perform this element successfully you need to:

A	Operate a petty cash system, including imprest system	20
B	Reconcile petty cash control account with cash in hand and petty cash book	20
C	Make adjustments through the journal	23
D	Reconcile sales and purchase ledger control accounts with subsidiary ledgers	22
E	Update cash book from source documents	21
F	Balance cash book and compare with bank statement	21
G	Reconcile bank statement	21
H	Prepare an initial trial balance	23
I	Create a suspense account when necessary and subsequently clear it	23

Range statement

Performance in this element relates to the following contexts:

Adjustments:
· Correct errors
· Write-off bad debts

Source documents:
· Bank statement
· Standing order and dorect debit schedules
· Credit transfer

DOUBLE ENTRY BOOKKEEPING – INTRODUCTION

INTRODUCTION

This chapter introduces the basic concepts and rules of bookkeeping. In particular, we study:
· the dual effect principle;
· the separate entity principle; and
· the accounting equation.

Together these will show how the assets of a business will always equal its liabilities and pave the way for studying double entry bookkeeping in the next chapter.

KNOWLEDGE & UNDERSTANDING

· Business transactions and documents involved (Elements 1,2 and 3)
· Double entry bookkeeping, including balancing accounts (Elements 1, 2 and 3)
· Operation of manual accounting systems (Element 1, 2 and 3)
· Relationship between the accounting system and the ledger (Element 1, 2 and 3)

CONTENTS

1 Types of accounting
2 Basic principles of double entry bookkeeping
3 The accounting equation: examples

1 Types of accounting

1.1 Management accounting and financial accounting

Depending on why the accounts are being produced, we can describe them as being either **management accounts** or **financial accounts**.

Financial accounts

These are prepared annually, mainly for the benefit of people outside the management of the business, such as the owners of the business, HM Revenue and Customs, banks, customers, suppliers and government.

In this text we focus on financial accounting principles, though most of the ideas would also apply to management accounting.

Management accounts

These are usually prepared on a monthly basis to enable the managers to run the business effectively.

1.2 The two main financial statements

The objective of financial accounting is to provide financial information about a business. This information is given in a set of financial statements (or accounts), which consists of two principal statements:

· The **profit and loss account**. This is a summary of the business's transactions for a given period.
· The **balance sheet**. This is a statement of the financial position of the business at a given date (usually the end of the period covered by the profit and loss account).

These financial statements are the final product of the accounting system of a business and it is useful to be aware of where all of the double entry bookkeeping that you will study in this chapter is leading. However, you do not need to know anything about the format or rules governing the preparation of the financial statements.

□ DEFINITIONS   □□□□

· An **asset** is something owned by a business, available for use in the business.
· **Fixed asset** – an asset which is to be used for the long term in the business and not resold as part of the trading activities.
· **Current asset** – a short-term asset of the business which is to be used in the business in the near future.
· A **debtor** is an example of a current asset. A debtor is someone who owes the business money.

- · A **liability** is an amount **owed** by the business, i.e. an obligation to pay money at some future date.
- · A **creditor** is an example of a liability. A creditor is someone the business owes money to.
- · **Capital** is the amount which the owner has invested in the business; this is owed back to the owner and is therefore a special liability of the business.

1.3 The difference between 'cash' and 'bank'

A possible confusion in terminology is caused by the apparent interchange-able use of the words 'cash' and 'bank'.

The normal use of the words suggests that a bank account operates by paying money out of the account with a cheque and paying either cash or cheques into the account. In practice you cannot pay 'cash' out of a bank account.

However, accounting terminology does not stick to this distinction, and the terms cash and bank are for the most part interchangeable. Thus the bank account is often referred to as the 'cash book'. Similarly we will often refer to someone 'taking cash out of the bank' or we will say things like 'John bought a car for £5,000 cash', whereas in reality John would have paid for the car using a cheque.

For the early part of your studies all movements of cash/cheques shall be made through the bank account and references to 'cash' or 'cheques' effectively mean the same thing.

1.4 The difference between 'cash transactions' and 'credit transactions'

☐ DEFINITIONS
A cash transaction means a transaction which is paid for immediately.

☐ DEFINITIONS
A credit transaction is a transaction that is only paid after an agreed period of time, eg 30 days.

Thus if John buys a car for £4,000 and pays immediately with a cheque or cash, that is a cash transacation.

If John buys a car for £4,000 on credit, he will not pay for, say, 30 days. This is a credit transaction. When he pays he can pay with either cash or a cheque – it makes no difference – it will be a credit transaction.

2 Basic principles of double entry bookkeeping

2.1 Introduction

Double entry bookkeeping is based upon three basic principles:
- the dual effect principle
- the separate entity principle
- the accounting equation.

2.2 The dual effect principle

This states that every transaction has two financial effects.

(a) For example, if you spend £2,000 on a car and pay for it by a cheque, one effect is that you have £2,000 less money in the bank, the second effect is that you have acquired an asset worth £2,000.

(b) Again, if you owe a creditor £100 and send him a cheque for that amount, one effect is that you owe £100 less than before, the second effect is that you have £100 less money in the bank.

2.3 The separate entity principle

This states that the owner of a business is, for accounting purposes, a completely separate entity from the business itself. Therefore the money that the owner pays into the business as initial capital has to be accounted for as an amount that the business owes back to the owner. In just the same way, any money that the owner takes out of the business, known as drawings, is treated as a reduction of the initial capital that is owed back to the owner.

The dual effect principle works here as well. If the owner of the business pays £5,000 into his business, one effect is that the business has £5,000 more cash and the second effect is that the business has a £5,000 liability (called 'capital').

Note that we look at this from the point of view of the business, not from the owner's point of view. This is because when studying bookkeeping we are only interested in the business - we are not considering the owner's personal finances.

2.4 The accounting equation

At its simplest, the accounting equation simply says that:
Assets = Liabilities

If we treat the owner's capital as a special form of liability then the accounting equation is:
Assets = Liabilities + Capital

KAPLAN PUBLISHING

Or, rearranging:

Assets – Liabilities = Capital

Profit will increase the proprietor's capital and drawings will reduce it, so that we can write the equation as:

Assets – Liabilities = Capital + Profit – Drawings

3 The accounting equation: examples

○ EXAMPLE 1   ○ ○ ○ ○

John starts his business on 1 July and pays £2,000 into his business bank account.

(a)   What is the dual effect of this transaction?

(b)   What is the accounting equation after this transaction?

Solution

(a)   **The dual effect**
        The business bank account has increased by £2,000 (an asset). The business capital has increased by £2,000 (a liability).

(b)   **The accounting equation**
        Assets   – Liabilities   = Capital
        £2,000   – £0   = £2,000

○ EXAMPLE 2   ○ ○ ○ ○

Percy started business on 1 January by paying £20,000 into a business bank account. He then spent £500 on a secondhand van by cheque, £1,000 on purchases of stock for cash, took £500 cash for his own use and bought goods on credit costing £400.

What are the two effects of each of these transactions?

What would the accounting equation look like after each of these transactions?

Solution

(a)   **Percy pays £20,000 into a business bank account**

        The bank balance increases from zero to £20,000 (an asset) and the business now has capital of £20,000 (a liability); capital is the amount that is owed back to the owner of the business, Percy.

Accounting equation:

Assets	– Liabilities	=	Capital
£20,000	– £0	=	£20,000

(b)   **Percy buys a secondhand van for £500 by cheque**

The bank balance decreases by £500 (a reduction of assets) but the business has acquired a new £500 asset, the van.

The van is a specific type of asset known as a fixed asset as it is for long-term use in the business rather than an asset that is likely to be sold in the trading activities of the business.

The assets of the business are now:

	£
Van	500
Bank (20,000 – 500)	19,500
	20,000

The liabilities and capital are unchanged.

Accounting equation:

Assets	– Liabilities	=	Capital
£20,000	– £0	=	£20,000

(c)   **Percy spends £1,000 on purchases of goods for cash**

The bank balance goes down by £1,000 but the business has another asset, stock of £1,000.

Stock is a short-term asset as it is due to be sold to customers in the near future and is known as a current asset.

The assets of the business are now:

	£
Van	500
Stock	1,000
Bank (19,500 – 1,000)	18,500
	20,000

Accounting equation:

Assets	– Liabilities	=	Capital
£20,000	– £0	=	£20,000

(d)   **Percy took £500 of cash out of the business**

The bank balance has decreased by £500 and capital has also decreased as the owner has taken money out of the business – this is known as drawings.

Remember that the owner is a completely separate entity from the business itself and if he takes money out of the business in the form of drawings then this means that the business owes him less.

The assets of the business are now:

	£
Van	500
Stock	1,000
Bank (18,500 – 500)	18,000
	19,500

The capital of the business is now £(20,000 – 500) = £19,500.

Accounting equation:

Assets	– Liabilities	=	Capital
£19,500	– £0	=	£19,500

(e) **Purchased goods on credit for £400**

The asset of stock increases by £400 and the business now has a liability of £400, the amount that is owed to the credit supplier. A liability is an amount that is owed by the business.

The assets of the business are now:

	£
Van	500
Stock (1,000 + 400)	1,400
Bank	18,000
	19,900

The liability of the business is £400.

The capital is unchanged.

Accounting equation:

Assets	– Liabilities	=	Capital
£19,900	– £400	=	£19,500

General notes

1   Each and every transaction that a business undertakes has two effects. The accounting equation reflects the two effects of each transaction and the accounting equation should always balance.

2   The owner is a completely separate entity from the business, any money the owner puts into the business is known as capital and any amounts taken out by the owner are known as drawings.

▷ ACTIVITY 1   ▷ ▷ ▷ ▷

State whether each of the following are assets or liabilities:
(i)   Money in the business bank account
(ii)   A creditor
(iii)   Stock of goods for resale
(iv)   A computer used in the accounts department
(v)   A debtor
(vi)   A salesman's car   [Answer on p. 13]

▷ ACTIVITY 2   ▷ ▷ ▷ ▷

A WORKED EXAMPLE

1   **Introduce capital**

Example 1
You win £10,000 and use it to create a retail business (called TLC) selling hearts and roses. What is the effect?

Answer 1
Dual effect
          The business has cash of   £10,000   (asset)
          The business owes you   £10,000   (capital)

TLC's position is:

Assets	Capital
£	£

(In this first example, we recorded the dual effect for you just to get you started. In later examples you will need to enter the dual effect yourself, as well as TLC's position after the transaction.)

2   **Buy stock with cash**

Example 2
TLC buys 500 chocolate hearts. The cost of each heart is £5. What is the effect?

Answer 2
Dual effect

TLC's position is:

Assets	Capital
£	£

3   Buy stock on credit

In reality a business will not always pay for its purchases with cash but is more likely to buy items on credit.

Example 3
TLC buys stock of 200 red roses on credit. Each red rose costs £10. What is the effect?

Answer 3
Dual effect

TLC's position is:

Net assets	Capital
£	£

4   Buy a delivery van

The delivery van is bought for ongoing use within the business rather than for resale. Such assets are known as **fixed assets**.

Example 4
TLC buys a delivery van for £1,000 cash. What is the effect?

Answer 4
Dual effect

TLC's position is:

Net assets	Capital
£	£

5   Sell stock for profit

Example 5
TLC sells 200 red roses for £15 cash each. What is the effect?

Answer 5
Dual effect

TLC's position is:

	Net assets £	Capital £

6 Sell stock (on credit) for profit

It is equally likely that a business will sell goods on credit. When goods are sold on credit, an asset of the business called a debtor is generated.

Example 6
TLC sells 400 chocolate hearts to Valentino for £12.50 each on credit. What is the effect?

Answer 6
Dual effect

TLC's position is:

	Net assets £	Capital £

7 Pay expenses

Example 7
In reality, TLC will have been incurring expenses from its commencement. TLC received and paid a gas bill for £500. What is the effect?

Answer 7
Dual effect

TLC's position is:

	Net assets £	Capital £

8 Take out a loan

In order to fund your future expansion plans for TLC, you persuade your Aunt to lend TLC £2,000.

Example 8
TLC is lent £2,000 cash by your Aunt. She expects to be repaid in two years' time. What is the effect?

Answer 8
Dual effect

TLC's position is:

	Net assets	Capital
	£	£

9 **Payment to creditors for purchases**

Example 9
TLC pays cash of £1,500 towards the £2,000 owed to the supplier. What is the effect?

Answer 9
Dual effect

TLC's position is:

	Net assets	Capital
	£	£

10 **Receive cash from debtors**

Example 10
TLC's debtor sends a cheque for £3,000. What is the effect?

Answer 10
Dual effect

TLC's position is:

	Net assets	Capital
	£	£

11 **Drawings**

Example 11
You withdraw £750 from the business. Such a withdrawal is merely a repayment of the capital you introduced. Your withdrawal is called **drawings.** What is the effect?

Answer 11
Dual effect

TLC's position is:

Net assets	*Capital*
£	£

[Answer on p. 13]

4 **Test your knowledge** ▷ ▷ ▷

1 What is an asset?

2 What is a liability?

3 Why is the owner's capital a liability?

4 Write down the accounting equation when the owner of a business introduces £10,000 capital.

5 Write down the accounting equation for the same business when it buys a van for £1,000.

[Answers on p. 16]

5 **Summary**

You must understand the basic definitions covered in this chapter. You must also understand the principles of dual effect and separate entity. The accounting equation underlies the whole of bookkeeping and you should re-work the examples in this chapter if you do not fully understand how it works.

KAPLAN PUBLISHING

Answers to chapter activities & 'test your knowledge' questions

△ ACTIVITY 1 △ △ △ △

(i)	Asset
(ii)	Liability
(iii)	Asset
(iv)	Asset
(v)	Asset
(vi)	Asset

△ ACTIVITY 2 △ △ △ △

Answer 1

	Assets £		Capital £
Cash	10,000	Capital introduced	10,000

Answer 2

Dual effect

Increase stock	£2,500	(↑ asset)
Decrease cash	£2,500	(↓ asset)

	Assets £		Capital £
Stock	2,500	Capital introduced	10,000
Cash	7,500		
	10,000		10,000

Answer 3

Dual effect

Increase stock	£2,000	(↑ asset)
Increase creditor	£2,000	(↑ liability)

	Net assets £		Capital £
Stock	4,500	Capital introduced	10,000
Cash	7,500		
	12,000		
Less: Creditors	(2,000)		
	10,000		10,000

Answer 4

Dual effect

Increase fixed asset	£1,000	(↑ asset)
Decrease cash	£1,000	(↓ asset)

	Net assets £		Capital £
Fixed asset	1,000	Capital introduced	10,000
Stock	4,500		
Cash	6,500		
	12,000		
Less: Creditors	(2,000)		
	10,000		10,000

Answer 5

Dual effect

Increase cash	£3,000	(↑ asset)
Decrease stock	£2,000	(↓ asset)
Increase profit	£1,000	(↑profit)

	Net assets £		Capital £
Fixed asset	1,000	Capital introduced	10,000
Stock	2,500	Profit	1,000
Cash	9,500		
	13,000		
Less: Creditors	(2,000)		
	11,000		11,000

Answer 6

Dual effect

Increase debtors	£5,000	(↑ asset)
Decrease stock	£2,000	(↓ asset)
Increase profit	£3,000	(↑ profit)

	Net assets £		Capital £
Fixed asset	1,000	Capital introduced	10,000
Stock	500	Profit	4,000
Debtors	5,000		
Cash	9,500		
	16,000		
Less: Creditors	(2,000)		
	14,000		14,000

Answer 7

Dual effect

Decrease cash	£500	(↓ asset)
Decrease profit	£500	(↓ profit)

KAPLAN PUBLISHING

Net assets	£		Capital	£
Fixed asset	1,000	Capital introduced		10,000
Stock	500	Profit		3,500
Debtors	5,000			
Cash	9,000			
	15,500			
Less: Creditors	(2,000)			
	13,500			13,500

Answer 8

Dual effect

Increase cash	£2,000	(↑ asset)	
Increase creditors	£2,000	(↑ liability)	

Net assets	£		Capital	£
Fixed asset	1,000	Capital introduced		10,000
Stock	500	Profit		3,500
Debtors	5,000			
Cash	11,000			
	17,500			
Less: Creditors	(2,000)			
Loan	(2,000)			
	13,500			13,500

The loan will be shown separately from creditors for purchases, which are known as trade creditors.

Answer 9

Dual effect

Decrease cash	£1,500	(↓ asset)	
Decrease creditors	£1,500	(↓ liability)	

Net assets	£		Capital	£
Fixed asset	1,000	Capital introduced		10,000
Stock	500	Profit		3,500
Debtors	5,000			
Cash	9,500			
	16,000			
Less: Creditors	(500)			
Loan	(2,000)			
	13,500			13,500

KAPLAN PUBLISHING

Answer 10

Dual effect

Decrease debtors	£3,000	(↓ asset)
Increase cash	£3,000	(↑ asset)

	Net assets £		Capital £
Fixed asset	1,000	Capital introduced	10,000
Stock	500	Profit	3,500
Debtors	2,000		
Cash	12,500		
	16,000		
Less: Creditors	(500)		
Loan	(2,000)		
	13,500		13,500

Answer 11

Dual effect

Decrease cash	£750	(↓ asset)
Increase drawings	£750	(↓ capital)

	Net assets £		Capital £
Fixed asset	1,000	Capital introduced	10,000
Stock	500	Profit	3,500
Debtors	2,000		
Cash	11,750		
	15,250		13,500
Less: Creditors	(500)	Less: Drawings	(750)
Loan	(2,000)		
	12,750		12,750

We do not simply deduct drawings from profit as we want to show separately the profit or loss for the period before any drawings were made.

Test your knowledge

1   An asset is something owned by the business.

2   A liability is something owed by the business.

3   The owner's capital is a liability of the business because it represents money/assets that are owed to the owner.

KAPLAN PUBLISHING

4	Assets		=	Capital	
	Cash	£10,000		Capital	£10,000

5	Assets		=	Capital	
	Van	£1,000		Capital	£10,000
	Cash	£9,000			
		£10,000			£10,000

KAPLAN PUBLISHING

LEDGER ACCOUNTING

INTRODUCTION

Now that we have looked at the basic theory of bookkeeping, it is time to learn and practise how to make the correct double entries for the sorts of transactions that are relevant for the AAT standards.

We shall start with accounting for cash transactions, and will study a series of the different sorts of things that a business can buy or sell (or pay for or receive) in cash.

We shall then study how to deal with purchases and sales made for credit.

KNOWLEDGE & UNDERSTANDING
· Business transactions and documents involved (Elements 1, 2 and 3)
· Double entry bookkeeping, including balancing accounts (Elements 1, 2 and 3)
· Operation of manual accounting systems (Elements 1, 2 and 3)
· Relationship between the accounting system and the ledger (Elements 1, 2 and 3)

CONTENTS

1 Ledger accounts
2 Introducing capital into the business
3 Purchasing goods for resale
4 Expenditure
5 Receiving income for services provided – Examples
6 Credit purchases
7 Credit sales

1   Ledger accounts

1.1 Introduction

In practice it would be far too time consuming to write up the accounting equation each time that the business undertook a transaction. Instead the two effects of each transaction are recorded in ledger accounts.

1.2 The ledger account

A typical ledger account is shown below:

Title of account							
DEBIT				**CREDIT**			
Date	*Details*	*Folio*	*Amount £*	*Date*	*Details*	*Folio*	*Amount £*

It is often called a 'T' account.

The important point to note is that it has two sides. The left hand side is known as the **debit** side and the right hand side is known as the **credit** side.

· The date column contains the date of the transaction.
· The details column contains the title of the other account that holds the second part of the dual effect. It may also have a brief description of the nature of the entry (e.g. 'rent 1.1.X3 to 31.3.X3').
· The folio column contains a reference to the source of the information. We shall see some of these sources later on but it could be, for example, 'sales day book p17' or 'payroll month 6'.
· The amount column simply contains the value of the transaction.
· The title of the account is a name that reflects the nature of the transaction ('van account', 'bank account', 'electricity account', etc).

1.3 Simplified account

The ledger account in 1.2 is very detailed and in much of this book we use a simpler form of the account. Part of the reason for this is that it is easier to 'see' the entries being made if there is less detail in the accounts. Thus, we sometimes do without the date or the full description or folio to keep things clear and simple.

For example, we will often use accounts which look like this:

Bank account

	£			£
		Van		500

Van account

	£		£
Bank	500		

It is simple and clearly shows the two sides of the account and the entries that have been made.

1.4 The golden rule for making entries in the ledger accounts

There is a golden rule for making entries in ledger accounts:

Every debit entry must have an equal and opposite credit entry.

This reflects the dual effect of each transaction and causes the accounting equation to always balance.

It is also why we refer to double entry bookkeeping.

1.5 What goes on the debit or credit side?

Step 1

If John pays £2,000 into his business bank account as capital, how do we know on what side of the accounts we should enter the amount. For example, does the payment into the bank go on the debit or credit side of the bank account?

To know this you just have to learn a few simple connected rules.

(a) **The bank account**

Starting with the bank account, the rule is that:

Money paid into the bank is a debit : Money paid out of the bank is a credit.

All the other rules follow from this.

Thus, if John has paid £2,000 into the bank as capital, this is a debit in the bank account.

(b)   **The capital account**

The other half of the double entry must be a £2,000 credit entry in the capital account.

Bank account

	£			£
Capital	2,000			

Capital account

	£			£
		Bank		2,000

Step 2

If John's business now pays £1,000 out of the bank to buy a van, the double entry will be:

(a)   **The bank account**

Start with the bank account again. Money is paid out so we credit the bank account with £1,000.

(b)   **The van account**

The other half of the transaction must therefore be a debit of £1,000 to the van account.

Bank account

	£			£
Capital	2,000	Van		1,000

Capital account

	£			£
		Bank		2,000

Van account

	£			£
Bank	1,000			

KAPLAN PUBLISHING

1.6 Which accounts to debit and credit

There are some rules that can help you in finding the correct account to put the debit and credit entries into.

Ledger account

A **debit entry** represents:	A **credit entry** represents:
· money paid into the business bank account;	· money paid out of the business bank account;
· drawings by the owner;	· capital invested by the owner;
· an increase in the value of an asset;	· a reduction in the value of an asset;
· a reduction in the value of a liability; or	· an increase in the value of a liability; or
· an item of expenditure.	· an item of income (revenue).

2 Introducing capital into the business

2.1 Explanation

The owner of a business starts the business by paying money into the business bank account. This is the capital of the business. The business will need this money to 'get going'. It may need to pay rent, buy stock for sale or pay wages to its staff before it has actually sold anything or received any money.

○ EXAMPLE   ○ ○ ○ ○

Frankie starts a business and pays £5,000 into the business bank account.

What is the double entry for this transaction?

As we have already seen the general rule when dealing with cash transactions is to start with the bank account. Cash paid out of the bank is a credit in the bank account and cash paid into the bank is a debit in the bank account.

Solution

· £5,000 has been paid into the bank account.
  This is therefore a debit in the bank account.
  It represents an asset of the business.
· The business has a liability because it owes Frankie (the owner) £5,000.
  This liability will be a credit in the capital account.

Bank (or cash book)		Capital	
Capital £5,000		Bank £5,000	

---

3 Purchasing goods for resale

3.1 Explanation

A business buys goods for resale to customers – that is how most businesses (eg shops) make their money. These goods are assets which the business owns.

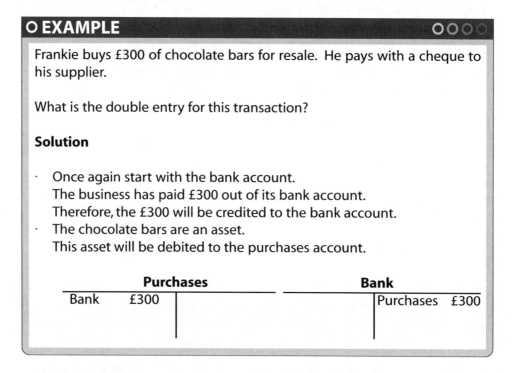

○ **EXAMPLE**　　　　　　　　　　　　　　　○○○○

Frankie buys £300 of chocolate bars for resale. He pays with a cheque to his supplier.

What is the double entry for this transaction?

Solution

· Once again start with the bank account.
  The business has paid £300 out of its bank account.
  Therefore, the £300 will be credited to the bank account.
· The chocolate bars are an asset.
  This asset will be debited to the purchases account.

Purchases		Bank	
Bank　£300			Purchases　£300

4 Expenditure

4.1 Paying office rent

A business will typically rent office space in order to carry out its operations. It will pay rent to the landlord (owner) of the offices. Rent is an expense of the business.

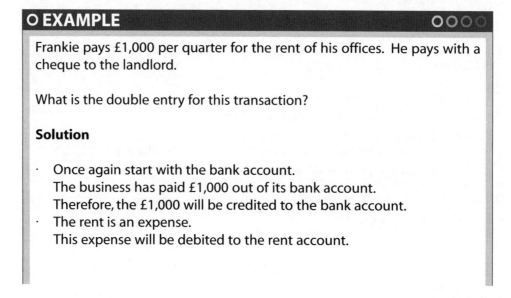

○ **EXAMPLE**　　　　　　　　　　　　　　　○○○○

Frankie pays £1,000 per quarter for the rent of his offices. He pays with a cheque to the landlord.

What is the double entry for this transaction?

Solution

· Once again start with the bank account.
  The business has paid £1,000 out of its bank account.
  Therefore, the £1,000 will be credited to the bank account.
· The rent is an expense.
  This expense will be debited to the rent account.

Rent		Bank	
Bank £1,000		Rent £1,000	

4.2 Buying stationery

A business will buy stationery in order to be able to operate. The items of stationery (pens, paper, etc) are not for resale to customers and are used quickly after they are purchased. Stationery is therefore an expense of the business.

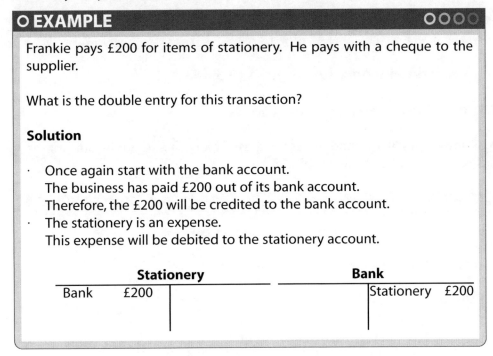

○ **EXAMPLE**   ○ ○ ○ ○

Frankie pays £200 for items of stationery. He pays with a cheque to the supplier.

What is the double entry for this transaction?

Solution

· Once again start with the bank account.
  The business has paid £200 out of its bank account.
  Therefore, the £200 will be credited to the bank account.
· The stationery is an expense.
  This expense will be debited to the stationery account.

Stationery		Bank	
Bank £200		Stationery £200	

4.3 Buying a computer

A business will buy computers in order to streamline its operations. These computers are not bought with a view to re-sale and are to be used in the business for the long term. They are therefore a fixed asset of the business.

○ **EXAMPLE**   ○ ○ ○ ○

Frankie pays £900 to purchase a computer. He pays with a cheque to the supplier.

What is the double entry for this transaction?

Solution

- Once again start with the bank account.
  The business has paid £900 out of its bank account.
  Therefore, the £900 will be credited to the bank account.
- The computer is a fixed asset.
  The £900 will be debited to the fixed asset computer account.

Computer		Bank	
Bank £900			Computer £900

5 Receiving income for services provided

5.1 Receiving income from sales of goods

A business will sell the goods it has purchased for re-sale. This is income for the business and is referred to as 'sales'.

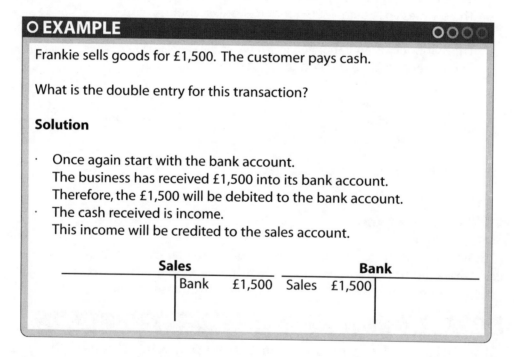

○ **EXAMPLE**   ○○○○

Frankie sells goods for £1,500. The customer pays cash.

What is the double entry for this transaction?

Solution

- Once again start with the bank account.
  The business has received £1,500 into its bank account.
  Therefore, the £1,500 will be debited to the bank account.
- The cash received is income.
  This income will be credited to the sales account.

Sales		Bank	
	Bank £1,500	Sales £1,500	

5.2 Receiving income for services provided

A business may provide services to its customers, e.g. it may provide consultancy advice. This is income for the business and will usually be referred to as 'sales'.

KAPLAN PUBLISHING

O **EXAMPLE** OOOO

Frankie provides consultancy services to a client who pays £2,000 in cash.

What is the double entry for this transaction?

Solution

· Once again start with the bank account.
  The business has received £2,000 into its bank account.
  Therefore, the £2,000 will be debited to the bank account.
· The cash received is income.
  This income will be credited to the sales account.

Sales			Bank		
	Bank	£2,000	Sales	£2,000	

O **EXAMPLE** OOOO

Percy started business on 1 January and made the following transactions.
1 Paid £20,000 into a business bank account.
2 Spent £500 on a secondhand van.
3 Paid £1,000 on purchases of stock.
4 Took £50 cash for his own use.
5 On 5 January bought goods for cash costing £500.
6 Made sales for cash of £2,000.
7 On 15 January paid £200 of rent.

Task 1

Show how the debit and credit entries for each transaction are determined.

Task 2

Enter the transactions into the relevant ledger accounts.

Solution

Task 1

(1) *Capital invested*

Percy has paid £20,000 into the bank account – therefore the bank account is debited.

Debit (Dr) Bank   £20,000

The business now owes the owner £20,000. Capital is the amount owed by the business to its owner – this is a liability, therefore a credit entry in the capital account.

Credit (Cr)   Capital   £20,000

(2)   *Purchase of van*

The business has paid £500 out of the bank account – therefore a credit entry in the bank account.

Cr   Bank   £500

The business now has a van costing £500 – this is an asset therefore a debit entry in the van account. This is a fixed asset of the business.

Dr   Van   £500

(3)   *Purchase of stock for cash*

The business has paid out £1,000 out of the bank account – therefore a credit to the bank account.

Cr   Bank   £1,000

The business has made purchases of stock costing £1,000 – this is an item of expenditure therefore a debit entry in the purchases account. Note that the debit entry is to a purchases account not a stock account. The stock account is a different account altogether and will be considered later in this study text.

Dr   Purchases   £1,000

(4)   *Drawings*

The business has paid £50 out of the bank account – therefore credit the bank account.

Cr   Bank   £50

The proprietor has made drawings of £50 – this is a reduction of capital and therefore a debit entry to the drawings account.

Dr   Drawings   £50

Drawings should not be directly debited to the capital account. A separate drawings account should be used.

(5)   *Purchase of goods for cash*

The business has paid out £500 – therefore credit the bank account.

Cr   Bank   £500

The business has made purchases of stock costing £500 – an expense therefore debit the purchases account.

Dr   Purchases   £500

(6)   *Sale for cash*

The business has paid £2,000 into the bank account – therefore a debit to the bank account.

Dr   Bank   £2,000

The business has made sales of £2,000 – this is income therefore a credit to the sales account.

Cr   Sales   £2,000

(7)   *Payment of rent*

The business now paid £200 out of the bank account – therefore a credit to the bank account.

Cr   Bank   £200

The business has incurred an expense of rent – as an expense item the rent account must be debited.

Dr   Rent   £200

General rule

When dealing with cash transactions think first of all about the cash side.
·   Money paid into the business bank account is a debit to the bank account therefore some other account must be credited.
·   Money paid out of the business bank account is a credit to the bank account therefore some other account must be debited.

Task 2

Bank

Date			£	Date			£
1 Jan	Capital	(1)	20,000	1 Jan	Van	(2)	500
5 Jan	Sales	(6)	2,000		Purchases	(3)	1,000
					Drawings	(4)	50
				5 Jan	Purchases	(5)	500
				15 Jan	Rent	(7)	200

Capital

Date	£	Date			£
		1 Jan	Bank	(1)	20,000

Van

Date			£	Date	£
1 Jan	Bank	(2)	500		

Purchases

Date			£	Date	£
1 Jan	Bank	(3)	1,000		
5 Jan	Bank	(5)	500		

Drawings

Date			£	Date	£
1 Jan	Bank	(4)	50		

Sales

Date	£	Date			£
		5 Jan	Bank	(6)	2,000

Rent

Date			£	Date	£
15 Jan	Bank	(7)	200		

▷ ACTIVITY 1 ▷▷▷▷

Write up the following cash transactions in the main ledger accounts.

Transaction	Details
1	Set up the business by introducing £150,000 in cash.
2	Purchase property costing £140,000. Pay in cash.
3	Purchase goods costing £5,000. Pay in cash.
4	Sell goods for £7,000. All cash sales.
5	Purchase goods costing £8,000. Pay in cash.
6	Pay a sundry expense of £100, by cheque.
7	Sell goods for £15,000. All cash sales.
8	Pay wages of £2,000 to an employee.
9	Pay postage costs of £100, by cheque. [Answer on p. 39]

6 Credit purchases

☐ DEFINITION ☐☐☐☐

A credit purchase occurs when goods are bought (or a service received) and the customer does not have to pay immediately but can pay after a specified number of days.

○ EXAMPLE ○○○○

We have already seen the double entry for a cash purchase and we shall now contrast this with the double entry for a credit purchase by means of an illustration.

John buys goods from Sam for £2,000.

(a) Record the double entry in John's books if John pays for the goods immediately with a cheque.

(b) Record the double entry in John's books if John buys the goods on credit and pays some time later.

Solution

(a) **Cash purchase**

The double entry is simply to:

Credit the bank account with £2,000 because £2,000 has been paid out.

Debit the purchases account with £2,000 because goods have been purchased with £2,000.

Bank

	£		£
		Purchases	2,000

Purchases

	£		£
Bank	2,000		

(b) **Credit purchase**

The double entry will be made at two separate times.

(i) *At the time the purchase is made*

At the time the purchase is made we debit £2,000 to the purchases account because a purchase has been made, but we cannot make any entry in the bank account at the time of the purchase because no cash is paid. However, the dual effect principle means that there must be another effect to this transaction, and in this case it is that the business has a creditor (the supplier to whom the £2,000 is owed).

The double entry is:

Debit the purchases account with £2,000 because expenses have increased by £2,000.

Credit creditors account with £2,000 (this is a liability of the business).

Purchases

	£		£
Creditor	2,000		

Creditors

	£		£
		Purchases	2,000

(ii)   *When John pays the £2,000*

The double entry now will be:

Credit the bank account with £2,000 because £2,000 has been paid out.

Debit the creditor account because John has paid and the creditor has been reduced by £2,000.

Creditors

	£		£
Bank	2,000	Purchases	2,000

Purchases

	£		£
Creditor	2,000		

Bank

	£		£
		Creditor	2,000

6.1 Summary

The net effect of the above credit purchase is that the creditor has a nil balance because John has paid, and we are left with a debit in the purchases account and a credit in the cash book. This is exactly as for a cash purchase – we just had to go through the intermediate step of the creditors account to get there.

7   Credit sales

□ DEFINITION   □□□□

A credit sale occurs when goods are sold (or a service provided) and the customer does not have to pay immediately but can pay after a specified number of days.

○ EXAMPLE   ○○○○

We have already seen the double entry for a cash sale and we shall now contrast this with the double entry for a credit sale by means of an illustration.

George sells goods to Harry for £1,000.

(a)   Record the double entry in George's books if Harry pays for the goods immediately with a cheque.

(b)   Record the double entry in George's books if Harry buys the goods on credit and pays some time later.

Solution

(a)   **Cash sale**

The double entry is simply to:

Debit the bank account with £1,000 because £1,000 has been paid in.

Credit the sales account with £1,000 because income has increased by £1,000.

Bank			
	£		£
Sales	1,000		

Sales			
	£		£
		Bank	1,000

(b) **Credit sale**

The double entry will be made at two separate times.

(i) *At the time the sale is made*

At the time the sale is made we credit £1,000 to the sales account because a sale has been made, but we cannot make any entry in the bank account at the time of the sale because no cash is received. However, the dual effect principle means that there must be another effect to this transaction, and in this case it is that the business has acquired a debtor.

The double entry is:

Debit debtors account with £1,000 (this is an asset of the business).

Credit the sales account with £1,000 because income has increased by £1,000.

Debtors

	£		£
Sales	1,000		

Sales

	£		£
		Debtor	1,000

(ii) *When Harry pays the £1,000*

The double entry now will be:

Debit the bank account with £1,000 because £1,000 has been paid in.

Credit the debtors account because Harry has paid and the debtor has been reduced by £1,000.

Debtors

	£		£
Sales	1,000	Bank	1,000

Sales

	£		£
		Debtor	1,000

	Bank		
	£		£
Debtor	1,000		

7.1 Summary

The net effect of the above credit sale is that the debtor has a nil balance because Harry has paid and we are left with a credit in the sales account and a debit in the cash book. This is exactly as for a cash sale – we just had to go through the intermediate step of the debtor account to get there.

▷ ACTIVITY 2   ▷ ▷ ▷ ▷

We shall now revisit our worked example from Chapter 1 and record the transactions with debits and credits to ledger accounts.

Date	Detail
1.1.X5	TLC commenced business with £10,000 introduced by you, the proprietor
2.1.X5	TLC bought stock of 500 chocolate hearts for £2,500 cash
3.1.X5	TLC bought stock of 200 red roses on credit for £2,000
4.1.X5	TLC bought a delivery van for £1,000 cash
5.1.X5	TLC sold all the red roses for £3,000 cash
6.1.X5	TLC sold 400 chocolate hearts for £5,000 on credit
7.1.X5	TLC paid a gas bill for £500 cash
8.1.X5	TLC took out a loan of £2,000
9.1.X5	TLC paid £1,500 to trade creditors
10.1.X5	TLC received £3,000 from debtors
11.1.X5	The proprietor withdrew £750 cash

Required:
Record these transactions in the relevant ledger accounts.
Make your entries in the ledger accounts below.

	Cash		
	£		£

Capital

	£		£

Purchases

	£		£

Creditors

	£		£

Delivery van

	£		£

Sales

	£		£

Debtors

	£		£

Gas

£	£

Loan

£	£

Drawings

£	£

[Answer on p. 40]

8 Test your knowledge

1 What is the difference between a cash and a credit transaction?

2 If a business buys goods for cash, is the entry in the bank account a debit or credit?

3 If the business buys a fixed asset for cash, is the entry in the fixed asset account a debit or credit?

4 If the business makes a sale for cash, what is the double entry?

5 If a business provides consultancy services for cash, what will be the entry in the bank account to record this?

6 If cash is paid into the bank account, is this a debit or credit entry in the bank ledger account?

7 Is an asset represented by a debit or credit entry in a ledger account?

8 The owner of a business pays in £1,000 as capital. What is the double entry for this?

9 Is income represented by a debit or credit entry in a ledger account?

[Answers on p. 41]

9 Summary

In this chapter we have studied cash and credit transactions. It is important to always start with the bank account and remember that cash received is a debit in the bank account and cash paid out is a credit in the bank account. If you get that right then the rest really does fall into place.

You should also be aware of the definitions of assets, expenses and income and the normal entries that you would make in the accounts for these.

Answers to chapter activities & 'test your knowledge' questions

△ ACTIVITY 1   △△△△

The figures in brackets are used here to indicate the transaction number in the activity. They can be used to match the debit entry for the transaction with the corresponding credit entry.

Capital

	£		£
		Cash at bank (1)	150,000

Property

	£		£
Cash at bank (2)	140,000		

Purchases

	£		£
Cash at bank (3)	5,000		
Cash at bank (5)	8,000		

Sales

	£		£
		Cash at bank (4)	7,000
		Cash at bank (7)	15,000

Sundry expenses

	£		£
Cash at bank (6)	100		

Wages payable

	£		£
Cash at bank (8)	2,000		

Postage

	£		£
Cash at bank (9)	100		

Cash at bank

	£		£
Capital (1)	150,000	Property (2)	140,000
Sales (4)	7,000	Purchases (3)	5,000
Sales (7)	15,000	Purchases (5)	8,000
		Sundry expenses (6)	100
		Wages payable (8)	2,000
		Postage (9)	100

KAPLAN PUBLISHING

△ ACTIVITY 2 △△△△

Cash

Date	Narrative	£	Date	Narrative	£
1.1.X5	Capital	10,000	2.1.X5	Purchases	2,500
5.1.X5	Sales	3,000	4.1.X5	Delivery van	1,000
8.1.X5	Loan	2,000	7.1.X5	Gas	500
10.1.X5	Debtors	3,000	9.1.X5	Creditors	1,500
			11.1.X5	Drawings	750

Capital

Date	Narrative	£	Date	Narrative	£
			1.1.X5	Cash	10,000

Purchases

Date	Narrative	£	Date	Narrative	£
2.1.X5	Cash	2,500			
3.1.X5	Creditors	2,000			

Creditors

Date	Narrative	£	Date	Narrative	£
9.1.X5	Cash	1,500	3.1.X5	Purchases	2,000

Delivery van

Date	Narrative	£	Date	Narrative	£
4.1.X5	Cash	1,000			

Sales

Date	Narrative	£	Date	Narrative	£
			5.1.X5	Cash	3,000
			6.1.X5	Debtors	5,000

Debtors

Date	Narrative	£	Date	Narrative	£
6.1.X5	Sales	5,000	10.1.X5	Cash	3,000

Gas

Date	Narrative	£	Date	Narrative	£
7.1.X5	Cash	500			

Loan

Date	Narrative	£	Date	Narrative	£
			8.1.X5	Cash	2,000

Drawings

Date	Narrative	£	Date	Narrative	£
11.1.X5	Cash	750			

Test your knowledge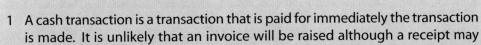

1   A cash transaction is a transaction that is paid for immediately the transaction is made. It is unlikely that an invoice will be raised although a receipt may be provided.

A credit transaction is one that is paid for at a specified time after the transaction. An invoice will generally be raised.

2   Credit

3   Debit

4   Debit the bank account; credit the sales account

5   Debit

6   Debit

7   Debit

8   Debit bank £1,000; credit capital £1,000

9   Credit

BALANCING THE LEDGER ACCOUNTS

INTRODUCTION

At the end of a period of time, for example a month of trading, the owner of the business might wish to know some details about the performance of the business in the period. For example how much sales revenue was earned, how much does the business owe to its creditors, how much money is left in the bank?

These figures can be found by balancing the ledger accounts. So in this chapter we will look at the procedure for balancing a ledger account.

KNOWLEDGE & UNDERSTANDING

· Double entry bookkeeping, including balancing accounts (Elements 1, 2 and 3)
· Operation of manual accounting systems (Elements 1, 2 and 3)
· Relationship between the accounting system and the ledger (Elements 1, 2 and 3)

CONTENTS

1 Procedure for balancing a ledger account
2 Casting and cross-casting

1 Procedure for balancing a ledger account

1.1 Steps to follow

Step 1 Total both the debit and the credit side of the ledger account and make a note of each total.

Step 2 Insert the higher of the two totals as the total on both sides of the ledger account leaving a line beneath the final entry on each side of the account.

Step 3 On the side with the smaller total insert the figure needed to make this column add up to the total. Call this figure the balance carried down (or 'Bal c/d' as an abbreviation).

Step 4 On the opposite side of the ledger account, below the total insert this same figure and call it the balance brought down (or 'Bal b/d' as an abbreviation).

○ EXAMPLE ○○○○

The bank account of a business has the following entries:

Bank

	£		£
Capital	1,000	Purchases	200
Sales	300	Drawings	100
Sales	400	Rent	400
Capital	500	Stationery	300
Sales	800	Purchases	400

Calculate the balance on the account and bring the balance down as a single amount.

Solution

Step 1 Total both sides of the account and make a note of the totals. (Note that these totals that are asterisked below would not normally be written into the ledger account itself. They are only shown here to explain the process more clearly.)

Bank

	£		£
Capital	1,000	Purchases	200
Sales	300	Drawings	100
Sales	400	Rent	400
Capital	500	Stationery	300
Sales	800	Purchases	400
*Sub-total debits**	*3,000*	*Sub-total credits**	*1,400*

Step 2   Insert the higher total as the total of both sides.

Bank

	£		£
Capital	1,000	Purchases	200
Sales	300	Drawings	100
Sales	400	Rent	400
Capital	500	Stationery	300
Sales	800	Purchases	400
Sub-total debits*	3,000	Sub-total credits*	1,400
Total	3,000	Total	3,000

Step 3   Insert a balancing figure on the side of the account with the lower sub-total. This is referred to as the 'balance carried down' or 'bal c/d' for short.

Bank

	£		£
Capital	1,000	Purchases	200
Sales	300	Drawings	100
Sales	400	Rent	400
Capital	500	Stationery	300
Sales	800	Purchases	400
Sub-total debits*	3,000	Sub-total credits*	1,400
		Bal c/d	1,600
Total	3,000	Total	3,000

Step 4   Insert the balance carried down figure beneath the total on the other side of the account. This is referred to as 'bal b/d' for short.

Bank

	£		£
Capital	1,000	Purchases	200
Sales	300	Drawings	100
Sales	400	Rent	400
Capital	500	Stationery	300
Sales	800	Purchases	400
Sub-total debits*	3,000	Sub-total credits*	1,400
		Bal c/d	1,600
Total	3,000	Total	3,000
Bal b/d	1,600		

The closing balance carried down at the end of the period is also the opening balance brought down at the start of the next period. This opening balance remains in the account as the starting position and any further transactions are then added into the account. In this case the balance brought down is a debit balance as there is money in the bank account making it an asset.

○ EXAMPLE   ○○○○

Consider again the ledger accounts from the example in the previous chapter which are reproduced below and balance them.

Bank

Date		£	Date			£
1 Jan	Capital	(1) 20,000	1 Jan	Van	(2)	500
5 Jan	Sales	(6) 2,000		Purchases	(3)	1,000
				Drawings	(4)	50
			5 Jan	Purchases	(5)	500
			15 Jan	Rent	(7)	200

Capital

Date		£	Date			£
			1 Jan	Bank	(1)	20,000

Van

Date			£	Date	£
1 Jan	Bank	(2)	500		

Purchases

Date			£	Date	£
1 Jan	Bank	(3)	1,000		
5 Jan	Bank	(5)	500		

Drawings

Date			£	Date	£
1 Jan	Bank	(4)	50		

Sales

Date		£	Date			£
			5 Jan	Bank	(6)	2,000

Rent

Date			£	Date	£
15 Jan	Bank	(7)	200		

Solution

(a)   **The bank account**

Bank

Date		£	Date		£
1 Jan	Capital	20,000	1 Jan	Van	500
5 Jan	Sales	2,000		Purchases	1,000
				Drawings	50
			5 Jan	Purchases	500
			15 Jan	Rent	200

Step 1 Total both the debit and the credit side of the ledger account and make a note of each total – debit side £22,000, credit side £2,250.

Step 2 Insert the higher of the two totals, £22,000, as the total on both sides of the ledger account leaving a line beneath the final entry on each side of the account.

Bank

Date		£	Date		£
1 Jan	Capital	20,000	1 Jan	Van	500
5 Jan	Sales	2,000		Purchases	1,000
				Drawings	50
			5 Jan	Purchases	500
			15 Jan	Rent	200
		22,000			22,000

Step 3 On the side with the smaller total insert the figure needed to make this column add up to the total. Call this figure the balance carried down (or Bal c/d as an abbreviation).

Step 4 On the opposite side of the ledger account, below the total insert this same figure and call it the balance brought down (or Bal b/d as an abbreviation).

Bank

Date		£	Date		£
1 Jan	Capital	20,000	1 Jan	Van	500
5 Jan	Sales	2,000		Purchases	1,000
				Drawings	50
			5 Jan	Purchases	500
			15 Jan	Rent	200
			31 Jan	Balance c/d	19,750
		22,000			22,000
1 Feb	Balance c/d	19,750			

This shows that the business has £19,750 left in the bank account at the end of January and therefore also on the first day of February. As the balance that is brought down to start the next period is on the debit side of the account this is known as a debit balance and indicates that this is an asset – money in the bank account.

(b) **Capital**

Capital

Date		£	Date		£
			1 Jan	Bank	20,000

As there is only one entry in this account there is no need to balance the account. The entry is on the credit side and is known as a credit balance. A credit balance is a liability of the business and this account shows that the business owes the owner £20,000 of capital.

(c)   **Van**

Van

Date		£	Date		£
1 Jan	Bank	500			

Again, there is no need to balance this account as there is only one entry. This is a debit balance as it is an asset – the fixed asset, the van, which cost £500.

(d)   **Purchases**

Purchases

Date		£	Date		£
1 Jan	Bank	1,000			
5 Jan	Bank	500	31 Jan	Balance c/d	1,500
		1,500			1,500
1 Feb	Balance b/d	1,500			

This now shows that during the month £1,500 of purchases were made. This is a debit balance as purchases are an expense of the business.

(e)   **Drawings**

Drawings

Date		£	Date		£
1 Jan	Bank	50			

This is a debit balance as drawings are a reduction of the capital owed to the owner which is a credit balance.

(f)   **Sales**

Sales

Date		£	Date		£
			5 Jan	Bank	2,000

There is no need to balance the account as there is only one entry – a £2,000 credit balance representing income.

(g)   **Rent**

Rent

Date		£	Date		£
15 Jan	Bank	200			

As there is only one entry there is no need to balance the account. This is a debit balance indicating that there has been an expense of £200 of rent incurred during the month.

▷ ACTIVITY 1   ▷ ▷ ▷ ▷

Given below is a bank ledger account for the month of March. Balance the account.

Bank

Date		£	Date		£
1 Mar	Capital	12,000	3 Mar	Purchases	3,000
7 Mar	Sales	5,000	15 Mar	Fixed asset	2,400
19 Mar	Sales	2,000	20 Mar	Purchases	5,300
22 Mar	Sales	3,000	24 Mar	Rent	1,000
			28 Mar	Drawings	2,000

[Answer on p. 51]

2   Casting and cross-casting

2.1 Introduction

Casting is the way accountants refer to adding a vertical column of figures and cross-casting is the way accountants refer to adding a horizontal row of figures.

It is worth very briefly doing a simple example of this just to show how a valuable check of the accuracy of your additions is provided by these two operations.

○ EXAMPLE   ○ ○ ○ ○

The following table of numbers is similar to the contents of accounting records such as the 'sales day book' or the 'analysed cash book' which you will come across in the next few chapters.

This table might represent the sales of products A to E in three geographical areas. We have deliberately chosen some awkward numbers to demonstrate the process.

You should calculate the totals yourself before looking at the solution.

	A	B	C	D	E	Total
UK	221,863	17,327	14,172	189,221	5,863	
USA	17,155	14,327	8,962	27,625	73,127	
Africa	18,627	33,563	62,815	1,003	57,100	
Total						

Solution

	A	B	C	D	E	Total
UK	221,863	17,327	14,172	189,221	5,863	**448,446**
USA	17,155	14,327	8,962	27,625	73,127	**141,196**
Africa	18,627	33,563	62,815	1,003	57,100	**173,108**
Total	**257,645**	**65,217**	**85,949**	**217,849**	**136,090**	**762,750**

If you managed to add the vertical columns and horizontal rows and then produced the overall total of 762,750 correctly for the overall table you have done very well.

This is a very useful technique and provides an excellent check on the accuracy of your addition.

3 Test your knowledge

1   In a ledger account, if the total debits are £6,323 and the total credits £5,816, what is the balance on the account and is this balance a debit or a credit?

2   In a ledger account, if the total debits are £4,825 and the total credits are £6,115, what is the balance on the account and is this balance a debit or a credit?

3   In a ledger account if you bring down a debit balance into the new period, were the total debits of the previous period larger or smaller than the total credits?

[Answers on p. 51]

4 Summary

Balancing an account is a very important technique which you must be able to master for these Units. You must understand how to bring the balance down onto the correct side.

Casting and cross-casting is a simple technique but provides a very useful check on the accuracy of your calculations.

KAPLAN PUBLISHING

Answers to chapter activities & 'test your knowledge' questions

△ **ACTIVITY 1**   △ △ △ △

Bank

Date		£	Date		£
1 Mar	Capital	12,000	3 Mar	Purchases	3,000
7 Mar	Sales	5,000	15 Mar	Fixed asset	2,400
19 Mar	Sales	2,000	20 Mar	Purchases	5,300
22 Mar	Sales	3,000	24 Mar	Rent	1,000
			28 Mar	Drawings	2,000
			31 Mar	Balance c/d	8,300
		22,000			22,000
1 Apr	Balance b/d	8,300			

Test your knowledge △ △ △

1   £507 debit

2   £1,290 credit

3   Larger

CREDIT SALES – DISCOUNTS AND VAT

INTRODUCTION

In this chapter we will be continuing with our studies of accounting for sales on credit, which were introduced in an earlier chapter, by considering the accounting for VAT and for discounts given to customers.

KNOWLEDGE & UNDERSTANDING

· General principles of VAT (Elements 1, 2 and 3)
· Types of discount (Elements 1 and 2)
· Double entry bookkeeping, including balancing accounts (Elements 1, 2 and 3)
· Operation of manual accounting systems (Elements 1, 2 and 3)
· Relationship between the accounting system and the ledger (Elements 1, 2 and 3)
· Accounting for receipts from credit customers and customers without credit accounts (Element 1)

CONTENTS

1 Discounts
2 Value added tax (VAT)
3 Cash (or settlement) discount and VAT
4 Accounting for credit sales and VAT

PERFORMANCE CRITERIA

· Enter sales invoices and credit notes into sales day book and sales returns day book (Element 30.1)
· Post sales invoices and credit notes into the subsidiary (sales) ledger and main (general) ledger (Element 30.1)

1 Discounts

1.1 Introduction

There are two main types of discount that a business might offer to its credit customers, a trade discount and a cash (or settlement) discount.

1.2 Trade discounts

A trade discount is a percentage of the list price of the goods being sold that is deducted from the list price for certain customers. This discount may be offered due to the fact that the customer is a frequent and valued customer or because the customer is another business rather than an individual.

A trade discount is deducted from the list price total of the invoice.

B2B (Business-to-business) customers buy the same things at lower (discounted) prices than B2C (Business-to-consumers) customers.

1.3 Cash or settlement discounts

A cash or settlement discount is offered to customers if they settle the invoice within a certain time period. It is up to the customer to decide whether or not to pay early and therefore take the settlement discount. The discount is expressed as a percentage of the invoice total but is not deducted from the invoice total as it is not certain when the invoice is sent out whether or not it will be accepted. Instead the details of the settlement discount will be noted at the bottom of the invoice.

A trade discount is a definite amount that is deducted from the list price of the goods. A settlement discount can be offered but it is up to the customer whether or not to take advantage of it.

2 Value added tax

2.1 The operation of VAT

VAT is a tax levied on **consumer** expenditure. However the procedure is that it is collected at each stage in the production and distribution chain. Most businesses (being **taxable persons** as defined later) avoid having to treat VAT as an expense as they may deduct the VAT they have paid on their purchases (**input tax**) from the VAT they charge to customers on their sales (**output tax**) and pay only the difference to HM Revenue and Customs.

2.2 How VAT works

Let us examine a simple illustration. We will assume a standard rate of 17.5%, and follow one article, a wooden table, through the production and distribution chain.

· A private individual cuts down a tree and sells it to a timber mill for £10.
  Tax effect – none. The individual is not a 'taxable person'.

· The timber mill saws the log and sells the timber to a furniture manufacturer for £100 + VAT.
  Tax effect – Being a taxable person, the mill is obliged to charge its customers VAT at 17.5% on the selling price (output tax). There is no input tax available for offset.
  Cash effect – The mill collected £117.50 from the customer (or has a debtor for this sum). Of this, £17.50 has to be remitted to HM Revenue and Customs, and therefore only £100 would be recognised as sales.

· The manufacturer makes a table from the wood, and sells this to a retailer for £400 + VAT.
  Tax effect – The manufacturer is obliged to charge VAT at 17.5% on the selling price (ie £70), but in this instance would be allowed to set off, against this output tax, the input tax of £17.50 charged on the purchase of wood from the mill.
  Cash effect – Tax of £52.50 is remitted to HM Revenue and Customs (output less input tax = £70 less £17.50). £400 is recognised as sales and £100 as purchases in the accounts.

· The retailer sells the table to a private customer for £851 plus VAT of £149.
  Tax effect – The retailer charges £149 of VAT to the customer but against this output tax may be set off the input tax of £70 charged on the purchase from the manufacturer.
  Cash effect – £79 (£149 – £70) is remitted to to HM Revenue and Customs. Purchases would be shown in the books at £400 and sales at £851.

· **The private customer** – VAT is a tax levied on consumer expenditure and the chain ends here. The customer is not a taxable person, and cannot recover the tax paid.

You will note that everybody else has passed the VAT on and, though the customer has paid his £149 to the retailer, to HM Revenue and Customs has received its tax by contributions from each link in the chain, as shown below:

	£
Timber mill	17.50
Manufacturer	52.50
Retailer	79.00
	149.00

☐ **DEFINITION** ☐☐☐☐

VAT is charged on the **taxable supply of goods and services** in the United Kingdom by a **taxable person** in the course of a business carried on by him.

2.3 Taxable supply of goods and services

Taxable supply is the supply of all items except those which are **exempt**. Examples of exempt items are as follows:

· certain land and buildings, where sold, leased or hired;
· insurance;
· Post Office postal services;
· betting, gaming and lotteries.

Input tax cannot be reclaimed where the trader's supplies are all exempt.

Betting, gaming and lotteries are exempt items

KAPLAN PUBLISHING

2.4 Rates of VAT

There are three rates of VAT on taxable supplies. Some items are 'zero-rated' (similar to exempt except that input tax can be reclaimed), there is a special rate of 5% for domestic fuel and power, and all other items are rated at the standard rate of 17.5%. Examples of 'zero-rated' supplies include:

· water and most types of food;
· books and newspapers;
· drugs and medicines;
· children's clothing and footwear.

2.5 Non-deductible VAT

Most types of food are 'zero-rated' supplies

VAT on some items is non-deductible. This means that VAT on any purchases of these items cannot be deducted from the amount of tax payable to HM Revenue and Customs. The business has to bear the VAT as an expense.

Non-deductible items include:
· motor cars;
· business entertaining.

In this book you will be dealing with taxable supplies at the standard rate of 17.5%.

2.6 Taxable person

A taxable person is any individual, partnership, company, etc who intends to make taxable supplies and is liable to register.

A person is liable to register if the value of his taxable supplies exceeds a specified amount in a 12-month period. Most companies and partnerships and many sole traders are liable to register.

2.7 Calculating the amount of VAT

If you are given the net price of goods, the price excluding VAT, then the amount of VAT is 17.5/100 of this price.

VAT is always rounded down to the nearest penny.

○ EXAMPLE ○○○○

A sale is made for £360.48 plus VAT. What is the amount of VAT to be charged on this sale?

Solution

VAT = £360.48 x 17.5/100 = £63.08

Remember to round down to the nearest penny.

2.8 VAT inclusive amounts

If a price is given that already includes the VAT then calculating the VAT requires an understanding of the price structure where VAT is concerned.

	%
Selling price including VAT (gross)	117.5
VAT	17.5
Selling price excluding VAT (net)	100.0

○ EXAMPLE ○○○○

Goods have a selling price of £2,350 inclusive of VAT. What is the VAT on the goods and the net price of these goods?

Solution

	£
Net price (£2,350 x 100/117.5)	2,000
VAT (£2,350 x 17.5/117.5)	350
Gross price	2,350

▷ ACTIVITY 1 ▷▷▷▷

What is the amount of VAT on each of the following transactions?

(i)   £145.37 net of VAT
(ii)   £285.47 net of VAT
(iii) £159.80 including VAT
(iv) £575.75 including VAT

[Answer on p. 68]

3 Cash (or settlement) discount and VAT

3.1 Introduction

When a cash/settlement discount is offered, this makes the VAT calculation slightly more complex.

Invoices should show the VAT payable as 17.5% of the discounted price. The amount paid by the customer is either:

(a)   taking discount – discounted amount (excluding VAT) plus discounted VAT; or

(b)   not taking discount – full amount (excluding VAT) plus discounted VAT.

The amount of VAT paid is always based on the discounted amount even though when the invoice is being prepared it is not known whether the customer will or will not take advantage of the cash or settlement discount.

○ EXAMPLE   ○○○○

A purchase is for 20 items @ £5 each. This totals £100.

A 2% discount is offered for settlement within 30 days.

(a)   Calculate the VAT.

(b)   Calculate the amount paid if the customer takes the discount.

(c)   Calculate the amount paid if the customer does not take the discount.

Solution

(a)   The VAT is therefore calculated as:
      (100 x 98%) x 17.5%; or
      (100 – (100 x 2%)) x 17.5%   = £17.15

The amount paid by the customer is either of the following:

(b)   *Taking discount*

		£
	Discounted amount	98.00
	Discounted VAT	17.15
	Total	115.15

(c)   *Not taking discount*

		£
	Full amount	100.00
	Discounted VAT	17.15
	Total	117.15

The difference between (b) and (c) is £2, the cash discount on £100.

The invoice looks as follows:

	£
20 items @ £5 each	100.00
VAT @ 17.5%	17.15
Total	117.15

If no settlement discount were offered the VAT would have been £17.50 and the total of the invoice £117.50.

You may be required to prepare a sales invoice where a cash or settlement discount has been offered and the VAT has to be calculated. You will be required to check invoices that the business has received and to ensure that the VAT has been correctly calculated given any settlement discount offered.

○ EXAMPLE   ○ ○ ○ ○

A sales invoice is to be prepared for two adult Fairisle sweaters at a cost of £50.00 each. A settlement discount of 5% for payment within 30 days is offered. What would the sales invoice look like?

Solution

INVOICE
Creative Clothing
3 The Mall, Wanstead, London, E11 3AY, Tel: 0208 491 3200, Fax: 0208 491 3220

Invoice to:	VAT Registration:	487 3921 12
Smith & Isaacs	Date/tax point:	14 February 20X0
23 Sloane Street	Invoice number:	149
London	Delivery note no:	41682
SW3	Account no:	SL43

Code	Description	Quantity	VAT rate %	Unit price (£)	Amount exclusive of VAT (£)
FW168	Fairisle Sweater (adult)	2	17.5	50.00	100.00
					100.00
VAT at 17.5%					16.62
Total amount payable					116.62

Terms: Deduct discount of 5% if paid within 30 days

The VAT is calculated as 17.5% x (£100 x 95%) = £16.62.

▷ ACTIVITY 2 ▷▷▷▷

A customer orders 10 Sansui radios priced at £25 each. The customer is given a 20% trade discount and a 10% cash discount for prompt payment. Calculate the VAT charged on the sale. [Answer on p. 68]

4 Accounting for credit sales and VAT

4.1 Accounting entries

We have already seen in this chapter that a business makes no profit out of any VAT charged on its sales. Instead this amount of output tax (less any related input tax) is paid over to HM Revenue and Customs. Therefore when a credit sale is recorded in the sales account it must be at the net of VAT amount.

However, when our customer eventually pays us he will pay the full amount due, i.e. the gross amount including the VAT. Therefore when we record a debtor in the ledger accounts it must be at the full gross amount of the invoice.

The difference between these two amounts, the VAT, is recorded in the VAT account.

4.2 Summary of entries

In summary the accounting entries for a credit sale with VAT are:
Debit   Debtors account with the gross amount
Credit   Sales account with the net amount
Credit   VAT account with the VAT

Work through the following examples to practise the double entry for credit sales.

○ EXAMPLE 1 ○○○○

A sells goods to X for £500 plus VAT on credit. X pays A in full. Record these transactions in the accounts.

Solution

Step 1   Calculate the VAT on the sale and enter the transaction in the debtors, sales and VAT accounts.

Calculation of VAT

	£
Net value of sale	500.00
VAT at 17.5%	87.50
Gross value of sale	587.50

Debtors

	£		£
Sales and VAT	587.50		

Sales

	£		£
		Debtors	500.00

VAT

	£		£
		Debtors	87.50

Step 2   Enter £587.50 paid by X in the debtors account and the bank account.

Debtors

	£		£
Sales and VAT	587.50	Bank	587.50

Sales

	£		£
		Debtors	500.00

VAT

	£		£
		Debtors	87.50

Bank

	£		£
Debtors	587.50		

Note 1   The VAT that has been credited to the VAT account is a liability of the business. The business has effectively collected this money from X on behalf of HM Revenue and Customs and will have to pay this money to HM Revenue and Customs.

○ **EXAMPLE 2**   ○○○○

B sells £1,000 of goods to Y net of VAT on credit. He gives Y a deduction of 20% trade discount from the £1,000 net value. Y pays his account in full. Enter these amounts in the accounts.

Solution

Step 1 Calculate the value of the sale net of discount and the VAT thereon.

	£
Sales value	1,000
Less: 20% discount	200
Net value	800
VAT at 17.5%	140
Total invoice value	940

Step 2 Enter the invoice value in the debtors, sales and VAT accounts.

Debtors

	£		£
Sales and VAT	940		

Sales

	£		£
		Debtors	800

VAT

	£		£
		Debtors	140

Note 1 Note that the trade discount does not feature at all in the accounts. The invoice value is expressed after deduction of the trade discount and it is this invoiced amount that is entered in the accounts.

Step 3 Enter the cash received from Y.

Debtors

	£		£
Sales and VAT	940	Bank	940

Sales

	£		£
		Debtors	800

	VAT		
	£		£
		Debtors	140

	Bank		
	£		£
Debtors	940		

O EXAMPLE 3   OOOO

C sells £2,000 of goods net of VAT to Z on credit. He offers Z a 5% settlement discount if Z pays within 30 days. Z does not pay his account within 30 days and so does not take the settlement discount. Z pays after 40 days. Enter these transactions in the accounts.

Solution

Step 1   Calculate the VAT on the sale.

	£
Sales value net of VAT	2,000.00
VAT = 17.5% x (2,000 – (5% x 2,000))	332.50
Invoice value	2,332.50

Note Remember that when a settlement discount is offered, the VAT is calculated on the sales value minus the settlement discount. In this case it turns out that Z does not take the settlement discount but at no stage do we go back to recalculate the VAT.

Step 2   Enter the invoice in the accounts.

	Debtors		
	£		£
Sales and VAT	2,332.50		

	Sales		
	£		£
		Debtors	2,000.00

	VAT		
	£		£
		Debtors	332.50

KAPLAN PUBLISHING

Step 3   Enter the payment by Z in the accounts.

Debtors

	£		£
Sales and VAT	2,332.50	Bank	2,332.50

Sales

	£		£
		Debtors	2,000.00

VAT

	£		£
		Debtors	332.50

Bank

	£		£
Debtors	2,332.50		

Note   As Z does not take the settlement discount, there is no entry for the settlement discount at all in the accounts.

○ **EXAMPLE 4**   ○ ○ ○ ○

Two months later C sells another £2,000 of goods net of VAT to Z on credit. He offers Z a 5% settlement discount if Z pays within 30 days. This time Z does pay his account within 30 days and takes the settlement discount. Enter these transactions in the accounts.

Solution

Step 1   Calculate the VAT on the sale.

> **Note** This is exactly the same as the previous example because the calculation of VAT with a settlement discount is the same whether the customer takes the settlement discount or not.

	£
Sales value net of VAT	2,000.00
VAT = 17.5% x (2,000 – (5% x 2,000))	332.50
Invoice value	2,332.50

Step 2   Enter the invoice in the accounts.

> **Note** This is exactly the same as the previous example because the value of the invoice is exactly the same as the previous example.

Debtors

	£		£
Sales and VAT	2,332.50		

Sales

	£		£
		Debtors	2,000.00

VAT

	£		£
		Debtors	332.50

Step 3   Calculate the amount paid by Z.

Note The amount paid by Z will be different from the previous example because Z does take the 5% discount.

	£
Sales value net of VAT	2,000.00
Less: settlement discount = 5% x 2,000	(100.00)
VAT (as per the invoice)	332.50
Amount paid by Z	2,232.50

Step 4   Enter this amount in the accounts.

Debtors

	£		£
Sales and VAT	2,332.50	Bank	2,232.50
		Discount allowed	100.00

The amount recorded as a debtor is larger than the amount eventually paid as the settlement discount has been taken by the customer. The difference, the discount allowed, must be credited to the debtors account in order to clear the account and show that nothing more is owed.

Sales

	£		£
		Debtors	2,000.00

VAT

	£		£
		Debtors	332.50

Bank

	£		£
Debtors	2,232.50		

Discount allowed		
	£	£
Debtors	100.00	

Note Because Z takes the settlement discount, he pays C £100 less than the invoice value. In order to clear the debtors account we have to credit that account with the £100 and debit a discount allowed account with £100. This £100 is an expense of the business as we have allowed our customer to pay less than the invoice value in order to have the benefit of receiving the money earlier.

5 Test your knowledge

1 What is a settlement discount?

2 If a customer is given a trade discount, does this discount appear anywhere in the ledger accounts?

3 If a customer takes a settlement discount of £100, what is the double entry to record this settlement discount in the accounts?

4 If goods are sold for £230 including VAT, what is the VAT on the sale?

5 If goods are sold for £230 excluding VAT, what is the VAT on the sale?

[Answers on p. 68]

6 Summary

We have covered some fairly tricky ideas in this chapter and it is very important that you really do understand them.

The calculations of VAT are fairly straightforward but do make sure that you can calculate the VAT element of a sale when you are given the sales value gross of VAT.

Also quite tricky is the treatment of settlement discounts. You have to be able to do two things.

(a) Calculate the VAT on a sale when a settlement discount is offered. Remember that it is irrelevant whether the customer takes the settlement discount or not.

(b) Calculate the amount paid by the customer if he takes a settlement discount. This will be less than the invoice value and you therefore have to account for the discount allowed.

Answers to chapter activities & 'test your knowledge' questions

△ ACTIVITY 1 △△△△

(i)	£145.37	x	17.5/100	=	£25.43
(ii)	£285.47	x	17.5/100	=	£49.95
(iii)	£159.80	x	17.5/117.5	=	£23.80
(iv)	£575.75	x	17.5/117.5	=	£85.75

△ ACTIVITY 2 △△△△

£31.50

Note: The answer is arrived at as follows:

	£
Sales price (10 x £25)	250.00
Less: Trade discount (250 x 20%)	(50.00)
	200.00
Less: Cash discount (200 x 10%)	(20.00)
	180.00
VAT @ 17.5%	31.50

Test your knowledge

1 A settlement discount is a percentage reduction from the sales value excluding VAT offered to a customer if he pays within a specified number of days.

2 No

3 Credit Debtors £100; debit discounts allowed £100

4 £34.25

Sales value including VAT	230.00
VAT = 230 ÷ 117.5 x 17.5	34.25

5 £230 x 17.5 = £40.25

THE SALES DAY BOOK
– MAIN AND SUBSIDIARY LEDGERS

INTRODUCTION

We have already seen how to calculate the amount of a credit sale, including VAT and any relevant discounts. In this chapter we will deal with the initial recording of credit sales before they are entered into the ledger accounts.

KNOWLEDGE & UNDERSTANDING

- Double entry bookkeeping, including balancing accounts (Elements 1, 2 and 3)
- Operation of manual accounting systems (Elements 1, 2 and 3)
- Relationship between accounting system and ledger (Elements 1, 2 and 3)

CONTENTS

1 Accounting for credit sales
2 The analysed sales day book
3 Sales returns
4 The sales returns day book

PERFORMANCE CRITERIA

- Enter invoices and credit notes into the sales day book and sales returns day book (Element 30.1)
- Post sales invoices and credit notes into the subsidiary (sales) ledger and main (general) ledger (Element 30.1)

1   Accounting for credit sales

1.1 Introduction

In a typical business there will be a great number of sales transactions to be recorded. We have to record each of these transactions individually but the accounts would be very cluttered if we entered every transaction individually in the main ledger accounts.

In order to simplify the process (and exercise greater control) we divide the recording of the transactions into three parts (we are studying sales invoices here, but similar systems apply to purchases, sales returns, etc as we shall see).

(a) The first part is the books of prime entry. We shall study here the sales day book.

(b) The second part is the main ledger itself where the double entry takes place.

(c) The third part is the subsidiary (sales) ledger which contains the individual debtor accounts.

Sales invoices and cheques are the source documents which will form the basis of accounting entries in all these three parts. Later in this book we study in more detail how invoices and cheques are dealt with.

1.2 Books of prime entry – the sales day book (SDB)

The sales day book is simply a list of the sales invoices that are to be processed for a given period (e.g. a week).

In its simplest form, the sales day book will comprise just the names of the customers and the amount of the invoices issued in the week.

The SDB is not part of the double entry; it is not part of the ledger accounts. It is just a list but we shall use it to perform the double entry. It will look something like this:

Week 1	
Customer	**Amount £**
X	1,000
Y	2,000
Z	3,000
Total	6,000

1.3 The main ledger

The main ledger is the place where the double entry takes place in the appropriate ledger accounts. The main ledger contains all the accounts you have become familiar with so far, for example:

Capital
Drawings
Van
Rent
Electricity
Purchases
Bank
etc

One of these typical accounts is the debtors account but now we will call this the sales ledger control account.

This account contains (for a given period) the **total** value of all the invoices issued to customers and the **total** of all the cash received. It does not contain any detail.

[Note that the AAT refers to this ledger as the main ledger. In some businesses it is referred to as the 'general ledger' or the 'nominal ledger'.]

1.4 The subsidiary (sales) ledger

However as well as information about our debtors in total we have to keep track of each individual debtor. How much have we invoiced him with? What has he paid? How much does he owe?

We do this in the subsidiary (sales) ledger. This ledger is **not** part of the main ledger and it is **not** part of the double entry.

The subsidiary (sales) ledger contains a separate ledger account for each individual debtor. Every individual invoice and cash receipt is posted to an individual's account in the subsidiary (sales) ledger.

1.5 Fitting it all together

We have now looked at the three elements of a typical accounting system. We must now see how it all fits together.

Consider three credit sales invoices

Customer	Amount
A	£1,500
B	£2,000
C	£2,500

Step 1

Each invoice is recorded in the sales day book and in the personal account of each debtor in the subsidiary sales ledger. The entry required for each invoice is a debit in each debtor account to indicate that this is the amount that each one owes us.

Step 2

At the end of the period the sales day book is totalled and the total is entered into the sales ledger control account (SLCA) (total debtors account) in the main ledger.

The full double entry is as we saw in the previous chapter (ignoring VAT at the moment):

Debit   Sales ledger control account
Credit   Sales

Step 3

Now consider the following cheques being received against these debts.

Customer	Amount
A	£1,000
B	£2,000

Each receipt is recorded in the cash book (see later chapter) and in the personal account of each debtor in the subsidiary sales ledger. The entry for cash received in the individual accounts is a credit entry to indicate that they no longer owe us these amounts.

Step 4

At the end of the period the cash book is totalled and the total is entered into the sales ledger control account (total debtors account) in the main ledger.

The full double entry is:

Debit   Cash account (money in)
Credit   Sales ledger control account

This is illustrated on the next page.

Notes

1   The invoices are entered into the SDB and the cheques are entered into the cash book.

2   The totals from the cash book and SDB are posted to the SLCA.

3   The individual invoices and cash received are posted to the subsidiary (sales) ledger.

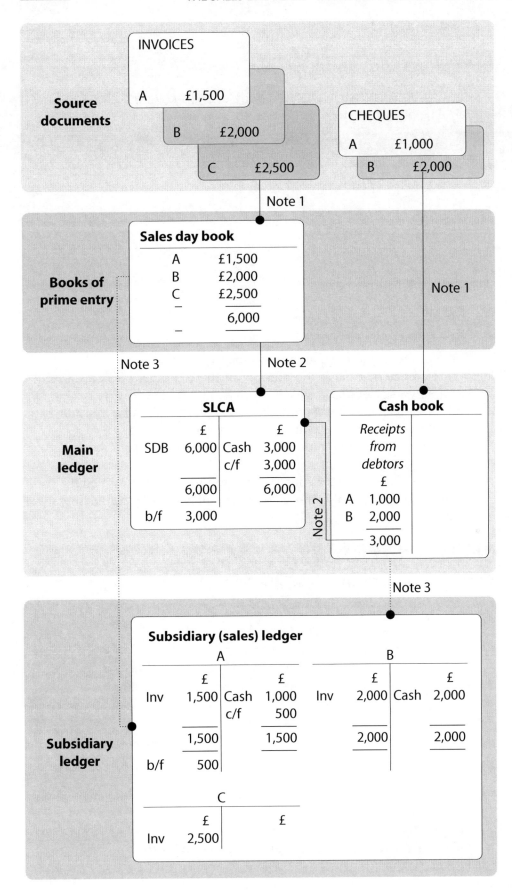

2 The analysed sales day book

2.1 Layout

The sales day book is usually analysed with 'analysis columns' showing how the total value of each customer's invoice is made up.

SALES DAY BOOK								
Date	Customer	Reference	Invoice number	Total £	VAT £	Product 1 £	Product 2 £	Product 3 £
			TOTALS					

(a) The date and customer columns are self explanatory.

(b) The reference number is the number of the customer's account in the subsidiary sales ledger.

(c) The invoice number is the number of the invoice issued for this sale.

(d) The total column is the value of the goods sold:
- after deducting any trade discount that may have been offered;
- including VAT;
- and including (i.e. not deducting) any settlement discount that may be offered (we shall not complicate things at this stage by considering this further).

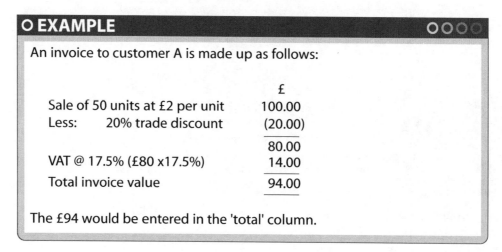

O EXAMPLE OOOO

An invoice to customer A is made up as follows:

	£
Sale of 50 units at £2 per unit	100.00
Less: 20% trade discount	(20.00)
	80.00
VAT @ 17.5% (£80 x17.5%)	14.00
Total invoice value	94.00

The £94 would be entered in the 'total' column.

(e) The VAT column – this column is the value of the VAT on the invoice – in this case £14.00.

(f) Product 1, 2, etc columns – these are columns that analyse the net sales value (i.e. the total value after deducting VAT) into groupings that are of interest to the business.

In this introductory section we shall not complicate things by considering more than one type of product so that there will only be one column for sales.

In this case the entry in the sales column would be £80.

(g)   The total boxes – at the end of a period (say a week or a month) the sales day book is totalled and the total values of each column are written in the total boxes.

The sales day book would therefore look as follows for the example above:

SALES DAY BOOK								
Date	Customer	Reference	Invoice number	Total £	VAT £	Product 1 £	Product 2 £	Product 3 £
	A			94	14	80		
			TOTALS	94	14	80		

Note: In the pages that follow we shall concentrate on the basic entries in the sales day book using only the customer, total, VAT and one sales column. This will enable us to concentrate on the simple double entry.

Later in this book we shall look at more realistic situations which will involve scenario type material such as you will meet in your skills test or examination.

○ EXAMPLE ○○○○

Posting the sales day book to the accounts in the ledgers

Consider the following sales transactions made by Roberts Metals.

Customer	Sales value (ex VAT) £	Trade discount %	Net sales value £	VAT £	Total £
A	1,000	10%	900	157.50	1,057.50
B	2,000	20%	1,600	280.00	1,880.00
C	3,000	30%	2,100	367.50	2,467.50

Enter this information in the ledger accounts using the following three steps.

Step 1   Write up the sales day book, and total the columns.

Step 2   Post the totals to the accounts in the main ledger.

Step 3   Post the individual invoices to the subsidiary sales ledger.

Solution

Step 1

SALES DAY BOOK						
Date	Customer	Reference	Invoice number	Total £	VAT £	Sales £
	A			1,057.50	157.50	900.00
	B			1,880.00	280.00	1,600.00
	C			2,467.50	367.50	2,100.00
			TOTALS	5,405.00	805.00	4,600.00

Step 2

Main ledger

Sales			VAT			SLCA	
£	£		£	£		£	£
	SDB 4,600.00			SDB 805.00	SDB 5,405.00		

Step 3

Subsidiary (sales) ledger

A			B			C	
£	£		£	£		£	£
SDB 1,057.50			SDB 1,880.00			SDB 2,467.50	

Note to solution

(a) The totals of the SDB are entered in the main ledger.

(b) The individual invoices (total value including VAT) are entered in the individual debtors accounts in the subsidiary ledger. This is the amount that the debtor will pay.

(c) Note that there are no entries for trade discounts either in the SDB or in the ledger accounts.

KAPLAN PUBLISHING

▷ ACTIVITY 1 ▷ ▷ ▷ ▷

An analysed sales day book has the following totals for a week.

Date	Invoice no	Customer name	Code	Total	VAT	Europe	Asia	America
				£	£	£	£	£
23/04/X0		Total		63,979	9,529	21,250	15,400	17,800

How would the totals be posted to the main ledger accounts?

[Answer on p. 85]

3 Sales returns

3.1 Introduction

When customers return goods, the accounting system has to record the fact that goods have been returned. If the goods were returned following a cash sale then cash would be repaid to the customer. If goods were returned following a credit sale then the customer's debtors ledger account will need to be credited with the value of the goods returned.

○ EXAMPLE ○○○○

Returns following a cash sale

X sells £500 of goods to A for cash plus £87.50 VAT.

X subsequently agrees that A can return £200 worth of goods (excluding the VAT).

Record these transactions in the ledger accounts.

Solution

Step 1

First of all we need to set up a new account called the 'sales returns account' in the main ledger. This will be used in addition to the sales account and cash book with which you are familiar.

Step 2

Enter the cash sale in the accounts.

Debit bank account for cash received	£587.50
Credit sales with net amount	£500.00
Credit VAT account with VAT	£87.50

Bank account

	£		£
Sales	587.50		

Sales

	£		£
		Cash book	500.00

Sales returns

	£		£

VAT

	£		£
		Cash book	87.50

Step 3

X will repay A £200 plus VAT of (£200 x 17.5%) = £35. We therefore need to enter the sale return, the cash and the VAT in the accounts.

Debit sales returns account	£200.00
Debit VAT account £200 17.5%	£35.00
Credit bank account with cash paid out	£235.00

Bank account

	£		£
Sales	587.50	Sales returns	235.00

Sales

	£		£
		Cash book	500.00

Sales returns

	£		£
Cash book	200.00		

VAT

	£		£
Cash book	35.00	Cash book	87.50

3.2 Sales returns for credit sales

When a credit customer returns goods, he does not receive cash for the return. Instead the seller will issue a credit note to record the fact that goods have been returned. This credit note is sent to the customer and is entered in the seller's books.

○ EXAMPLE   ○○○○

X sells goods on credit to A for £500. A returns goods worth £200. X sends a credit note for £200 to A. Enter these transactions in the main ledger of X's books. There is no VAT.

Solution

Step 1

Record the invoice issued for the credit sale for £500:

Debit the SLCA in the main ledger with £500.

Credit the sales account in the main ledger with £500.

SLCA

	£		£
Sales	500.00		

Sales

	£		£
		SLCA	500.00

Step 2

Record the credit note for £200. The return is debited to a 'sales returns account' to reflect the reduction in sales. The SLCA is credited to show that the debtor has been reduced.

SLCA

	£		£
Sales	500.00	Sales returns	200.00

Sales

	£		£
		SLCA	500.00

Sales returns

	£		£
SLCA	200.00		

3.3 Sales returns with VAT

When a return is made and we include VAT, the VAT has to be accounted for both on the invoice when the sale is made, and on the credit note when the goods are returned. This VAT has to be entered in the books.

○ **EXAMPLE**   ○○○○

X sells goods on credit to B for £1,000 + VAT.

B returns goods worth £400 + VAT.

Enter these transactions in the main ledger of X's books.

Solution

Step 1

Enter the invoice in the usual way, including the VAT.

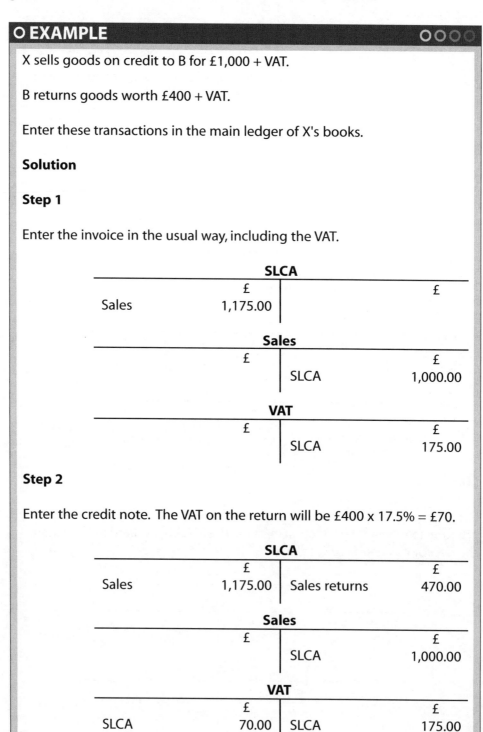

	SLCA		
	£		£
Sales	1,175.00		

	Sales		
	£		£
		SLCA	1,000.00

	VAT		
	£		£
		SLCA	175.00

Step 2

Enter the credit note. The VAT on the return will be £400 x 17.5% = £70.

	SLCA		
	£		£
Sales	1,175.00	Sales returns	470.00

	Sales		
	£		£
		SLCA	1,000.00

	VAT		
	£		£
SLCA	70.00	SLCA	175.00

Sales returns

	£		£
SLCA	400.00		

The books will reflect the position after the return. The balance on the SLCA is £705. This is made up as:

	£
Sale	1,000
Sale return	400
	600
VAT 600 x 17.5%	105
	705

4 The sales returns day book

4.1 The sales returns day book

Sales returns are in practice entered in a 'sales returns day book'. This is similar to the sales day book, and the columns are used in the same way. The only difference is that instead of having a column for the invoice number, there is a column for the 'credit note number'. This is because when the goods are received back the business will issue a credit note.

SALES RETURNS DAY BOOK						
Date	Customer	Reference	Credit note number	Total £	VAT £	Sales returns £

○ EXAMPLE ○○○○

A and B are credit customers of Ellis Electricals. The balances on their accounts in the subsidiary sales ledger are £1,175 and £2,350 because both A and B have made earlier purchases which have not yet been paid.

A returns goods which cost £600 excluding VAT.

B returns goods which cost £400 excluding VAT.

Enter the above returns in the sales returns day book and in the main and subsidiary ledgers of Ellis Electricals.

Solution

Step 1

Enter the original sales invoices in the main ledger.

	SLCA		
	£		£
SDB	3,525.00		

	Sales		
	£		£
		SDB	3,000.00

	VAT		
	£		£
		SDB	525.00

Step 2

Write up the sales returns day book.

SALES RETURNS DAY BOOK						
Date	Customer	Reference	Credit note number	Total £	VAT £	Sales returns £
	A B			705.00 470.00	105.00 70.00	600.00 400.00
				1,175.00	175.00	1,000.00

Step 3

Enter the SRDB totals in the main ledger accounts.

	SLCA		
	£		£
SDB	3,525.00	SRDB	1,175.00

	Sales		
	£		£
		SDB	3,000.00

	VAT		
	£		£
SRDB	175.00	SDB	525.00

Sales returns

	£		£
SRDB	1,000.00		

Step 4

Enter the individual amounts in the subsidiary sales ledger.

A

	£		£
SDB	1,175.00	SRDB	705.00

B

	£		£
SDB	2,350.00	SRDB	470.00

4.2 Sales returns in sales day book

In some businesses the level of sales returns are fairly low and therefore it is not justified to keep a separate sales returns day book. In these cases any credit notes that are issued for sales returns are recorded as negative amounts in the sales day book.

▷ ACTIVITY 2   ▷ ▷ ▷ ▷

Given below are the totals of an analysed sales returns day book for a week.

Date	Customer name	Credit note no	Code	Total £	VAT £	Europe £	Asia £	America £
23/04/X0				3,290	490	1,458	650	692

Post these totals to the main ledger accounts.   [Answer on p. 86]

5 Test your knowledge

1 Does the double entry bookkeeping take place in the main ledger or the subsidiary ledgers?

2 When a credit sale is made, is the debit part of the double entry entered in the sales ledger control account or the individual debtors account?

3 If a supplier gives his customer a trade discount, does this appear in the sales day book?

4 Does the total column of the analysed sales day book include or exclude VAT?

[Answers on p. 86]

6 Summary

The sales day book, analysed sales day book, and the sales returns day book, are fairly straightforward. Remember that they are simply lists of invoices/credit notes which simplify posting entries to the main ledger.

You should make sure that you are familiar with the material in this chapter and fully understand how the various parts of the accounting system relate to each other. You will often be required to enter invoices and credit notes into the books of prime entry and then to post the entries to the main ledger and subsidiary ledger.

Answers to chapter activities & 'test your knowledge' questions

△ ACTIVITY 1 △ △ △ △

The required double entry is as follows:

Debit	Sales ledger control account	£63,979
Credit	VAT	£9,529
	Europe sales	£21,250
	Asia sales	£15,400
	America sales	£17,800

Note carefully that it is the net amount that is credited to each sales account and the gross amount (including VAT) that is debited to the sales ledger control account. The VAT total is credited to the VAT account.

The ledger entries would appear as follows:

Sales ledger control account

	£		£
SDB	63,979		

VAT

	£		£
		SDB	9,529

Europe sales

	£		£
		SDB	21,250

Asia sales

	£		£
		SDB	15,400

America sales

	£		£
		SDB	17,800

KAPLAN PUBLISHING

△ ACTIVITY 2   △ △ △ △

Sales returns – Europe account

	£		£
SRDB	1,458		

Sales returns – Asia account

	£		£
SRDB	650		

Sales returns – America account

	£		£
SRDB	692		

VAT account

	£		£
SRDB	490		

Sales ledger control account

	£		£
		SRDB	3,290

Note carefully that it is the net amount that is debited to each returns account and the gross amount to the sales ledger control account. The difference, the VAT, is debited to the VAT account.

Test your knowledge △ △ △

1   Main ledger

2   Sales ledger control account

3   No

4   It includes VAT

THE ANALYSED CASH RECEIPTS BOOK

INTRODUCTION

In this chapter we will look in more detail at the recording of cash receipts from customers and in particular from credit customers.

KNOWLEDGE & UNDERSTANDING

- Double entry bookkeeping including balancing accounts (Elements 1, 2 and 3)
- Operation of manual accounting systems (Elements 1, 2 and 3)
- Relationship between the accounting system and the ledger (Elements 1, 2 and 3)
- Accounting for receipts from credit customers and customers without credit accounts (Element 1)
- The use of the petty cash book and cash book as part of the double entry system or as books of prime entry (Element 3)

CONTENTS

1 The analysed cash receipts book
2 Settlement discounts allowed to customers
3 Cash and credit sales contrasted

PERFORMANCE CRITERIA

- Enter receipts into the cash book, subsidiary ledger and main ledger (Element 30.1)

1   The analysed cash receipts book

1.1 Layout

A proforma analysed cash receipts book is shown below.

CASH RECEIPTS BOOK							
Date	Narrative	Reference	Total	VAT	Debtors	Cash sales	Discount allowed
			£	£	£	£	£
		TOTALS					

Notes

(a)   The date column contains the date of the transaction.

(b)   The narrative column describes the transactions - typically the name of the customer who is paying. It would also contain the subsidiary (sales) ledger code of the debtor.

(c)   The reference column contains any other information that may be helpful e.g. 'cash', 'cheque', 'BACS' etc.

(d)   The total column contains the total cash received (including any VAT).

(e)   The VAT column contains the VAT on the transaction but not if the VAT has already been entered in the sales day book. This is a tricky point and is dealt with later.

(f)   The debtors column contains any cash received that has been received from a debtor. The total received including VAT is entered in this column.

(g)   The cash sales and discount allowed columns will be dealt with later.

○ **EXAMPLE**   ○ ○ ○ ○

The following is from the example of Roberts Metals in the previous chapter.

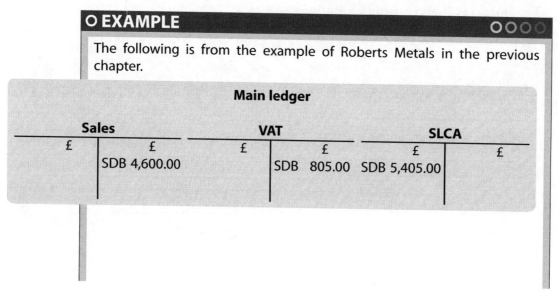

Main ledger

Sales		VAT		SLCA	
£	£	£	£	£	£
	SDB 4,600.00		SDB 805.00	SDB 5,405.00	

Subsidiary (sales) ledger

A		B		C	
£	£	£	£	£	£
SDB 1,057.50		SDB 1,880.00		SDB 2,467.50	

The following transactions took place:
Debtor A pays £1,057.50
Debtor B pays £1,000.00

Enter this information in the cash receipts book and in the ledger accounts given above.

Solution

The following steps are needed.

Step 1   Enter these transactions in the cash book.

Step 2   Total the cash book and post the totals to the main ledger.

Step 3   Post the individual amounts of cash paid by debtors to the subsidiary ledger.

Step 1

CASH RECEIPTS BOOK

Date	Narrative	Reference	Total	VAT	Debtors	Cash sales	Discount allowed
			£	£	£	£	£
	A		1,057.50	See Note 2 of Step 2	1.057.50		
	B		1,000.00		1,000.00		
		TOTALS	2,057.50		2,057.50		

Step 2

We have brought forward the balances from the main ledger in the earlier example and now post the cash received book (CRB) totals to the main ledger.

Main ledger

Sales		VAT		SLCA	
£	£	£	£	£	£
	b/f 4,600.00		b/f 805.00	b/f 5,405.00	CRB 2,057.50

Note 1

We have posted the total of the debtors column of the CRB to the sales ledger control account. This is the same as the total column in this example, but in more complex examples it need not be. The entry to the sales ledger control account is a credit entry as this is reducing the amount owed by our debtors.

Note 2

A common confusion is for people to wonder about the VAT – surely some of the money paid by A and B is actually paying the VAT part of the invoice. Yes it is, but we have already accounted for this VAT element when we entered the invoices themselves into the ledger accounts via the sales day book. Look back at Chapter 5 – the invoices were debited to the debtor accounts **including the VAT** (the VAT and sales entries are the corresponding credits). We therefore now post the total cash including VAT to the sales ledger control account but nothing is posted to the VAT account as this has already been done when dealing with the invoices.

Note 3

This is now the full double entry for the cash received completed.

Debit   Bank account (cash receipts book)
Credit   Sales ledger control account

We have credited the sales ledger control account and the entry in the cash receipts book itself is the related debit entry. So there is no need for any further debit entry.

Step 3

We have brought forward the balance from the subsidiary ledger in the earlier example and now post the cash received to the individual debtor accounts. Again, as with the sales ledger control account, this is a credit entry in each case as the cash received is reducing the amount owed by each debtor.

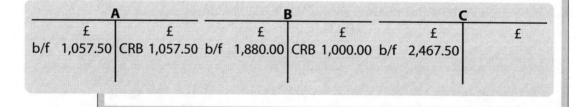

A		B		C	
£	£	£	£	£	£
b/f 1,057.50	CRB 1,057.50	b/f 1,880.00	CRB 1,000.00	b/f 2,467.50	

1.2 Balancing the accounts

Below we reproduce the accounts as they have been written up above and we then balance the accounts and bring down the balances.

Main ledger

Sales			VAT			SLCA		
£	£		£	£		£	£	
	SDB 4,600.00			SDB 805.00		SDB 5,405.00	CRB 2,057.50	
							c/f 3,347.50	
						5,405.00	5,405.00	
						b/f 3,347.50		

Subsidiary sales ledger

A			B			C		
£	£		£	£		£	£	
SDB 1,057.50	CRB 1,057.50		SDB 1,880.00	CRB 1,000.00		SDB 2,467.50		
				c/f 880.00				
1,057.50	1,057.50		1,880.00	1,880.00				
			b/f 880.00					

Note

The balance on the sales ledger control account in the main ledger (£3,347.50) is the same as the total balances of the individual accounts in the subsidiary sales ledger (£880.00 + £2,467.50 = £3,347.50). We will come back to this important point later in the Study Text.

2 Settlement discounts allowed to customers

2.1 Introduction

Settlement discounts are a small but tricky complication when dealing with the analysed sales day book and cash book.

We shall consider the same example as before with only one change – debtor A is offered an additional 5% settlement discount if he pays his invoice within 30 days.

○ EXAMPLE 1   ○○○○

The sales day book with settlement discounts

Consider again the following sales transactions made by Roberts Metals.

Customer	Sales value (ex VAT) £	Trade discount £	Net sales value £	VAT £	Total £
A	1,000	10%	900	149.62	1,049.62
B	2,000	20%	1,600	280.00	1,880.00
C	3,000	30%	2,100	367.50	2,467.50

In addition to the trade discount, customer A has been offered an additional 5% discount if he pays his invoice within 30 days.

Enter this information in the sales day book and ledger accounts.

Solution

The following steps are needed.

Step 1   Write up the sales day book.

Step 2   Post the totals to the accounts in the main ledger.

Step 3   Post the individual invoices to the subsidiary ledger.

The solution is the same as before except that the VAT for customer A has been recalculated to take account of the settlement discount (W1).

SALES DAY BOOK						
Date	Customer	Reference	Invoice number	Total £	VAT £	Sales £
	A			1,049.62	149.62 (W1)	900.00
	B			1,880.00	280.00	1,600.00
	C			2,467.50	367.50	2,100.00
			TOTALS	5,397.12	797.12	4,600.00

Workings

	£
Sales value	1,000.00
Trade discount	100.00
Net sale value	900.00
VAT £(900 – (900 x 5%)) x 17.5%	149.62
	1,049.62

Step 2

Main ledger

Sales		VAT		SLCA	
£	£	£	£	£	£
	SDB 4,600.00		SDB 797.12	SDB 5,397.12	

Step 3

Subsidiary (sales) ledger

A		B		C	
£	£	£	£	£	£
SDB 1,049.62		SDB 1,880.00		SDB 2,467.50	

As you can see the offering of the settlement discount has had no effect on the entries to the sales day book or the ledgers other than the calculation of the VAT.

○ EXAMPLE 2   ○○○○

The analysed cash receipts book with settlement discounts

Now we will look at the cash receipts book.

Debtor A pays his debt within 30 days and therefore takes the 5% discount and debtor B pays £1,000 on account.

Enter these transactions in the cash receipts book and the ledger accounts.

Solution

Notes

The entries in the cash receipts book are different when a debtor takes a settlement discount because a new column is added to the CRB – the 'discount allowed' column. In addition, a new account is opened in the main ledger – the 'discount allowed ledger account'.

The four steps are now:

Step 1   Calculate the cash that A pays after allowing for the discount.

Step 2   Enter the cash received in the CRB (with the additional column for 'discounts allowed'). Total the columns.

Step 3   Enter the totals in the main ledger (including the 'discount allowed account').

Step 4   Enter the individual cash received from debtors A and B in the subsidiary ledger account.

Step 1

Calculate the cash paid by A.

	£
Sale value after trade discount	900.00
VAT (900 – (5% x 900)) x 17.5%	149.62
Invoice value (as entered in SDB)	1,049.62
Less: 5% settlement discount (900 x 5%)	(45.00)
Cash paid by A	1,004.62

Step 2

Enter cash received in the CRB.

CASH RECEIPTS BOOK						
Date	Narrative	Total	VAT	Debtors		Discount allowed
		£	£	£		£
	A	1,004.62		1,004.62		45.00
	B	1,000.00		1,000.00		
		2,004.62		2,004.62		45.00

Note

The CRB does not 'cross-cast', i.e. if you add the totals across (debtors + discounts) this does not equal the total column.

The discount allowed column is known as a 'memorandum column' – it is not really part of the cash book – it is simply there to remind the bookkeeper to make an entry in the main ledger as we shall see below.

Step 3 – posting the CRB totals

The CRB totals are posted as follows to the main ledger.

KAPLAN PUBLISHING

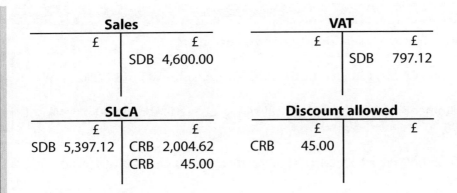

Sales		VAT	
£	£	£	£
	SDB 4,600.00		SDB 797.12

SLCA		Discount allowed	
£	£	£	£
SDB 5,397.12	CRB 2,004.62	CRB 45.00	
	CRB 45.00		

Note that the discount allowed figure in the CRB is entered in the SLCA (to acknowledge the fact that discount has been taken) and is debited to the discount allowed account.

This debit is an expense of the business – allowing the discount has cost the business £45.

Step 4 – posting to the subsidiary ledger

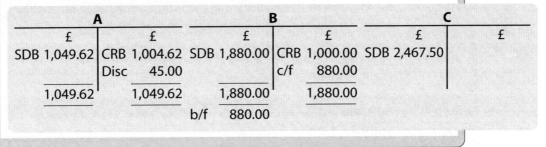

A		B		C	
£	£	£	£	£	£
SDB 1,049.62	CRB 1,004.62	SDB 1,880.00	CRB 1,000.00	SDB 2,467.50	
	Disc 45.00		c/f 880.00		
1,049.62	1,049.62	1,880.00	1,880.00		
		b/f 880.00			

Note again that the discount is credited to the account of A to show that he has taken the £45 discount which clears his account.

Note also that there is no corresponding debit entry of £45 to a discount account in the subsidiary ledger. The subsidiary sales ledger is simply there to show the detail in the main ledger SLCA. The double entry for the £45 discount only takes place in the main ledger as we have seen between the SLCA and the discounts allowed account.

3 Cash and credit sales contrasted

3.1 Introduction

We studied cash sales at the very start of double entry bookkeeping and saw that the entries were very simple – Debit cash and credit sales. Nothing has happened to change that but it is worth looking at cash and credit sales 'side by side' to appreciate the difference in their treatment, when we consider the sales day book and cash receipts book.

○ EXAMPLE ○○○○

Linda's Electricals sells goods to three customers.

Customer A buys an electric fire for £100 cash plus VAT of £17.50.

Customer B buys rolls of electrical wiring on credit for £1,000 plus VAT of £175.00.

Customer C buys 100 switches on credit for £200 plus VAT of £35.00.

Customer B pays his debt in full.

There are no trade or settlement discounts.

Write up the books in the following steps.

Step 1	Enter the cash sale in the analysed cash receipts book in the main ledger.
Step 2	Enter the credit sales in the SDB and cash received in the analysed cash receipts book in the main ledger.
Step 3	Post the totals of the SDB and cash book to the accounts in the main ledger.
Step 4	Post the individual amounts in the SDB and cash book to the subsidiary (sales) ledger.

Solution

Step 1

Enter the cash sale in the cash book.

CASH RECEIPTS BOOK

Date	Narrative	Total £	VAT £	Debtors £	Cash sales £		Discount allowed £
	A	117.50	17.50		100.00		

This is a very simple entry. At the moment of course it is only half of the double entry (the debit side of the entry). We have yet to do the credit entries (see Step 3).

Step 2

Enter the credit sales into the SDB and the cash received into the analysed cash receipts book (which already has the cash received from A per Step 1).

SALES DAY BOOK

Date	Customer	Reference	Invoice number	Total £	VAT £	Net sales value £
	B			1,175.00	175.00	1,000.00
	C			235.00	35.00	200.00
			TOTALS	1,410.00	210.00	1,200.00

CASH RECEIPTS BOOK

Date	Narrative	Total £	VAT £	Debtors £	Cash sales £		Discount allowed £
	A	117.50	17.50		100.00		
	B	1,175.00		1,175.00			
		1,292.50	17.50	1,175.00	100.00		

Note the different treatment of VAT for a cash and credit sale. For the cash sale, the VAT paid by A is entered in the VAT column of the cash book. For the credit sales of B and C, the VAT is entered in the VAT column of the SDB, and because it has already been 'captured' in the books it is not entered again in the cash book when the debt is paid by B.

In Step 3, we will see how the double entry is completed to ensure that all amounts are correctly treated.

Step 3

Post the SDB totals and cash book totals to the main ledger.

Sales			
£		£	
	SDB	1,200.00	
	CRB	100.00	

VAT			
£		£	
	SDB	210.00	
	CRB	17.50	

SLCA			
£		£	
SDB 1,410.00	CRB	1,175.00	

Note 1

The VAT on the three sales are all now correctly credited to the VAT account, either by way of the SDB for credit sales or the CRB for cash sales.

Note 2

Remember that the CRB is part of the double entry. The total column in the CRB is the debit entry that tells us how much cash has been paid in (£1,292.50), and the entries from the CRB to the other main ledger accounts are the balancing credit entries.

	£
Sales	100.00
VAT	17.50
SLCA	1,175.00
Total credits	1,292.50

▷ ACTIVITY 1

Ellis Electricals makes the following credit sales to A and B giving a 20% trade discount plus a 5% settlement discount if customers pay their invoices within 30 days.

	Customer A	Customer B
	£	£
Sales value	1,000	4,000
Trade discount (20%)	200	800
Net sales value	800	3,200
VAT (calculated on the net sales value after allowing for the settlement discount)		
Customer A: (800 − (800 x 5%)) x 17.5%	133	
Customer B: (3,200 − (3,200 x 5%)) x 17.5%		532
Total invoice value	933	3,732

Ellis Electricals also makes a cash sale to C for £300 plus VAT.

Remember that the VAT is calculated as if the settlement discount is taken whether the customer pays within 30 days and takes it or not – there is no going back to recalculate the VAT.

Customer A pays his invoice in full within 30 days and takes the settlement discount. Customer B pays £2,000 on account.

Task

Write up the SDB and the CRB and post the entries to the main and sub-sidiary ledgers. [Answer on p. 100]

4 Test your knowledge

1   When a business receives cash from a debtor, is any entry made in the VAT column of the analysed cash book?

2   When a business receives cash from a cash sale, is any entry made in the VAT column of the analysed cash book?

3   When a business raises an invoice offering a settlement discount to the customer, is any entry made to reflect this discount in the analysed sales day book?

4   When a customer pays an invoice having taken a settlement discount, is any entry made in the analysed cash book?

5   What is the double entry in the main ledger to reflect a customer taking a settlement discount?   [Answers on p. 101]

5   Summary

This has been quite a difficult chapter which has addressed some of the trickier topics in the standards for these Units. There are two points which typically cause trouble and which you should get to grips with.

(a)   Accounting for VAT on cash received from debtors and cash received from cash sales.

(b)   Accounting for discounts allowed in the analysed cash book and main ledger accounts.

If you have any doubt at all about the treatment of these you should go back and study these two points in the chapter.

Answers to chapter activities & 'test your knowledge' questions

△ ACTIVITY 1   △ △ △ △

Step 1

Write up the sales day book.

SALES DAY BOOK				
Date	Customer	Total £	VAT £	Sales £
	A	933.00	133.00	800.00
	B	3,732.00	532.00	3,200.00
		4,665.00	665.00	4,000.00

Step 2

Write up the cash receipts book.

CASH RECEIPTS BOOK							
Date	Narrative	Total £	VAT £	Sales ledger £	Cash sales £		Discount allowed £
	A (W)	893.00		893.00			40.00
	B	2,000.00		2,000.00			
		352.50	52.50		300.00		
		3,245.50	52.50	2,893.00	300.00		40.00

Working

Cash paid by A:

	£
Sale value net of VAT	800
VAT	133
	933
Less: Settlement discount (800 x 5%)	(40)
	893

KAPLAN PUBLISHING

Step 3

Post the totals to the main ledger.

Sales			
£		£	
		SDB	4,000.00
		CRB	300.00

VAT			
£		£	
		SDB	665.00
		CRB	52.50

SLCA			
£		£	
SDB	4,665.00	CRB	2,893.00
		CRB	40.00

Discount allowed			
£		£	
CRB	40.00		

Step 4

Post individual amounts for the SDB and CRB to the subsidiary sales ledger.

A			
£		£	
SDB	933.00	CRB	893.00
		CRB	40.00

B			
£		£	
SDB	3,732.00		2,000.00

Test your knowledge △ △ △

1   No. Entries relating to the VAT on the sale were initially entered in the sales day book and from there entered in the VAT account in the main ledger.

2   Yes. There are no books of prime entry for a cash sale and therefore no entries regarding VAT will have been made.

3   No. The sales day book simply lists the value of the invoice which the customer owes and (apart from an adjustment to the calculation of VAT) this is not affected by the settlement discount. If the customer takes the settlement discount and therefore pays less than the books show he owes, this is adjusted for by an entry in the discount allowed account.

4   Yes, the amount of the cash received and the amount of the discount taken.

5   Debit discount allowed account: Credit sales ledger control account.

CREDIT PURCHASES – DISCOUNTS AND VAT

INTRODUCTION

In this chapter we move on from considering the accounting entries for sales and look here at the equivalent accounting entries for purchases.

KNOWLEDGE & UNDERSTANDING

- Double entry bookkeeping, including balancing accounts (Elements 1, 2 and 3)
- Operation of manual accounting systems (Elements 1, 2 and 3)
- Relationship between the accounting system and the ledger (Elements 1, 2 and 3)
- Accounting for payments to credit suppliers, and to suppliers where a credit account is not available (Element 2)

CONTENTS

1 Discounts and VAT
2 Credit purchases – double entry

PERFORMANCE CRITERIA

- Post invoices and credit notes into the subsidiary (purchases) ledger and main (general) ledger (Element 30.2)
- Enter payments in the cash book and ledgers (Element 30.2)

1 Discounts and VAT

1.1 Introduction

We studied discounts and VAT when studying sales. The calculation of VAT and discounts are **exactly** the same when considering purchases. Remember that it is the seller who offers the discounts and it is the seller who charges the VAT, so the fact that we are now studying purchases does not change how these things are calculated.

The purchaser will receive a 'sales invoice' from the seller. This will have details of discounts and VAT exactly as we saw before when studying sales. The purchaser will call this a 'purchase invoice' and enter it in the books accordingly as we shall see.

We shall not therefore go through all the details of VAT and discounts but will simply revise this with a short example.

○ EXAMPLE ○○○○

Carl buys £1,000 of goods from Susan on credit. Susan sends a sales invoice with the goods offering a 5% discount if Carl pays within 30 days. Carl pays within 30 days.

Calculate:
(a)   the VAT;
(b)   the total value of the invoice; and
(c)   the amount that Carl will pay.

Solution

(a)   VAT = (£1,000 – (5% x £1,000)) x 17.5% = £166.25

(b)   **Total value of invoice**

	£
Goods	1,000.00
VAT	166.25
Invoice value	1,166.25

(c)   **Amount Carl will pay**

	£
Goods	1,000.00
Less settlement discount	50.00
	950.00
VAT	166.25
	1,116.25

Note: Remember that if Carl does not pay within 30 days the VAT is not recalculated.

KAPLAN PUBLISHING

2 Credit purchases – double entry

2.1 Basic double entry

The basic double entry for credit purchases with VAT is as follows:

Debit   Purchases account with the net amount
Debit   VAT account with the VAT
Credit   Creditors account with the gross amount

Purchases have been debited with the net amount as the VAT is not a cost to the business. Instead the VAT is an amount that can be set off against the amount of VAT due to HM Revenue and Customs and therefore the VAT is a debit entry in the VAT account. The creditors account is credited with the gross amount as this is the amount that must be paid to the supplier.

As with debtors and the sales ledger control account we will now be calling the creditors account the purchases ledger control account (PLCA).

Work through the following examples to practise the double entry for credit purchases.

○ EXAMPLE 1   ○○○○

B sells goods on credit to Y for £500 plus VAT. Y pays B the full amount due. Record these transactions in the accounts of Y.

Solution

Step 1   Calculate the VAT on the purchase and enter the transaction in the PLCA, purchases and VAT accounts.

Calculation of VAT

	£
Net value of sale	500.00
VAT at 17.5%	87.50
Gross value of purchase	587.50

PLCA

	£		£
		Purchases and VAT	587.50

Purchases

	£		£
PLCA	500.00		

VAT

	£		£
PLCA	87.50		

Step 2   Enter £587.50 paid by Y in the PLCA and the bank account.

PLCA

	£		£
Bank	587.50	Purchases and VAT	587.50

Purchases

	£		£
PLCA	500.00		

VAT

	£		£
PLCA	87.50		

Bank

	£		£
		PLCA	587.50

○ EXAMPLE 2   ○○○○

B sells £1,000 of goods to Y net of VAT on credit. He gives Y a deduction of 20% trade discount from the £1,000 net value. Y pays his account in full. Enter these amounts in the accounts of Y.

Solution

Step 1   Calculate the value of the sale net of discount and the VAT thereon.

	£
Sales value	1,000
Less: 20% discount	200
Net value	800
VAT at 17.5%	140
Total invoice value	940

Step 2   Enter the invoice in the PLCA, purchases and VAT accounts.

PLCA

	£		£
		Purchases and VAT	940

Purchases

	£		£
PLCA	800		

VAT

	£		£
PLCA	140		

Note 1   Note that the trade discount does not feature at all in the accounts. The invoice value is expressed after deduction of the trade discount and it is this invoiced amount that is entered in the accounts.

Step 3   Enter the cash paid by Y.

PLCA

	£		£
Bank	940	Purchases and VAT	940

Purchases

	£		£
PLCA	800		

VAT

	£		£
PLCA	140		

Bank

	£		£
		PLCA	940

○ EXAMPLE 3   ○○○○

C sells £2,000 of goods net of VAT to Z on credit. He offers Z a 5% settlement discount if Z pays within 30 days. Z pays his account within 30 days and takes the settlement discount. Enter these transactions in the accounts of Z.

Solution

Step 1   Calculate the VAT on the purchase.

	£
Invoice value net of VAT	2,000.00
VAT = 17.5% x (2,000 – (5% x 2,000))	332.50
Invoice value	2,332.50

Step 2   Enter the invoice in the accounts of Z.

PLCA

	£		£
		Purchases and VAT	2,332.50

Purchases

	£		£
PLCA	2,000.00		

VAT

	£		£
PLCA	332.50		

Step 3   Calculate the amount paid by Z.

	£
Invoice value net of VAT	2,000.00
Less: settlement discount = 5% x 2,000	(100.00)
VAT (as per the invoice)	332.50
Amount paid by Z	2,232.50

Step 4   Enter this amount in the accounts.

PLCA

	£		£
Bank	2,232.50	Purchases and VAT	2,232.50
Discount received	100.00		

Purchases

	£		£
PLCA	2,000.00		

VAT

	£		£
PLCA	332.50		

Bank

	£		£
		PLCA	2,232.50

Discount received

	£		£
		PLCA	100.00

Note   Because Z takes the settlement discount, he pays C £100 less than the invoice value. In order to clear the creditors account (the PLCA) we have to debit that account with the £100 and credit a discount received account with £100. This £100 is income (reduction of an expense) of the business as the business is paying less than the face value of the invoice.

3 Test your knowledge

1   A business purchases goods worth £500 including VAT. What is the VAT on the purchase?

2   A business receives an invoice for goods purchased for £100 plus VAT. The invoice offers the business a 5% settlement discount for payment within 30 days. What is the total value of the invoice including VAT?

3   In the above question the business pays the invoice within 30 days. How much does the business pay the supplier?

4   A business receives £100 settlement discount from a supplier for early payment. What is the double entry in the main ledger?

5   A business receives a trade discount of £200 from a supplier. What is the double entry in the main ledger?

[Answers on p. 110]

4   Summary

The topics covered in this chapter will have been familiar to you as you have already studied the similar topics for sales.

Make sure you understand the point about VAT when there is a settlement discount offered. You must also understand the double entry for settlement discounts.

Answers to 'test your knowledge' questions

Test your knowledge △ △ △

1 500 x 17.5 ÷ 117.5 = £74.46

2	£
Value of goods	100.00
VAT (100 − (100 x 5%)) x 17.5%	16.62
Invoice value	116.62

3	£
Value of goods	100.00
Less 5% discount	(5.00)
	95.00
VAT (per invoice)	16.62
Total payment	111.62

4 Debit purchase ledger control account £100; credit discounts received £100.

5 There are no entries for trade discounts in the main ledger.

THE PURCHASES DAY BOOK
– MAIN AND SUBSIDIARY LEDGERS

INTRODUCTION

Just as we did for sales on credit we will now consider how purchases on credit are recorded in the books of prime entry and the ledger accounts.

KNOWLEDGE & UNDERSTANDING

- Double entry bookkeeping, including balancing accounts (Elements 1, 2 and 3)
- Operation of manual accounting system (Elements 1, 2 and 3)
- Relationship between the accounting system and the ledger (Elements 1, 2 and 3)

CONTENTS

1 Accounting for credit purchases
2 The analysed purchases day book
3 Purchase returns – cash customers
4 Purchase returns – credit customers
5 The purchase returns day book

PERFORMANCE CRITERIA
- Enter purchase invoices and credit notes into the purchases day book and purchases day returns day book (Element 30.2)
- Post invoices and credit notes into the subsidiary (purchases) ledger and main (general) ledger (Element 30.2)

1   Accounting for credit purchases

1.1 Introduction

When we studied accounting for sales in the earlier chapters of this book, we dealt with the three parts of the accounting records as they affected sales.

In the case of purchases, the parts are exactly the same except that instead of a 'sales day book' we have the 'purchases day book', and instead of the 'subsidiary sales ledger' we have the 'subsidiary purchases ledger'. The third part, namely the main ledger, is exactly the same and contains all the main ledger accounts with which you are familiar.

Below we will illustrate how these parts fit together with a diagram.

1.2 Fitting it all together

Consider these three credit purchases invoices

Supplier	Amount
X	£4,000
Y	£5,000
Z	£6,000

Step 1

Each invoice is recorded in the purchases day book by the purchaser.

Step 2

At the end of the period the purchases day book is totalled and the total is entered into the purchases ledger control account in the nominal ledger. The individual entries are recorded in the individual creditor accounts in the subsidiary purchases ledger.

Now consider these cheques being paid to the creditors.

Customer	Amount
X	£2,000
Y	£3,000

Step 1

Each payment is recorded in the cash book.

Step 2

At the end of the period the cash book is totalled and the total is entered into the purchases ledger control account in the nominal ledger. The individual entries are recorded in the individual creditor accounts in the subsidiary purchases ledger.

This is illustrated below.

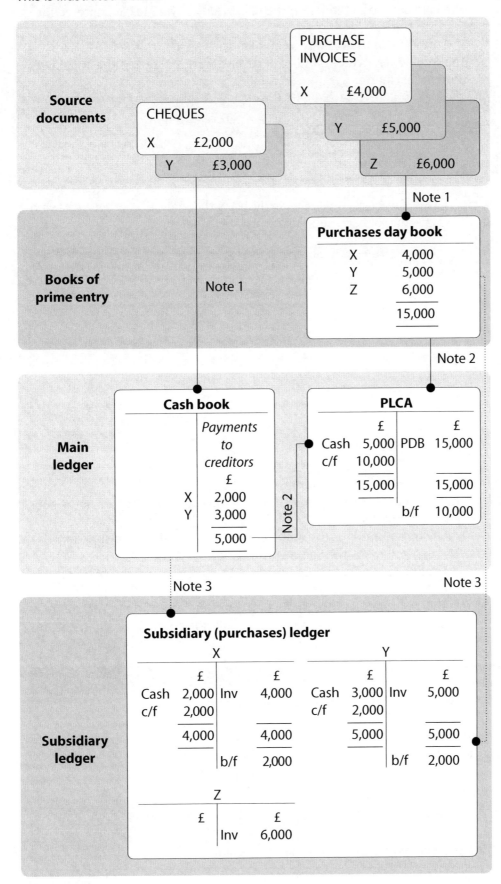

Notes

1   The invoices are entered into the PDB and the cheques are entered into the cash book.

2   The totals from the cash book and PDB are posted to the PLCA.

3   The individual invoices and cash received are posted to the subsidiary (purchases) ledger.

2   The analysed purchases day book

2.1 Layout

The purchases day book is usually analysed with 'analysis columns' showing how the total value of each supplier's invoice is made up.

PURCHASES DAY BOOK

Date	Supplier	Reference	Invoice number	Total £	VAT £	Product 1 £	Product 2 £	Product 3 £
			TOTALS					

(a)   The date and supplier columns are self explanatory.

(b)   The reference number is the number of the supplier's account in the subsidiary purchases ledger.

(c)   The invoice number is the number of the invoice from the supplier.

(d)   The total column is the value of the goods purchased:
·   after deducting any trade discount that may have been offered;
·   including VAT;
·   and including (i.e. not deducting) any settlement discount that may be offered to the purchaser (we shall not complicate things at this stage by considering this further).

○ EXAMPLE   ○○○○

Customer B receives an invoice as follows from supplier X:

	£
50 units at £6 per unit	300
Less: 20% trade discount	60
	240
VAT @ 17.5% (£240 x 17.5%)	42
Total invoice value	282

The £282 would be entered in the 'total' column.

(e) The VAT column – this column is the value of the VAT on the invoice – in this case £42.

(f) Product 1, 2, etc columns – these are columns that analyse the net purchases value (ie the total value after deducting VAT) into groupings that are of interest to the business.

In this introductory section we shall not complicate things by considering more than one type of product so that there will only be one column for purchases.

In this case the entry in the purchases column would be £240.

(g) The total boxes – at the end of a period (say a week or a month) the purchases day book is totalled and the total values of each column are written in the total boxes.

The purchases day book would therefore look as follows for the example above:

PURCHASES DAY BOOK

Date	Supplier	Reference	Invoice number	Total £	VAT £	Product 1 £	Product 2 £	Product 3 £
	X			282	42	240		
			TOTALS	282	42	240		

Note: In the pages that follow we shall concentrate on the basic entries in the purchases day book using only the supplier, total, VAT and one purchases column. This will enable us to concentrate on the simple double entry.

O EXAMPLE OOOO

Posting the purchases day book to the accounts in the ledgers

Consider the following purchase invoices received from suppliers by Roberts Metals.

Supplier	Purchases value (ex VAT) £	Trade discount %	Net purchases value £	VAT £	Total £
X	500	10%	450	78.75	528.75
Y	1,750	20%	1,400	245.00	1,645.00
Z	5,000	30%	3,500	612.50	4,112.50

The following three steps are needed to enter this information in the ledger accounts.

Step 1 Write up the purchases day book, and total the columns.

Step 2 Post the totals to the accounts in the main ledger.

Step 3 Post the individual invoices to the subsidiary purchases ledger.

Solution

Step 1

PURCHASES DAY BOOK						
Date	Supplier	Reference	Invoice number	Total £	VAT £	Sales £
	X			528.75	78.75	450.00
	Y			1,645.00	245.00	1,400.00
	Z			4,112.50	612.50	3,500.00
			TOTALS	6,286.25	936.25	5,350.00

Step 2

Main ledger

Purchases		VAT		PLCA	
£	£	£	£	£	£
PDB 5,350.00		PDB 936.25			PDB 6,286.25

Step 3

Subsidiary (purchases) ledger

X		Y		Z	
£	£	£	£	£	£
	PDB 528.75		PDB 1,645.00		PDB 4,112.50

Note to solution

(a) The totals of the PDB are entered in the main ledger.
(b) The individual invoices (total value including VAT) are entered in the individual creditor accounts in the subsidiary ledger. This is the amount that will be paid to the creditor.
(c) Note that there are no entries for trade discounts either in the PDB or in the ledger accounts.

▷ **ACTIVITY 1** ▷▷▷▷

An analysed purchases day book has the following totals for a week.

Date	Invoice no	Supplier	Code	Total £	VAT £	Dept 1 £	Dept 2 £	Dept 3 £
		Total		88,125	13,125	20,000	15,000	40,000

How would the totals be posted to the main ledger accounts?

[Answer on p. 124]

3 Purchases returns – cash customers

3.1 Introduction

When a business buys and then returns goods to a supplier, the accounting system has to record the fact that goods have been returned. If the goods were returned following a cash purchase then cash would be repaid by the supplier to the customer who had bought the goods. If goods were returned following a credit purchase then the supplier's ledger account will need to be debited with the value of the goods returned.

○ **EXAMPLE** ○○○○

Returns following a cash purchase

Y buys £1,000 of goods from B for cash plus £175 VAT.

B subsequently agrees that Y can return £500 worth of goods (excluding VAT).

Record these transactions in the ledger accounts of Y.

Solution

Step 1

First of all we need to set up a new account called the 'purchases returns account' in the main ledger.

Step 2

Enter the cash purchases in the accounts of Y.

Credit cash book for cash paid	£1,175.00
Debit purchases with expense	£1,000.00
Debit VAT account with VAT	£175.00

Cash book

	£		£
		Purchases + VAT	1,175.00

Purchases

	£		£
Cash book	1,000.00		

Purchases returns

	£		£

VAT

	£		£
Cash book	175.00		

Step 3

B will repay Y £500 plus VAT of £87.50. We therefore need to enter the purchase return, the cash and the VAT in the accounts.

Cash book

	£		£
Purchases return + VAT	587.50	Purchases + VAT	1,175.00

Purchases

	£		£
Cash book	1,000.00		

Purchases returns

	£		£
		Cash book	500.00

VAT

	£		£
Cash book	175.00	Cash book	87.50

4   Purchases returns – credit customers

4.1 Introduction

When a credit customer returns goods, he does not receive cash for the return; the seller will issue a credit note to record the fact that goods have been returned. This credit note is sent to the customer and is entered in the customer's books.

KAPLAN PUBLISHING

4.2 Purchases returns with VAT

When a return is made and we include VAT, the VAT has to be accounted for both on the invoice when the purchase is made, and on the credit note when the goods are returned. This VAT has to be entered in the books.

○ **EXAMPLE**   ○○○○

D buys goods from Z for £800 + VAT (= £940).

D returns goods worth £200 + VAT.

Enter these transactions in the main ledger of D's books.

Solution

Step 1

Enter the invoice in the usual way, including the VAT.

PLCA

	£		£
		Purchases	940.00

Purchases

	£		£
PLCA	800.00		

VAT

	£		£
PLCA	140.00		

Step 2

Enter the credit note. The VAT on the return will be £200 x 17.5% = £35. This gives a total credit note of £235.

PLCA

	£		£
Purchases returns	235.00	Purchases	940.00

Purchases

	£		£
PLCA	800.00		

VAT

	£		£
PLCA	140.00	PLCA	35.00

	Purchases returns		
£			£
	PLCA		200.00

The books will reflect the position after the return. The balance on the PLCA is £705. This is made up as:

	£
Purchase	800
Purchase return	200
	600
VAT 600 x 17.5%	105
	705

5 The purchases returns day book

5.1 Introduction

Purchases returns are in practice entered in a 'purchases returns day book'. This is similar to the purchases day book, and the columns are used in the same way. The only difference is that instead of having a column for the invoice number, there is a column for the 'credit note number'. This is because when the goods are sent back the business will receive a credit note from the supplier.

PURCHASES RETURNS DAY BOOK						
Date	Supplier	Reference	Credit note number	Total £	VAT £	Purchases returns £

O EXAMPLE   ○○○○

John bought goods for £750 + VAT from X and £1,000 + VAT from Y.

John returns goods which cost £200 excluding VAT to X, and goods which cost £400 excluding VAT to Y.

Enter the above purchases and returns in the main and subsidiary ledgers of John, using a purchases returns book.

Solution

Step 1

Enter the original purchases invoices in the main ledger.

PLCA

	£		£
		PDB	2,056.25

Purchases

	£		£
PDB	1,750.00		

VAT

	£		£
PDB	306.25		

Step 2

Write up the purchases returns day book.

PURCHASES RETURNS DAY BOOK						
Date	Supplier	Reference	Credit note number	Total £	VAT £	Purchases returns £
	X			235.00	35.00	200.00
	Y			470.00	70.00	400.00
				705.00	105.00	600.00

Step 3

Enter the PRDB totals in the main ledger accounts.

PLCA

	£		£
PRDB	705.00	PDB	2,056.25

Purchases

	£		£
PDB	1,750.00		

VAT

	£		£
PDB	306.25	PRDB	105.00

Purchases returns

	£		£
		PRDB	600.00

Step 4

Enter the individual amounts in the subsidiary purchases ledger. The amounts that will be debited to the individual creditor accounts as the return is reducing the amount that is owed to the creditor.

	X		
	£		£
PRDB	235.00	PDB (£750 + VAT)	881.25

	Y		
	£		£
PRDB	470.00	PDB (£1,000 + VAT)	1,175.00

5.2 Purchases returns in purchases day book

In some businesses the level of purchases returns are fairly low and therefore it is not justified to keep a separate purchases returns day book. In these cases any credit notes that are received for purchases returns are recorded as negative amounts in the purchases day book. In simulations if this is the case then you will be told that this is the policy of the business. Care should be taken, however, when adding up the columns in the purchases day book as any credit notes must be deducted rather than added in.

▷ ACTIVITY 2 ▷▷▷▷

Given below are the totals of an analysed purchases returns day book for a week.

Date	Supplier	Credit note no	Code	Total £	VAT £	Dept 1 £	Dept 2 £	Dept 3 £
23/04/X0				9,400	1,400	1,000	2,000	5,000

Post these totals to the main ledger accounts.   [Answer on p. 125]

6 Test your knowledge ▷ ▷ ▷

1 Does the total column in the analysed purchases day book include or exclude VAT?

2 Why is there no discount received column for settlement discounts in the purchases day book?

3 An analysed purchases day book has the following totals for a week.

Date	Invoice no	Supplier	Code	Total £	VAT £	Dept 1 £	Dept 2 £	Dept 3 £
				19,975	2,975	2,000	5,000	10,000

How would the totals be posted to the main ledger accounts?

4 Given below are the totals of an analysed purchases returns day book for a week.

Date	Supplier	Credit note no	Code	Total £	VAT £	Dept 1 £	Dept 2 £	Dept 3 £
23/04/X0				5,287.50	787.50	500	1,000	3,000

Post these totals to the main ledger accounts.   [Answers on p. 125]

7 Summary

The purchases day book and the purchases returns day book are simple devices for grouping together purchases invoices for goods purchased and credit notes for goods returned. The topics you need to practise are:

(a) posting the total of these day books to the main ledger accounts; and

(b) posting the individual invoices and credit notes to the creditors accounts in the subsidiary purchases ledger.

It is also useful if you understand how the accounts fit together as shown in the diagram in Section 1.2 of this chapter.

Answers to chapter activities & 'test your knowledge' questions

△ **ACTIVITY 1**   △ △ △ △

The required double entry is as follows:

Debit	VAT	£13,125
	Department 1 purchases	£20,000
	Department 2 purchases	£15,000
	Department 2 purchases	£40,000
Credit	Purchases ledger control account	£88,125

Note carefully that it is the net amount that is debited to each purchases account and the gross amount (including VAT) that is credited to the purchases ledger control account. The VAT total is debited to the VAT account.

The ledger entries would appear as follows:

Purchases ledger control account

	£			£
			PDB	88,125

VAT

	£			£
PDB	13,125			

Department 1 purchases

	£			£
PDB	20,000			

Department 2 purchases

	£			£
PDB	15,000			

Department 3 purchases

	£			£
PDB	40,000			

KAPLAN PUBLISHING

△ ACTIVITY 2 △△△△

Purchases returns – Department 1 account

	£		£
		PRDB	1,000

Purchases returns – Department 2 account

	£		£
		PRDB	2,000

Purchases returns – Department 3 account

	£		£
		PRDB	5,000

VAT account

	£		£
		PRDB	1,400

Purchases ledger control account

	£		£
PRDB	9,400		

Note carefully that it is the net amount that is credited to each returns account and the gross amount to the purchases ledger control account. The difference, the VAT, is credited to the VAT account.

Test your knowledge △ △ △

1   Include.

2   There is no discount received column in the purchases day book because for each invoice the amount entered is the total value of the invoice. The value of the invoice which is entered in the day book does not depend on whether the settlement discount is taken or not. Discount received is only accounted for when the payment is made and if the settlement discount is taken it is at this stage that the double entry is put through the main ledger.

3   The required double entry is as follows:

Debit	VAT	£2,975
	Department 1 purchases	£2,000
	Department 2 purchases	£5,000
	Department 2 purchases	£10,000
Credit	Purchases ledger control account	£19,975

Note carefully that it is the net amount that is debited to each purchases account and the gross amount (including VAT) that is credited to the purchases ledger control account. The VAT total is debited to the VAT account.

The ledger entries would appear as follows:

Purchases ledger control account

	£			£
		PDB		19,975

VAT

	£			£
PDB	2,975			

Department 1 purchases

	£			£
PDB	2,000			

Department 2 purchases

	£			£
PDB	5,000			

Department 3 purchases

	£			£
PDB	10,000			

4

Purchases returns – Department 1 account

	£			£
		PRDB		500

Purchases returns – Department 2 account

	£			£
		PRDB		1,000

Purchases returns – Department 3 account

	£			£
		PRDB		3,000

VAT account

	£			£
		PRDB		787.50

Purchases ledger control account

	£			£
PRDB	5,287.50			

THE ANALYSED CASH PAYMENTS BOOK

INTRODUCTION
In this chapter we will consider how cash payments for cash purchases and to credit suppliers are recorded in the cash payments book and in the ledger accounts.

KNOWLEDGE & UNDERSTANDING

- Double entry bookkeeping, including balancing accounts (Elements 1, 2 and 3)
- Operation of manual accounting systems (Elements 1, 2 and 3)
- Relationship between the accounting system and ledger (Elements 1, 2 and 3)
- Accounting for payments to credit suppliers, and to suppliers where a credit account is not available (Element 2)
- The use of the petty cash book and cash book as part of the double entry system or as books of prime entry (Element 3)

CONTENTS
1 The analysed cash payments book
2 Settlement discounts received from suppliers

PERFORMANCE CRITERIA
- Post invoices and credit notes into the subsidiary (purchases) ledger and main (general ledger (Element 30.2)
- Enter payments in cash book and ledgers (Element 30.2)

1 The analysed cash payments book

1.1 Layout

A proforma analysed cash payments book is shown below

CASH PAYMENTS BOOK								
Date	Narrative	Reference	Total £	VAT £	Suppliers £	Cash Purchases £	Admin £	Rent and rates £	Discount received £
		TOTALS							

Notes

(a) The date column contains the date of the transaction.

(b) The narrative column describes the transactions.

(c) The total column contains the total cash received (including any VAT).

(d) The VAT column contains the VAT on the transaction but not if the VAT has already been entered in the purchases day book. This is a tricky point but is in principle exactly the same as the treatment of VAT that we studied for the cash receipts book.

(e) The suppliers column contains any cash paid that has been paid to a supplier. The total paid including VAT is entered in this column.

(f) The cash purchases column contains cash paid for purchases that are not bought on credit.

(g) We saw with the analysed cash receipts book that nearly all receipts come from debtors or cash sales. In the case of payments, there is a great variety of suppliers who are paid through the cash book; rent and rates, telephone, electricity, marketing, etc. The business will have a separate column for the categories of expense that it wishes to analyse.

1.2 Main ledger payments not entered in the PDB

The PDB is often used only for invoices from suppliers of purchases, i.e. goods for resale. Invoices for rent, electricity, telephone, etc will typically not be entered in the PDB. They will be paid by cheque, and the double entry will be made directly between the cash payments book and the relevant expense account in the main ledger.

One reason for this is that the purchases day book (like the sales day book) is used because the business will typically have a large number of similar transactions (e.g. purchases of goods for resale). To simplify the accounting these are all listed in the PDB and posted in total to the main ledger. Payment of rent or telephone only happens once every three months so there is no need to group these together; they are easily dealt with on an individual basis.

O EXAMPLE   OOOO

Parma Products buys goods for resale from two suppliers on credit. The business buys £1,000 + VAT of goods from X and £3,000 + VAT of goods from Y. Parma receives an invoice and pays £500 + VAT rent to their land-lord. Parma also pays X's invoice in full. Enter these transactions in the accounts of Parma Products. The rent invoice is not entered in the PDB.

Solution

Step 1   Enter the invoices for goods in the PDB

PURCHASES DAY BOOK						
Date	Supplier	Reference	Invoice number	Total £	VAT £	Purchases £
	X			1,175	175	1,000
	Y			3,525	525	3,000
				4,700	700	4,000

Step 2   Enter the totals of the PDB in the main ledger.

Purchases

	£		£
PDB	4,000.00		

VAT

	£		£
PDB	700.00		

PLCA

	£		£
		PDB	4,700.00

Step 3   Enter the cash paid in the analysed cash payments book.

CASH PAYMENTS BOOK							
Date	Narrative	Reference	Total £	VAT £	Suppliers £	Rent £	Discount received £
	X		1,175.00		1,175.00		
	Rent		587.50	87.50		500.00	
		TOTALS	1,762.50	87.50	1,175.00	500.00	

Note that the VAT on the payment to the supplier has already been accounted for in the main ledger via the entries in the PDB. However, the rent invoice was not entered in the PDB and so the VAT has to be entered in the VAT column of the cash book from where it will be posted to the VAT account (see Step 4).

Step 4   Post the cash paid totals from the cash book to the main ledger.

Purchases

	£		£
PDB	4,000.00		

VAT

	£		£
PDB	700.00		
CPB	87.50		

PLCA

	£		£
CPB	1,175.00	PDB	4,700.00

Rent

	£		£
CPB	500.00		

Note 1:   All the VAT paid is now debited to the VAT account. You must make sure that you understand how some is posted via the PDB and some via the cash book.

Note 2:   All of the entries made from the cash payments book are debit entries. The credit entry is the total of the cash payments (£1,762.50) since the cash payments book is part of the double entry.

Step 5   Enter the amounts in the subsidiary purchases ledger.

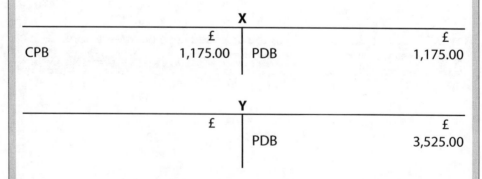

X

	£		£
CPB	1,175.00	PDB	1,175.00

Y

	£		£
		PDB	3,525.00

The entries to the subsidiary ledger from the cash payments book are debit entries in the individual creditor accounts as the payment means that less is owed to the creditor.

2 Settlement discounts received from suppliers

2.1 Introduction

Settlement discounts are a tricky complication when dealing with the analysed purchases day book and cash book.

○ **EXAMPLE** ○○○○

Consider a business run by Francis which buys goods costing £2,000 + VAT from Z. Z offers a 5% settlement discount if Francis pays within 30 days. Francis pays within 30 days.

Enter these new transactions in the books of Francis.

Solution

Step 1 Calculate the value of the invoice.

	£
Cost of goods	2,000.00
VAT (2,000 – (5% x 2,000)) x 17.5%	332.50
Total invoice value	2,332.50

Step 2 Enter the invoice from Z in the purchases day book.

PURCHASES DAY BOOK

Date	Supplier	Reference	Invoice number	Total £	VAT £	Purchases £
	Z			2,332.50	332.50	2,000.00
				2,332.50	332.50	2,000.00

Step 3 Enter the totals of the purchases day book in the main ledger.

Purchases

	£		£
PDB	2,000.00		

VAT

	£		£
PDB	332.50		

PLCA

	£		£
		PDB	2,332.50

Step 4   Calculate the cash paid by Francis.

	£
Cost of goods	2,000.00
5% settlement discount	(100.00)
	1,900.00
VAT (2,000 – (5% x 2,000)) x 17.5%	332.50
Total cash paid	2,232.50

Step 5   Enter the cash paid in the analysed cash payments book.

CASH PAYMENTS BOOK

Date	Narrative	Reference	Total	VAT	Suppliers	Rent	Discount received
			£	£	£	£	£
	Z		2,232.50		2,232.50		100.00
		TOTALS	2,232.50		2,232.50		100.00

Note: Remember that the discount received column is a 'memorandum' account. The cash book only cross-casts if you ignore the discount received column.

Step 6   Post the cash payments book totals to the main ledger.

Purchases

	£		£
PDB	2,000.00		

VAT

	£		£
PDB	332.50		

PLCA

	£		£
CPB	2,232.50	PDB	2,332.50
Discount received	100.00		

Discount received

	£		£
		PLCA	100.00

▷ ACTIVITY 1   ▷ ▷ ▷ ▷

FFP makes the following payments in respect of various credit invoices and other items:

· Payment of £4,230 on 23/7/X4 to N Hudson for credit purchases. A settlement discount of £130 was taken. This was paid by cheque (cheque number 1003). The purchase ledger reference code is P4153.

· On 24/7/X4, £2,350 to G Farr in respect of an outstanding invoice, by cheque (cheque number 1004). The subsidiary (purchases) ledger reference code is P4778.

· On 28/7/X4, purchase of stock, not on credit, of £940 including VAT of £140 (cheque number 1005).

· On 30/7/X4, payment of a salary by cheque of £2,500, using cheque number 1006. (There is no VAT on wages and salaries.)

Task 1   Enter these transactions in the cash payments book and total the columns.

Task 2   Post the totals to the main ledger.

Task 3   Post the payments to N Hudson and G Farr to the subsidiary (purchases) ledger. The opening balances are N Hudson £10,327.00 and G Farr £8,263.00.   [Answer on p. 135]

3   Test your knowledge   ▷ ▷ ▷

1 Supplier B offers his customer X a 5% settlement discount on an invoice of £1,000 plus VAT if X pays within 30 days. What is the VAT on the invoice?

2 Following on from the question above, if X takes the settlement discount, how much will he pay B?

3 We take a settlement discount of £75 from a supplier when paying an invoice. What is the double entry for this discount?

4 John makes two transactions.

(a) He pays a rent bill of £150 including VAT which has not been entered in the PDB.

(b) He pays a supplier £1,175 for an invoice which was entered in the purchases day book.

Enter these transactions in the cash payments book.   [Answers on p. 136]

4   Summary

The two main areas covered in this chapter which cause problems are:
(a)   the treatment of VAT in the cash payments book; and
(b)   the treatment of discount received.

Regarding VAT, remember that if an invoice has been entered in the purchases day book, the VAT will have been captured in the PDB and posted to the VAT account from there. If, however, an invoice is not entered in the purchases day book, the VAT has to be entered in the VAT column of the cash book and posted to the VAT account from there.

Regarding discounts, remember that the discount column in the cash book is simply a memorandum column. The double entry for discount received is entered in the main ledger as: debit PLCA; credit discount received. Remember also that in the subsidiary purchases ledger, the discount received is entered in the suppliers account but there is no corresponding double entry in the discount received account (it has already been posted from the PLCA).

Answers to chapter activities & 'test your knowledge' questions

△ ACTIVITY 1   △△△△

Task 1

ANALYSED CASH PAYMENTS BOOK (CPB)

Date	Cheque number	Payee/ account number	Total	Creditors	VAT	Wages and salaries	Purchases	Discount received
			£	£	£	£	£	£
23/7/X4	1003	N Hudson, P4153	4,230	4,230				130
24/7/X4	1004	G Farr, P4778	2,350	2,350				
28/7/X4	1005	Purchases	940		140		800	
30/7/X4	1006	Salary	2,500			2,500		
			10,020	6,580	140	2,500	800	130

Task 2

Creditors control account   2001

Date	Details	Folio	£	Date	Details	Folio	£
31/7/X4	Bank	CPB	6,580				
31/7/X4	Discounts received	CPB	130				

VAT account   3215

Date	Details	Folio	£	Date	Details	Folio	£
31/7/X4	Bank	CPB	140				

Wages and salaries account   4100

Date	Details	Folio	£	Date	Details	Folio	£
31/7/X4	Bank	CPB	2,500				

Purchases account   4200

Date	Details	Folio	£	Date	Details	Folio	£
31/7/X4	Bank	CPB	800				

Discount received account   1000

Date	Details	Folio	£	Date	Details	Folio	£
				31/7/X4	Creditors	CPB	130

Task 3

N Hudson account   P4153

Date	Details	Folio	£	Date	Details	Folio	£
23/7/X4	Bank	CPB	4,230		b/f		10,327
23/7/X4	Discounts received	CPB	130				

G Farr account   P4778

Date	Details	Folio	£	Date	Details	Folio	£
24/7/X4	Bank	CPB	2,350		b/f		8,263

Test your knowledge △ △ △

1   $(£1,000 – (5\% \times £1,000)) \times 17.5\% = £166.25$

2

	£
Cost of goods	1,000.00
Less 5% discount	(50.00)
	950.00
Add VAT	166.25
	1,116.25

3

Purchases ledger control account

	£		£
Discount received	75.00		

Discount received account

	£		£
		PLCA	75.00

4

CASH PAYMENTS BOOK

Date	Narrative	Reference	Total	VAT	Suppliers	Rent	Discount received
			£	£	£	£	£
			150.00	22.34		127.66	
			1,175.00		1,175.00		
			1,325.00	22.34	1,175.00	127.66	

CREDIT SALES: DOCUMENTS

INTRODUCTION

For this part of the AAT Syllabus you will be required to deal with many aspects of the sales that a business makes. This will involve the procedure for making the sale and the procedures for receiving the money for the sale.

In this chapter we will take an outline look at the documents required when making a sale.

KNOWLEDGE & UNDERSTANDING

· Business transactions and document involved (Elements 1,2 and 3)
· General principles of VAT (Elements 1, 2 and 3)
· Types of discounts (Elements 1 and 2)
· Credit limits (Element 1)
· Methods of coding data (Elements 1, 2 and 3)

CONTENTS

1 The sales documents
2 Summary of a credit sale
3 Setting up a credit sale
4 Supplying the goods
5 Issuing credit notes
6 Coding sales invoices

PERFORMANCE CRITERIA

· Prepare sales invoices from source documents (Element 30.1)
· Prepare sales credit notes from correspondence or other relevant source documents and ensure authorisation (Element 30.1)
· Code sales invoices and credit notes (Element 30.1

1 The sales documents

1.1 Introduction

We will now consider the processes involved in making sales to customers. Cash sales are relatively straightforward but credit sales are more involved. The details of all of the aspects covered here will be dealt with in greater depth in later chapters.

1.2 Cash sales

A cash sale will normally be made in a retail environment. A customer will enter the shop, choose the goods they wish to buy then come to the till in order to pay for them. The seller will tell the customer the price of the goods and the customer then offers payment for them.

This may be in the form of notes and coins, in which case it is possible that change will need to be calculated and given to the customer, if they have given more cash than the price of the goods. Most electronic tills calculate the amount of change required and therefore it is a fairly simple task to ensure that the correct amount of change is given.

The customer may alternatively offer to pay for the goods by cheque or by credit or debit card. The detailed procedures for accepting payment by these methods will be considered in later chapters.

Finally, once the customer has paid for the goods, a receipt of some sort will be given to the customer. This may be printed automatically by the till or may be a handwritten receipt in some businesses. The transaction is now complete!

1.3 Credit sales

The procedure for a sale on credit can be rather more involved. The sale process will normally be initiated by the receipt of an order from a customer. This order may be in writing, by fax, over the telephone or by e-mail. When your business receives the order, the first decision that must be made is whether or not to allow the customer credit for this sale.

1.4 Offering credit

Selling goods on credit always involves an element of risk. The goods are being taken away or delivered to the customer now with the promise of payment in the future. Therefore your business must be confident that the payment will be received. The decision process as to whether or not to make the sale on credit will be different depending upon whether this is a sale to an existing credit customer or a new customer.

1.5 Existing customers

If an existing credit customer wishes to make a further purchase on credit, it would be normal practice to carry out some basic checks. When the customer was originally taken on as a credit customer, a credit limit will have been set which should not be exceeded. This means that at any time the amount owing from that customer should not exceed the credit limit. Therefore the amount currently owing from the customer should be checked to ensure that the new sale will not take that figure over the credit limit.

It would also be sensible to check that there have been no problems recently with receiving payment from this customer. If the checks are satisfactory then the credit sale can go ahead.

1.6 New customer

If a new customer asks for credit from your business then it would be normal practice to ask the customer to supply some trade references – names of other businesses that they trade with on credit who can vouch for their creditworthiness. Your business may also wish to check the customer's creditworthiness through an agency such as Dun and Bradstreet, or by asking for references from the customer's bank.

If the references and checks are satisfactory then a credit limit will be set for this customer and the sale can go ahead.

2 Summary of a credit sale

The main document flows for a credit sale are illustrated below. The various documents are described in the paragraphs that follow.

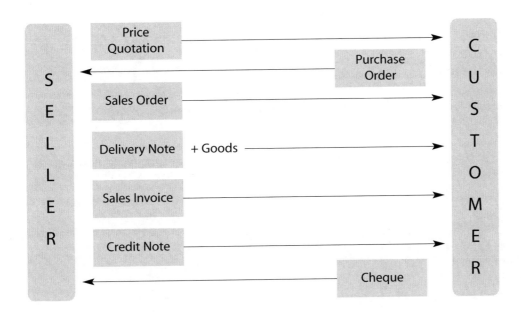

3 Setting up a credit sale

3.1 Price enquiry

The first stage of the process of a credit sale may be the receipt of a price enquiry from a customer.

The price enquiry may be a formal written document or more likely a telephone call. When responding to a price enquiry it is important that you make sure that the price you quote is the correct one as if it is incorrect you may find that you are contracted to sell the goods at that price under contract law (see later chapter in this Study Text).

3.2 Price quotation

In some organisations it is common practice to quote prices to customers over the telephone particularly if there is a catalogue or price list from which there are no deviations in price. However, some businesses will be prepared to offer certain customers goods at different prices. Therefore it is often the case that a price quotation is sent out to a customer showing the price at which the goods that they want can be bought.

A typical price quotation is shown below

City Woods Suppliers

192 Old Kent Road
London ← *Name and address of*
SE1 8QT *business quoting price*

Tel: 020 7248 7009 - Fax: 020 7248 7890

QUOTATION

TO: Alpha Limited   Date: 14 Sept 20X3
Mountjoy Street ← *Name and address of*
London W12 6RS   *customer*   ↖ *Today's date*

Thank you for your telephone enquiry of 10 September. We are pleased to quote the following price:

Chipboard sheeting 6' x 4'   Code CB0351   £23.00 per unit, excluding VAT

Details of   ↘ *Price being*
Goods   *quoted*

J Kramer ← *Authorisation*
Sales manager   *Signature*

KAPLAN PUBLISHING

The price quotation is an important document as this is the price that your organisation is now contracted to sell the goods at. Therefore it is important that it is authorised by the appropriate person in the organisation.

3.3 The purchase order

If the customer is happy with the price quotation that they have received from your business then they will place a firm order with you. The order may be by telephone or it may be in writing. Whatever method is used for the purchase order, it is important to check all of the details carefully.

· Is the price that which was quoted to the customer?
· Are the delivery terms acceptable?
· Are any discounts applicable?

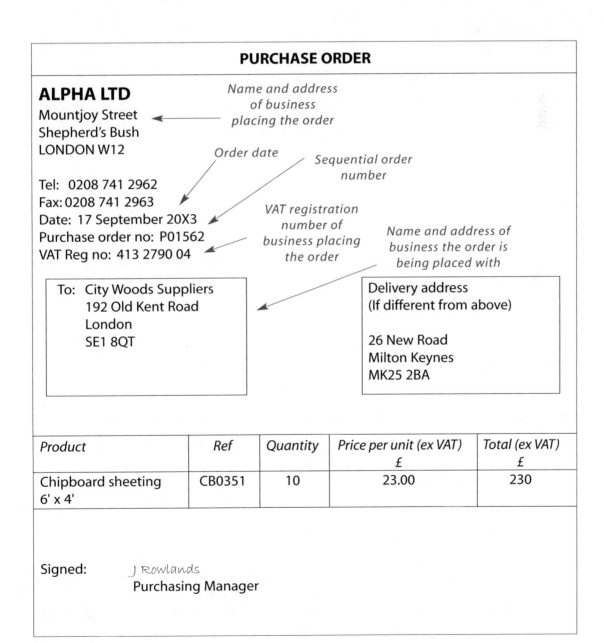

3.4 Confirming sales orders

To avoid misunderstandings, a supplier will normally confirm a customer's order by completing a **sales order**, even if the customer has already sent a written purchase order.

A **sales order** is a document confirming:
· quantity/type of goods or service;
· date of supply;
· location of supply;
· price and terms.

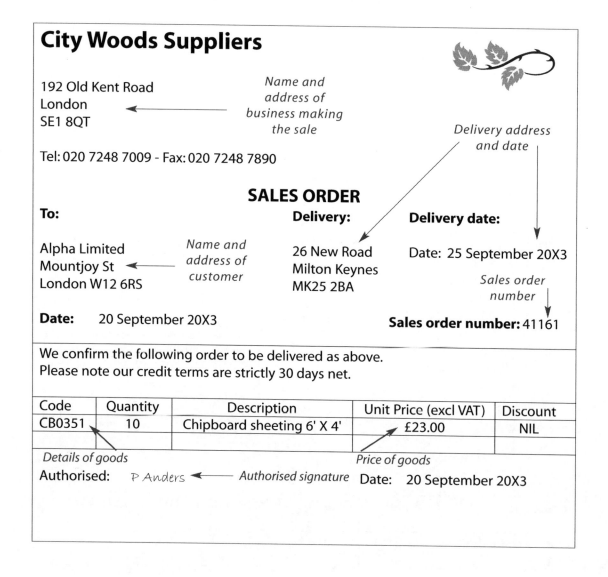

City Woods Suppliers

192 Old Kent Road
London
SE1 8QT

Name and address of business making the sale

Delivery address and date

Tel: 020 7248 7009 - Fax: 020 7248 7890

SALES ORDER

To:

Delivery:

Delivery date:

Alpha Limited
Mountjoy St
London W12 6RS

Name and address of customer

26 New Road
Milton Keynes
MK25 2BA

Date: 25 September 20X3

Sales order number

Date: 20 September 20X3

Sales order number: 41161

We confirm the following order to be delivered as above.
Please note our credit terms are strictly 30 days net.

Code	Quantity	Description	Unit Price (excl VAT)	Discount
CB0351	10	Chipboard sheeting 6' X 4'	£23.00	NIL

Details of goods

Price of goods

Authorised: P Anders ← *Authorised signature*   Date: 20 September 20X3

4 Supplying the goods

4.1 Introduction

Once all of the negotiations over the price and terms of the credit sale have been completed, then the goods themselves must be delivered.

4.2 Delivery notes

Delivery note – a document accompanying goods despatched to a customer.

Delivery notes should have **sequential numbers** that are either pre-printed for a manual system or computer generated in a computer system, and should be used in order. Spoiled delivery notes should be cancelled and kept.

There will normally be three parts to a delivery note:

Part one – This is kept by the customer in order to compare to the purchase order to ensure that the goods that have been delivered were ordered and then to the sales invoice when they receive it.

Part two – Signed and returned to the supplier of the goods as evidence that they have been received by the customer.

Part three – Signed and kept by the delivery organisation as evidence that they have delivered the goods and that the customer has received them.

City Woods Suppliers

192 Old Kent Road
London
SE1 8QT

Tel: 020 7248 7009 - Fax: 020 7248 7890   DN 005673

DELIVERY NOTE

To: **Delivery:**   **Delivery date:**

Alpha Limited   26 New Road   Date: 25 September 20X3
Mountjoy St   Milton Keynes
London W12 6RS   MK25 2BA

Date: 20 September 20X3   **Sales order number:** 41161

We confirm the following order to be delivered as above.

Product	Code	Quantity
Chipboard 6' x 4'	CB0351	10

Received in good condition: *A Patel*

4.3 The sales invoice

The next stage is to prepare and send out the sales invoice.

In a manual system, sales invoices must be prepared from the details shown on delivery notes. Delivery notes do not normally show details of prices, discounts or VAT. (This is because the customer might mistake the delivery note for a sales invoice.) Price, discounts and VAT are shown on the sales invoice.

Sales invoices should have **pre-printed sequential numbers** and should be used in order. Spoiled sales invoices should be cancelled and kept.

In a computer system, the sales invoice will generally be produced at the same time as the delivery note and will be identical except that the delivery note may not have details of price, etc.

City Woods Suppliers

192 Old Kent Road
London
SE1 8QT

Tel: 020 7248 7009 - Fax: 020 7248 7890

Invoice no:	I005673
Tax point:	20 September 20X3
VAT reg no:	618 2201 63
Delivery note:	DN005673
Account no:	AL6215

INVOICE

To:

Alpha Limited
Mountjoy St
London W12 6RS

Delivery:

26 New Road
Milton Keynes
MK25 2BA

Delivery date:

Date: 25 September 20X3

Date: 20 September 20X3

Sales order number: 41161

We confirm the following order to be delivered as above.

Product	Code	Quantity	Price per unit £	Total £
Chipboard 6' x 4'	CB0351	10	23.00	230.00
			VAT	40.25
				270.25

4.4 Pricing goods and services

Unit prices for goods or services are kept in master files which must be updated regularly. If a price quotation has been sent to a customer then this must be used to find the price to use on the invoice.

Prices will normally be quoted exclusive of value added tax (VAT), as this is the true selling price to the business.

4.5 Customer details

In order to prepare the sales invoice the customer master file must be found. This will show the details of any discounts, etc offered to this customer (see later in this chapter).

4.6 The effect of value added tax

If the selling business is registered for VAT, VAT must be charged on taxable supplies.

Most goods and services are standard-rated (i.e. 17.5% rate of VAT must be charged). This will be considered in more detail later in the chapter.

▷ **ACTIVITY 1**   ▷ ▷ ▷ ▷

(AAT CA J92)
List six items of data which you would expect an invoice to contain.

[Answer on p. 156]

○ **EXAMPLE**   ○ ○ ○ ○

Preparing a sales invoice

Thelma Goody is the sales invoicing clerk for a clothing wholesaler which trades as a limited company. Thelma prepares the sales invoices to be sent to the customer from the price list and a copy of the delivery note sent up to her by the sales department.

The business is registered for VAT.

Today she has received the following delivery note from the sales department

---

Delivery note: 2685

To: Kids Clothes Ltd
9 Port Street
MANCHESTER
M1 5EX

A B Fashions Ltd

3 Park Road
Parkway
Bristol
BR6 6SJ
Tel: 01272 695221
Fax: 01272 695222

Delivery date: 20 August 20X6

Quantity	Code	DESCRIPTION	Colour
90	SSB 330	Shawls (babies)	Assorted
30	CJA 991	Cashmere jumpers (adult)	Cream
30	GGC 442	Gloves (children)	Assorted

Received by: ....

Signature: .... Date: ....

Print name: ....

Code	Description	Colour	Unit price £	VAT rate
SSG 001	Skirt (girls)	Black	13.50	Zero
SSW 002	Skirt (women)	Navy	15.90	Standard
TTW 037	Trousers (women)	Black	21.00	Standard
TTW 038	Trousers (women)	Navy	15.60	Standard
TTW 039	Trousers (women)	Red	15.60	Standard
SSB 330	Shawl (babies)	Assorted	11.50	Zero
SSB 331	Shawl (babies)	White	11.50	Zero
CJA 991	Cashmere jumper (adult)	Cream	65.00	Standard
CJA 992	Cashmere jumper (adult)	Pink	65.00	Standard
CJA 993	Cashmere jumper (adult)	Blue	65.00	Standard
CJA 994	Cashmere jumper (adult)	Camel	65.00	Standard
HHB 665	Hat (babies)	White	3.50	Zero
HHB 666	Hat (babies)	Blue	3.50	Zero
GGC 442	Gloves (children)	Assorted	6.20	Zero
GGC 443	Gloves (children)	White	6.50	Zero
GGC 444	Gloves (children)	Black	6.50	Zero

The customer file shows that Kids Clothes Ltd's account number is KC 0055 and that a trade discount of 10% is offered to this customer.

Thelma must now prepare the sales invoice. Today's date is 22 August 20X6.

Solution

INVOICE

AB Fashions Ltd

Invoice to:

Kids Clothes Ltd
9 Port Street
Manchester
M1 5EX

3 Park Road
Parkway
Bristol   BR6 6SJ
Tel: 01272 695221
Fax: 01272 695222

Deliver to:

As above

Invoice no:	95124
Tax point:	22 August 20X6
VAT reg no:	488 7922 26
Delivery note no:	2685
Account no:	KC 0055

Code	Description	Quantity	VAT rate %	Unit price £	Amount excl of VAT £
SSB 330	Shawls (babies) assorted	90	0	11.50	1,035.00
CJA 991	Cashmere Jumper (adult) cream	30	17.5	65.00	1,950.00
GGC 442	Gloves (children) assorted	30	0	6.20	186.00
					3,171.00
Trade discount 10%					(317.10)
					2,853.90
VAT at 17.5%					307.12
Total amount payable					3,161.02

Step 1 Enter today's date on the invoice and the invoice number which should be the next number after the last sales invoice number.

Step 2 Enter the customer details – name, address and account number.

Step 3 Refer now to the delivery note copy and enter the delivery note number and the quantities, codes and descriptions of the goods.

Step 4 Refer to the price list and enter the unit prices of the goods and the rate of VAT (note that the VAT rate for children's clothes is zero).

Step 5 Now for the calculations – firstly multiply the number of each item by the unit price to find the VAT exclusive price – then total these total prices – finally calculate the trade discount as 10% of this total, £3,171 x 10% = £317.10 and deduct it.

Step 6 Calculate the VAT – in this case there is only standard rate VAT on the cashmere jumpers but you must remember to deduct the trade discount (£1,950 – £195) before calculating the VAT amount £1,755 x 17.5% = £307.12 – add the VAT to the invoice total after deducting the trade discount.

▷ ACTIVITY 2   ▷ ▷ ▷ ▷

A business sells 38 units of a product that is sold for £16.50 per unit and 24 units of a product that is sold for £19.80. The customer is given a 15% trade discount and all of the goods are chargeable to VAT at the standard rate.

Show the figures that would appear on the sales invoice for this sale.

[Answer on p. 156]

4.7 Other terms found on invoices

You may also find other terms and conditions shown on invoices or other documents. Here are some of the more common:

E & OE – Errors and omissions excepted. The seller is claiming the right to correct any genuine errors on the invoice (e.g. prices) at a later date.

Carriage paid – The invoice value includes delivery of the goods to the customer's premises.

Ex works – Prices quoted do not include delivery to the customer's premises. The customer must organise and pay for the delivery of the goods.

Cash on delivery – The customer is expected to pay for the goods when they are delivered.

▷ ACTIVITY 3   ▷ ▷ ▷ ▷

A purchase order, number 28596, has been received from J Hardy Construction for the following:
- 3 Cotswold panels
- 5 insulation bricks
- 1 red brick roof tile

The file for this customer shows that trade discounts are offered to this customer of 2% and settlement discounts of 3% if payment is within 14 days. The file also includes the customer's address: Poplar Works, Poplar Street, Oldham, OL4 6QB and account number SL07.

An extract from the price list is given.

Description	Code	Unit price £
Insulation bricks	159 SO4	195.50
Red brick roof tiles	874 KL5	56.65
Cotswold panels	950 BB3	300.00

The goods are to be despatched along with despatch note number 68553. The next sales invoice number is 69472. Today's date is 23 August 20X3.

Prepare the sales invoice for this sale on the blank invoice given below.

INVOICE

A.J. Broom & Company Limited

Invoice to:

59 Parkway
Manchester
M2 6EG
Tel: 0161 560 3392
Fax: 0161 560 5322

Deliver to:

Invoice no:
Tax point:
VAT reg no: 625 9911 58
Order no:
Delivery note no:
Account no:

Code	Description	Quantity	VAT rate %	Unit price £	Amount excl of VAT £

Trade discount   %

VAT at 17.5%
Total amount payable
Deduct discount of   % if paid within

[Answer on p. 157]

5 Issuing credit notes

5.1 Introduction

Credit notes are issued as documentary evidence that goods have been returned and that all or part of a previous sales invoice is cancelled. Therefore a business must keep strict control over the credit notes it issues.

Credit note – Document issued by a supplier to a customer cancelling part or all of a sales invoice. Business normally issues a credit note:

· when a customer has returned faulty or damaged goods;
· when a customer has returned perfect goods by agreement with the supplier;
· to make a refund for short deliveries;
· to settle a dispute with a customer.

A credit note is the reversal of a previous invoice or part of the invoice value.

5.2 Return of goods

Returned goods must be inspected, counted and recorded on receipt. They would normally be recorded on a returns inwards note.

5.3 Authorising credit notes

All credit notes must be authorised by a supervisor prior to being issued.

Some credit notes may be issued without a returns inwards note. For example, an error may have been made in pricing on an invoice but the customer is satisfied with the goods and does not need to return them.

These credit notes must be issued only after written authorisation has been received and must be reviewed and approved before being sent to the customer or recorded.

5.4 Preparing credit notes

A credit note is effectively the reverse of an invoice and therefore will tend to include all the details that would normally appear on a sales invoice.

If Alpha Ltd returned two of the chipboard panels, the credit note would be as follows.

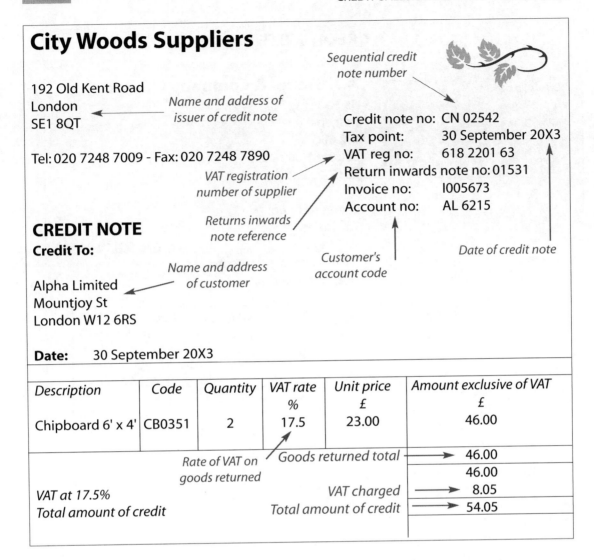

City Woods Suppliers

192 Old Kent Road
London
SE1 8QT

Name and address of issuer of credit note

Sequential credit note number

Credit note no: CN 02542
Tax point: 30 September 20X3
VAT reg no: 618 2201 63
Return inwards note no: 01531
Invoice no: I005673
Account no: AL 6215

Tel: 020 7248 7009 - Fax: 020 7248 7890

VAT registration number of supplier

Returns inwards note reference

Customer's account code

Date of credit note

CREDIT NOTE
Credit To:

Alpha Limited
Mountjoy St
London W12 6RS

Name and address of customer

Date: 30 September 20X3

Description	Code	Quantity	VAT rate %	Unit price £	Amount exclusive of VAT £
Chipboard 6' x 4'	CB0351	2	17.5	23.00	46.00
				Goods returned total	46.00
					46.00
VAT at 17.5%				VAT charged	8.05
Total amount of credit				Total amount of credit	54.05

Rate of VAT on goods returned

▷ **ACTIVITY 4** ▷ ▷ ▷ ▷

You work for A J Broom & Company Limited and have returns inwards note number 01532 in front of you and you have to prepare a credit note to send to K Phipps Builders for one insulation brick, code 159 SO4, that was damaged. The unit price of the insulation brick is £195.50.

The customer file shows that a trade discount of 5% is given to this customer but no settlement discount. The file also shows the customer's address: Hayward House, Manor Estate, Oldham, OL7 4HD, and the customer's account number SL35.

The next credit note number to use is CN 02543 and today's date is 25 August 20X3.

Prepare the credit note on the blank form provided.

CREDIT NOTE

Credit note to:

A.J. Broom & Company Limited

59 Parkway
Manchester
M2 6EG
Tel: 0161 560 3392
Fax: 0161 560 5322

Credit note no:
Tax point:
VAT reg no: 625 9911 58
Returns inwards note no:
Account no:

Code	Description	Quantity	VAT rate %	Unit price £	Amount exclusive of VAT £

Trade discount   %

VAT at 17.5%
Total amount of credit

[Answer on p. 158]

6 Coding sales invoices

6.1 Introduction

Sales invoices should be coded to show:
· product group/type for analysis of sales;
· customer account number.

There are several different systems of coding which can be used by a business and the main ones are outlined below.

6.2 Sequence codes

Allocate a number, or a letter, to items in a simple list.

For example:

Code	Name
01	ADAMS, Joan
02	AITKEN, James
03	ALCOCK, Freda
04	BROWN, Joe

6.3 Block codes

These allocate bands of numbers to particular categories.

For example, consider a tobacco manufacturer who produces several types of cigarettes, cigars and pipe tobaccos. He could assign a code to each particular brand as follows:

Product type	Block code
Cigarette	01 – 19
Cigar	20 – 29
Pipe tobacco	30 – 39

6.4 Significant digit codes

These are a particular type of group classification code where individual digits and letters are used to represent features of the coded item. The example given is one used to describe different kinds of vehicle tyres.

Code	Item
TT67015B	Tube Tyre 670 x 15 Blackwall
LT67015W	Tubeless Tyre 670 x 15 Whitewall

6.5 Faceted codes

Faceted codes are another type of group classification code by which the digits of the code are divided into facets of several digits and each facet represents some attribute of the item being coded. These codes are similar to significant digit codes but are purely numerical.

Example: faceted code for types of carpet

Facet 1	=	type of weave (1 digit)	1	=	cord
			2	=	twist
			3	=	short tufted, etc
Facet 2	=	material (1 digit)	1	=	all wool
			2	=	80% wool, 20% nylon
			3	=	50% wool, 50% nylon, etc
Facet 3	=	pattern (2 digits)	01	=	self colour (plain)
			02	=	self colour (embossed)
			03	=	fig leaf, etc
Facet 4	=	colour (2 digits)	01	=	off white
			02	=	bright yellow
			03	=	scarlet, etc

A typical code would be 220302 representing a twist carpet in 80% wool, 20% nylon, pattern fig leaf and colour bright yellow.

Note that a two-digit facet allows up to 100 different codings (00 to 99).

6.6 Decimal codes (or hierarchical codes)

These are yet another form of a group classification code. The most obvious example of a decimal code is the Universal Decimal Code (UDC) devised by Dewey and widely used for the classification of books in libraries. UDC divides all human knowledge into more and more detailed categories as shown.

Code	Item
3	Social science
37	Education
372	Elementary
372.2	Kindergarten
372.21	Methods
372.215	Songs and games

Whatever the coding system that is used it is important for further accounting purposes that the invoices and credit notes are coded according to type of sales and the particular customer.

You may be expected to code items included on sales invoices or credit notes according to a coding system that is given to you in an assessment.

▷ ACTIVITY 5 ▷▷▷▷

Is the cheque number used in a cheque book an example of a sequential code or a hierarchical code?

[Answer on p. 158]

KAPLAN PUBLISHING

7 **Test your knowledge** ▷ ▷ ▷

1   What are the key features that would appear on a sales order?

2   What is a settlement discount?

3   How is a trade discount treated on a sales invoice?

4   Goods have a list price of £268.45 exclusive of VAT. How much VAT at the standard rate should be charged on these goods?

5   Goods have a total VAT inclusive price of £138.65. How much VAT is included in this price?

6   23 items with a list price of £18.60 each have been sent to a customer. A 15% trade discount is allowed to this customer and the goods are all standard rated for VAT purposes. What is the invoice total?

7   14 items at a list price of £23.50 each have been delivered to a customer. The customer is offered a 3% settlement discount and the goods are standard rated for VAT purposes. What is the invoice total?

8   What does the phrase 'E&OE' mean on an invoice?

9   Give three examples of when a credit note might be issued.

10 What are the main items that should be coded on a sales invoice?

[Answers on p. 159]

8   Summary

In this chapter we have concentrated on the process of actually preparing sales invoices and credit notes. Before preparing an invoice it is necessary to ensure that this is for a valid sale by checking the order and delivery details. When preparing the invoice you need to understand the difference between trade discounts and settlement discounts and their treatment on the invoice and for VAT purposes. You also need to be able to correctly find the price of items from a price list and to correctly transfer this to the invoice together with correct multiplication to arrive at the total. No invoice or credit note should be sent out unless it has been properly authorised and it will also need to be coded to ensure that it is eventually correctly recorded in the accounting records.

Answers to chapter activities & 'test your knowledge' question

△ ACTIVITY 1 △ △ △ △

Any six from:	Date
	Invoice number
	Customer name and address
	Seller's name and address
	VAT details
	Terms of payment
	Purchase order number
	Number of items that were sold
	Price per item
	Description of goods
	Total amount payable

△ ACTIVITY 2 △ △ △ △

	£
38 units x £16.50	627.00
24 units x £19.80	475.20
	1,102.20
Less: Trade discount	165.33
	936.87
VAT	163.95
	1,100.82

KAPLAN PUBLISHING

INVOICE

Invoice to:	**A.J. Broom & Company Limited**
J Hardy Construction	59 Parkway
Poplar Works	Manchester
Poplar Street	M2 6EG
Oldham OL4 6QB	Tel: 0161 560 3392
	Fax: 0161 560 5322

Deliver to:	
As above	

Invoice no:	69472
Tax point:	23 August 20X3
VAT reg no:	625 9911 58
Order no:	28596
Delivery note no:	68553
Account no:	SL07

Code	Description	Quantity	VAT rate %	Unit price £	Amount excl of VAT £
950 BB3	Cotswold Panels	3	17.5	300.00	900.00
159 S04	Insulation Bricks	5	17.5	195.50	977.50
874 KL5	Red Brick Roof Tiles	1	17.5	56.65	56.65
					1,934.15

Trade discount 2%   38.68

1,895.47

VAT at 17.5% *   321.75

Total amount payable   2,217.22

Deduct discount of 3% if paid within 14 days

* VAT is calculated as 17.5% x (£1,895.47 x 0.97), i.e. assuming that the settlement discount is taken.

Note that the trade discount is deducted on the face of the invoice whereas the only effect of the settlement discount is in the calculation of the VAT.

△ **ACTIVITY 4**   △ △ △ △

CREDIT NOTE

Credit note to:
K Phipps Builders
Hayward House
Manor Estate
Oldham
OL7 4HD

A.J. Broom & Company Limited
59 Parkway
Manchester
M2 6EG
Tel: 0161 560 3392
Fax: 0161 560 5322

Credit note no:	CN02543
Tax point:	25 August 20X3
VAT reg no:	625 9911 58
Returns inwards note no:	01532
Account no:	SL35

Code	Description	Quantity	VAT rate %	Unit price £	Amount exclusive of VAT £
159 S04	Insulation Brick	1	17.5	195.50	195.50

Trade discount 5%	195.50
	9.77
	185.73
VAT at 17.5%	32.50
Total amount of credit	218.23

△ **ACTIVITY 5**   △ △ △ △

A sequential code (the numbers run in sequential order).

Test your knowledge △ △ △

1 · Quantity and type of goods
  · Date of supply
  · Location of supply
  · Price and terms
  · Delivery address
  · Name and address of seller
  · Name and address of buyer
  · Sales order number
  · Authorisation

2 A settlement discount is a discount that is offered to a customer for payment of the invoice within a certain time period.

3 A trade discount is deducted from the list price of the goods on a sales invoice.

4 £268.45 x 17.5/100   =   £46.97   (remember to round down)

5 £138.65 x 17.5/117.5   =   £20.65

6
	£
23 x £18.60	427.80
Trade discount@ 15%	(64.17)
	363.63
VAT @ 17.5%	63.63
Invoice total	427.26

7
	£
14 x £23.50	329.00
VAT (17.5% x (£329 x 97%))	55.84
Invoice total	384.84

8 Errors and omissions excepted.

9 · When a customer has returned faulty or damaged goods
  · As a refund for short delivery
  · To settle a dispute with a customer

10 · Type of product
  · Type of sale
  · Customer account number

THE BANKING SYSTEM

INTRODUCTION

You will have to deal with a variety of different types of receipts of money and the documents involved in paying this money into the bank. You must also be aware of many different payment methods and be able to use the most appropriate in each circumstance. Therefore in this chapter we introduce you to the banking system and the types of receipts and payments that you may come across.

KNOWLEDGE & UNDERSTANDING

- Cheques, including crossings and endorsements (Element 1 and 2)
- The function, form and use of banking documentation (Element 1, 2 and 3)
- Automated receipts and payments (Element 1 and 2)
- Credit card procedure (Element 1 and 2)
- General bank services and operation of the bank clearing system (Element 3)

CONTENTS

1 Bank and customer relationship
2 Bank accounts
3 Banking procedures
4 The clearing system
5 Cheques
6 Cheque crossings
7 Transferring money by different methods
8 Credit cards and debit cards
9 Banking documentation

1 Bank and customer relationship

1.1 Introduction

The relationship between the bank and the customer can be described best as that of a debtor and creditor.

1.2 Debtor/creditor relationship

This is the basic bank/customer relationship. If the bank holds money belonging to the customer, the money has to be repaid at some time, and therefore from the bank's point of view, the customer is the **creditor** (i.e. the bank owes money). From the customer's point of view the bank is the debtor (i.e. the customer is owed money by the bank).

However, when the customer borrows money from the bank the relationship is reversed. For the bank the customer is the **debtor** and for the customer the bank is the **creditor**.

This is the case not only if a business has a loan from the bank but also if the business has an overdraft with a bank. In this situation the business owes the bank money.

1.3 Banking terminology

The usual meanings of debit and credit in double entry bookkeeping in the context of cash are:

· debit – money into the bank account;
· credit – money out of the bank account.

On a bank statement these meanings are reversed as the statement is prepared from the bank's point of view, that is:

Debit Increase in a debtor (e.g. increase in overdraft)
or Decrease in a creditor (e.g. decrease in cash balance)

Credit Decrease in a debtor (e.g. decrease in overdraft)
or Increase in creditor (e.g. increase in cash balance)

When a customer has money in the bank account this is described by the bank as a credit balance. If the customer has an overdraft then this is described as a debit balance.

1.4 Customer's duties

The law states that if the bank holds the customer's money, it is up to the customer to ask for the money back. This is unusual, because normally the onus is on the person who owes the money to repay it.

The customer must be careful when writing cheques so as not to mislead the bank or make forgery easy.

The customer's request for repayment must be in writing (e.g. a cheque).

△ **ACTIVITY 1**   △ △ △ △

(AAT CA J93)

A credit balance on a ledger account normally denotes a liability. In view of this, explain briefly why, when the company has funds in the bank, it should receive a statement showing a credit balance.

[Answer on p. 181]

1.5 Legal relationship between banker and customer

In law there is technically a contract between the banker and his customer. This means that not only does the customer have duties to perform but also the bank has certain rights and duties within the relationship.

The duties of the bank include:
· paying a customer's cheques when there are sufficient funds in the account;
· keeping the details of a customer's account secret;
· sending bank statements to customers;
· to follow the customer's instructions for payment such as a standing order (see later in the chapter);
· to accept cash and cheques paid in by the customer and to credit the customer's account
· to exercise proper skill and care.

The legal nature of the relationship means that if the bank fails in these duties and the customer suffers losses then the customer could sue the bank. For example if a bank failed to pay a properly completed cheque to a supplier and that supplier cuts off supplies, the bank's customer who wrote the cheque could sue the bank for any losses suffered.

2 Bank accounts

2.1 Introduction

There are three main types of bank account:
· current accounts;
· deposit or savings accounts;
· loan accounts.

2.2 Current accounts

The current account is a business's normal working account. Cash and cheques received from customers are paid into this account and the business will be issued with a cheque book so that expenses and suppliers can be paid by writing cheques.

Current accounts are also the most common form of account for personal customers. A personal customer will normally be issued with a cheque book, a cheque guarantee card (see later in the chapter) and a card for use in the automated cash machines.

Many current accounts now pay a low rate of interest on any credit balances.

2.3 Overdraft

Most banks, on request, will allow a business (or indeed a personal customer) an agreed level of overdraft. This means that on occasions if the current account does not have enough funds to cover cheques written the bank will still honour those cheques up to the overdraft limit. The bank will charge interest on any overdrawn balances and often an arrangement fee for the setting up of the overdraft facility.

2.4 Deposit accounts

Deposit accounts, or savings accounts, are held by many business and personal customers. A business can use a deposit account to house short-term surplus funds as the interest earned on deposit account balances is often considerably higher than that on current account balances. Money in deposit accounts can then be transferred to the current account when required but some types of account do require a period of notice before funds can be transferred or removed from the account.

2.5 Loan accounts

Although an overdraft on a current account can be a useful method of short term borrowing in order to fund the everyday expenses of a business, if larger funds are required for example for the purchase of plant and machinery in a business, then a separate loan should be taken out.

A business loan can be made to all types of business and will normally be secured. This means that the bank will have rights over assets of the business if the loan is not repaid or alternatively the personal guarantee of the owner of the business will be required.

For the purchase of property a commercial mortgage can be provided. This is normally for a period of 25 years and is secured on the property itself. Therefore if the mortgage is not repaid, the bank can sell the property in order to get its money back.

3 Banking procedures

3.1 Getting payment for the customer

When a customer pays a cheque into their bank account which has been received from another person, the customer is asking the branch to obtain payment from the other person's bank account and credit it to (i.e. pay it into) his or her bank account.

The bank has a duty to:
· credit the customer's account with the value of the cheques presented by the customer;
· collect the money from the third party;
· credit the money to the correct account.

3.2 Paying in cash and cheques

The individual who is paying in monies takes the cash, cheques and paying in book to the bank and hands them to the cashier behind the counter.

The cashier:
· agrees the items to be paid in against the information on the paying-in slip;
· checks the other details on the paying-in slip (e.g. date, payee);
· stamps both copies;
· removes the bank's copy, leaving the paying-in stub as the customer's record;
· returns the paying-in book.

Any cash paid in will be credited direct to the business's account when the branch records all the transactions for the day.

Cheques paid in are sorted and put through the clearing system.

4 The clearing system

4.1 Introduction

The major banks have developed a system known as the clearing system which is the method by which the banks exchange cheques.

Most of the UK high street banks are involved in this system.

4.2 How the clearing system works

The whole process of clearing cheques takes three working days.

Day 1

The branch of the bank (the collecting bank) will have received cheques paid-in by customers written by third parties who have their accounts at:
· other clearing banks;
· other branches of the same bank.

At the end of the day these cheques are:
· sorted by the bank;
· stamped with details of the branch/bank;
· processed through a machine which puts the amount payable onto the bottom of the cheque in code.

The cheques are then sent by courier to the bank's own clearing department.

Day 2

The bank's clearing department receives cheques from all its branches. It will now:
· sort the cheques by bank;
· take other banks' cheques to the Central Clearing House;
· send the cheques relating to its own branches to those branches without sending them to the clearing house (this is inter-branch clearing).

The central clearing house arranges for all the banks involved to attend to 'swap' cheques and to arrange for any differences in the values of cheques swapped to be paid on the following day.

The clearing departments of the banks then receive the cheques which have been written by their customers. Each department will:
· sort the cheques by branch using a machine which reads the code on each cheque;
· record the cheque information into the bank computer (to debit customers' accounts by the amounts paid on the cheques);
· send the paid cheques to the paying customers' branches.

Day 3

Each branch receives the cheques written by its own customers. The branch has to check that the cheque is valid and to return any cheques that cannot be paid.

Any cheques which cannot be paid are sent by first class post to the branch that collected them (shown by the stamp placed on the cheque on day 1).

4.3 Clearing debts

The clearing process results in banks owing money to each other.

Each clearing bank maintains an account with the Bank of England. These accounts are known as **operational balances.** These balances are used to settle the debts which arise between the banks in the course of clearing.

Cheques which are written by an account holder at the same branch do not leave the branch.

Cheques which are written by an account holder of a different branch of the same bank go from the bank's own clearing department to the other branch.

The operation of the clearing system means that when cheques are paid into a bank account it will take three working days before they are credited to the organisation's bank account.

△ ACTIVITY 2

(AAT CA J93)

During the day Barclays Bank accepted £10 million of Lloyds' cheques and Lloyds Bank accepted £12 million of Barclays' cheques. Both banks use the banker's clearing house where the cheques are exchanged.

(a)   What settlement should now take place between the two banks?

(b)   How does the settlement take place?

[Answer on p. 181]

△ ACTIVITY 3

David Cater has received a cheque for £1,000 from MEL Motor Factors Limited and has paid it into his account at the Mid-West Bank. When he asks if he can draw out some cash against the cheque, he is told by the cashier that he will have to wait four days from the date that the cheque was paid in.

Explain briefly why the bank might ask David to wait before he can draw out some or all of the £1,000.

[Answer on p. 181]

---

5   Cheques

□ DEFINITION □□□□

Cheque – An unconditional order in writing signed by the drawer, requiring a bank to pay on demand a sum certain in money to a named person or to the bearer.

5.1 Detailed meaning of the definition

1	**Unconditional**	Payment cannot depend upon the outcome of events, e.g. 'pay Mr Brown £75 provided my salary cheque has been paid into my account'.
2	**Writing**	A cheque must be in writing. Pen, biro, print or pencil can be used. Details in pencil can, however, be changed easily, and should be avoided. Most banks insist their pre-printed cheques be completed in ink.
3	**Signed**	A cheque must be signed by the drawer, that is the person wanting to pay the money who draws up the cheque.
4	**On demand**	It is expected that the cheque will be paid as soon as it is presented to the bank.
5	**A sum certain**	The amount must be definite, in both words and figures.
6	**Named person or bearer**	The cheque must be payable to a named person or to the bearer, i.e. whoever has the cheque in his or her possession. A cheque made out to 'cash' will be treated as payable to bearer.

5.2 Parties to a cheque

The parties involved in a cheque are:

- the drawer – the person writing the cheque.
- the payee – the person the cheque is to be paid to.
- the drawee – the bank upon whom the cheque is drawn, i.e. the bank who has issued the cheque book.

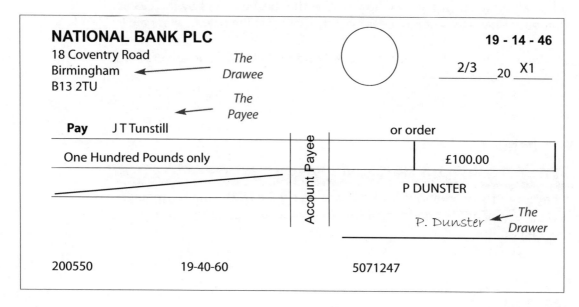

△ **ACTIVITY 4** △ △ △ △

(AAT CA D94)

The cheque shown below has been issued by Chang Fashions Limited.

Give the name of:

(a)   the drawer;

(b)   the drawee;

(c)   the payee.

ROYAL BANK PLC   19 - 40 - 60

61 Euston Road   25/5   20 X1
London
W12 6TH

Pay   K Mitchell   or order

One Hundred and Fifty Pounds only   £150.00

                                    Chang Fashions Limited

                                        Mary Chang

200550   19-40-60   5071247

[Answer on p. 181]

5.3 Checking cheques – the collecting bank

When the bank accepts a cheque which has been paid in by a customer, the bank must carefully review that cheque. Each item that the bank will check will be considered in turn.

5.4 Out of date cheque

A cheque can become out of date as it is only valid for six months from the date of issue. For example, a cheque dated 1 August 20X0 would be out of date if not paid into a bank account until 8 February 20X1.

5.5 Post-dated cheque

A cheque which is dated later than the day on which it is written cannot be paid in until that later date.

For example, a cheque written on 5 May 20X1 but dated 10 May 20X1 could not be paid into a bank account before 10 May 20X1.

5.6 Undated cheque

If a cheque is presented to the payee undated the payee can insert a date. The bank's cashier would normally ask the payee to do this.

If any undated cheques are accidentally accepted by the bank, the bank's date stamp can be used to insert it.

Once a date is entered on a cheque it cannot, however, be altered by the payee.

5.7 Payee's name

The payee's name should be the same as the one shown on the account that the cheque is being paid into.

If the name is different, then an endorsement is required (see below). If a cheque is presented with no payee's name then it cannot be accepted by the bank's cashier.

5.8 Words and figures

Both words and figures should be completed and should agree.
If they disagree the cheque should be returned by the bank to the drawer for amendment or for a new cheque to be issued.

A returned cheque will often be marked R/D or 'Return to drawer'.

5.9 Signature

The cheque must be signed by the drawer.

5.10   Crossings

If the cheque has a crossing (two parallel lines on the face of the cheque), it must be paid into a bank account. It cannot be exchanged for cash over the counter. Pre-printed cheques carry crossings (see later in the chapter).

The bank must carry out these checks when cheques are paid into a bank account. Therefore it is important that these details are checked by the appropriate person in the organisation before the cheques are paid in to the bank.

5.11   Stopped cheques

A customer has the right to stop a cheque right up until the banker pays it. The customer must write to the bank and give clear details of the payee's name, the cheque's number and the amount payable.

5.12 The sort code

The sort code is 6 numbers, normally presented in three pairs, e.g. 19-40-60

This is a number that is unique to each branch of every bank. It is printed on every cheque that the particular branch issues and can be read by a computer.

Its purpose is the enable the computer to recognise the branch on which the cheque is drawn (the drawee) so that the clearing process can allocate that cheque to the correct branch.

△ **ACTIVITY 5**   △△△△

(AAT CA J93)

A cheque for £374 has been accepted by one of the cashiers in payment for a washing machine. As you record the cheque, you notice that it has been dated 1 June 20X2. Today's date is 1 June 20X3.

(a)   Will payment of the cheque by the drawer's bank be affected by the incorrect date?

(b)   Having noticed the error, is it acceptable for you to alter the cheque to the correct date?

[Answer on p. 181]

---

6   Cheque crossings

6.1 Introduction

Given below is a typical example of a pre-printed cheque issued by a bank.

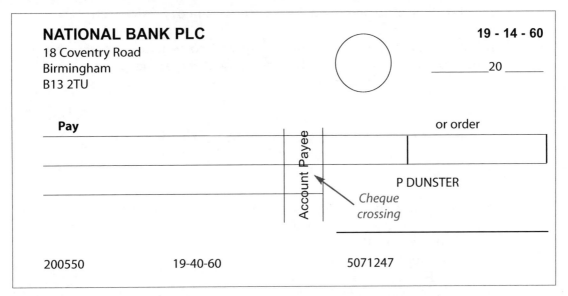

The words in the crossing will normally be in the short form 'A/c payee'.

You will see that it names:

(a)   the drawee: the bank paying the cheque, National Bank plc;

(b)   the drawer of the cheque: the account holder who is making the payment, P Dunster.

You will also see that the cheque has two vertical parallel lines with the words 'Account payee' printed in between them. This is known as an account payee or A/c payee crossing.

> **□ DEFINITION**   □□□□
>
> A cheque crossing is an instruction to the bank, the drawee, as to how to pay the cheque.

6.2 Account payee crossing

The account payee crossing means that this cheque can only be paid into the bank account of the person named on the cheque as the payee.

Legally this crossing must now always be printed on cheques therefore this is the type of cheque crossing that you are likely to come across in practice.

6.3 Cheque endorsements

In the past, before all cheques were crossed with the words 'A/c payee' it was possible to endorse a cheque by the payee signing the reverse of the cheque with an instruction to pay a different person. Such a cheque could then be paid into the bank account of that different person.

In practice we have already seen that all pre-printed bank cheques have an account payee crossing. As this means that the cheque can only be paid into the payee's bank account then these cheques cannot be endorsed.

It is most unlikely that in an assessment you will come across any other form of cheque crossing, and we do not therefore consider these other possible crossings or their endorsements further.

7   Transferring money by different methods

7.1 Introduction

A bank customer can transfer money from his account to another person's account by two other methods which do not involve the cheque clearing system or writing cheques. These are:

·   standing orders;

·   direct debits.

7.2 Standing order

This is an instruction to a customer's bank to make regular payments (usually fixed amounts).

To arrange a standing order all the customer needs to do is sign a **standing order mandate** which authorises the bank to make the payments.

Standing orders are ideal for paying regular monthly bills such as insurance premiums. They can also be used to transfer money between a customer's own different accounts, e.g. transferring surplus money each month from a current account into a deposit account where it will earn interest.

7.3 Standing order mandate

To	**FINANCIAL BANK PLC**	

_____ Branch	STANDING ORDER MANDATE

	Bank	Branch title (not address)	Sort code number
Please pay			
	Beneficiary's name		Account number
Credit			
	Amount in figures	Amount in words	
the sum of	£		
commencing	Date of first payment		Due date & frequency
	now/*	and thereafter every	
	Date and amount of last payment		
until		£	* until you receive further notice from me/us in writing
quoting the reference			and debit my/our account accordingly

Please cancel any previous standing order or direct debit in favour of the named beneficiary above.

Special instructions

Account to be debited	Account number

Signature (s)

_____   Date _____

_____

*Delete if not applicable

7.4 Direct debit

This is an instruction to a customer's bank to allow a third party to debit (ie collect money from) the customer's account at regular intervals.

Direct debits are better than standing orders when either:
·   the amount is uncertain; or
·   the date of payment is uncertain.

Direct debits are useful for paying items such as membership subscriptions which increase from year to year or monthly bills which alter in amount each month such as credit card bills.
Both direct debits and standing orders continue to be valid until the customer cancels or changes them.

> △ **ACTIVITY 6**   △△△△
>
> **(AAT CA D93)**
> Music World Limited needs to make regular monthly payments to Firmcare Finance Limited. The amount of the payment varies from month to month. Which service provided by the banks would appear to be the most appropriate?
>
> [Answer on p. 181]

7.5 Bank giro credit

An alternative method of transferring money into someone else's bank account is to use a bank giro credit (or credit transfer).

A **bank giro credit** is a method of transferring money into someone else's bank account in any bank in the country.

The system is commonly used to pay bills such as electricity, gas, credit cards, telephone.

Many businesses issue the credit transfer slip as part of their bill, or in a book. These payments are then cleared through a clearing system which is similar to the cheque clearing system.

7.6 Electronic clearing

To try to reduce the number of pieces of paper used to clear payments using the cheque clearing and giro clearing systems, a further service was introduced in 1968.

This service is known as BACS (Bankers Automated Clearing System) and is part of the clearing system.

BACS – A method of clearing payments in which transactions are recorded on magnetic tape or disks (rather than on paper). Transactions are then processed at the BACS computer centre instead of through the clearing house.

BACS can be used by banks or by companies which have been allowed to do so by the banks.

7.7 Use of BACS

BACS is used for:
- standing order payments;
- direct debits;
- salary payments;
- bank giro credits.

7.8 Telegraphic transfer

Telegraphic transfer or mail transfer may be used for large transactions that need to be processed quickly. These are electronic funds transfers between bank accounts and can be made to foreign bank accounts as well as to accounts within the UK.

To arrange an electronic funds transfer, a business must write to its bank requesting that the payment be made and enclosing details of the bank account to which the payment must be made.

7.9 CHAPS

A further service is also available to customers wishing to transfer large sums of money. This is CHAPS (Clearing House Automated Payments System).

CHAPS – Electronic clearing system for large sums. Payments are credited to the payee on the same day as instructions are received.

8 Credit cards and debit cards

8.1 Credit cards

Credit cards are issued by the credit card companies to allow customers to make purchases (without using cash or cheques) at certain shops, hotels, web-sites, etc.

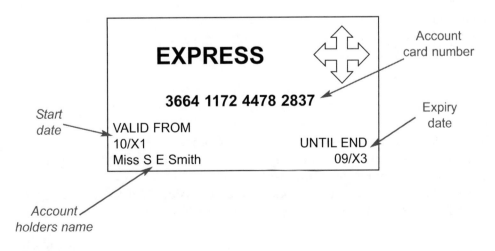

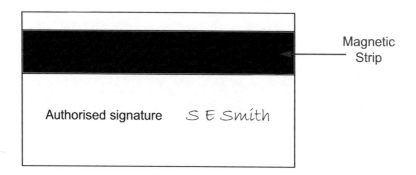

An individual opens an account with one of the credit card companies, filling in and posting off an application form. If accepted, the individual will receive a credit card.

This credit card can then be used in places which accept that particular card (they normally display a sign). The payment is recorded on a credit card sales voucher.

8.2 Payment of the credit card balance

Once a month, the credit cardholder receives a statement detailing how much he has 'spent' which is the amount he owes the credit card company.

The cardholder has a choice of:
· paying a minimum balance (set by the credit card company dependent upon the amount owed);
· paying off more than the minimum but less than the total balance outstanding;
· paying off the total balance outstanding.

If the cardholder does not pay off the total balance within 25 days of receiving the statement, he will have to pay interest on the unpaid amount.

8.3 Accepting credit cards

Businesses which make direct sales to the public are generally known as retailers. If a retailer is to be able to accept payment by credit cards, he or she must have the agreement of the credit card company to be allowed to accept payment by that particular credit card.

In return for this service the credit card company will normally charge a commission on each payment using that card.

To complete a sale the retailer needs the following.
· **Imprinter** – A machine which transfers the cardholder's and the retailer's details onto a credit card voucher.
· **Credit card sales voucher** – Voucher recording details of retailer, customer and sale. Normally three or four copies. At least one copy for each of

customer, retailer and bank/credit card company. Vouchers have a standard format with variations between credit card companies.

· **Cardholder's card.**
· **A pen** – To write in the details and for the cardholder to sign their signature.

3664 1172 4478 2837								EXPRESS			10/X1 09/X3	C
Miss S. E. Smith	DAY		MONTH		YEAR		DEPT	SALES NO	INITIALS			A
048 9133	0	8	0	8	X	2	020	115	ANO			R
CHESTERS	DESCRIPTION							AMOUNT				D
BOLTON												H
							Books	26	95			O
Cardholder's signature							Book Token	10	00			L
												D
S. E. Smith	AUTHORISATION CODE						TOTAL	POUNDS	PENCE			E
Cardholder's Declaration: I promise to pay the total amount shown as payable together with any charges thereon subject in the rules of issue.							3	6 :	9 5			R
	SALES VOUCHER											C
	Please keep this copy for your records											O
												P Y

8.4 Electronic acceptance of credit cards

Many retail organisations no longer use the mechanical imprinter in order to accept credit card payments. Instead they are electronically connected to the credit card companies and the credit card is swiped through a machine which then sends the details of the card and the payment to the credit card company. The payment is automatically authorised by the credit card company and at the end of the day the funds are automatically paid into the organisation's bank account. Even more recently the use of PIN numbers for credit card payments has been introduced. Here the customer is asked to key in their PIN number to the credit card machine and, if it is correct, then the payment is accepted by the credit card company.

8.5 Debit cards

In recent years the popularity of debit cards has increased dramatically. They are a plastic card which looks very similar to a credit card but unlike a credit card no credit is given to the cardholder.

A debit card is a method of making payment direct from a bank account without having to write out a cheque. Debit cards are issued by the main banks.

When a debit card is used to make a payment the cardholder's bank account is automatically debited with the amount of the payment. The payment then appears on the customer's bank statement along with cheque payments, standing orders and direct debits.

9   Banking documentation

9.1 Bank statement

A bank statement is a statement showing how money has gone into or left a bank account, and the amount of money held in that account at a certain date. There is a standard format with a few variations between banks.

FINANCIAL BANK plc   CONFIDENTIAL

fb

You can bank on us!

10 Yorkshire Street   Account   CURRENT   Sheet No.   103
Headingley   MISS ELIZABETH DERBY   *Name of account*
Leeds LS1 1QT   *Name and*   *holder*
Telephone: 0113 633061   *address of bank*

Statement date   31 July 20X5   Account Number   34786695

Date	Details		Withdrawals (£)	Deposits (£)	Balance (£)
28 June	*Balance from sheet no.* **102**				2670.91
1 July	000354		7.95		
	Security insurance	DD	10.15		
	Leeds Brigate	AC	50.00		
	NWWA	DD	13.03		2589.78
2 July	Supersaver	CP	12.63		2577.15
5 July	000349		40.00		2537.15
8 July	000348		18.80		2518.35
11 July	Sure Building Society	DD	327.74		
	000346		29.80		
	Deposit Account	TR	250.00		1910.81
14 July	English Gas	SO	12.50		1898.31
17 July	000355		30.95		1867.36
20 July	English Electricity	SO	5.00		1862.36
22 July	000356		50.00		1812.36
25 July	000351		11.29		1801.07
29 July	000352		5.29		
	000350		50.00		
	PAYROLL			340.99	2086.77
30 July	000358		26.51		
	Balance to Sheet no. **104**				2060.26

SO	Standing order	DD	Direct debit	CP	Card purchase
AC	Automated cash	OD	Overdrawn	TR	Transfer

closing balance

9.2 Paying money into the bank

Money may be paid into the bank account free of charge in any branch of that particular bank. Other banks may charge a small fee.

The money paid in can be:
· cash;
· cheques;
· postal orders.

The amounts to be paid in must be summarised on a paying-in slip.

9.3 Paying-in slip

A paying-in slip is a summary of details of money paid into a bank account. There is a standard format with a few variations between banks.

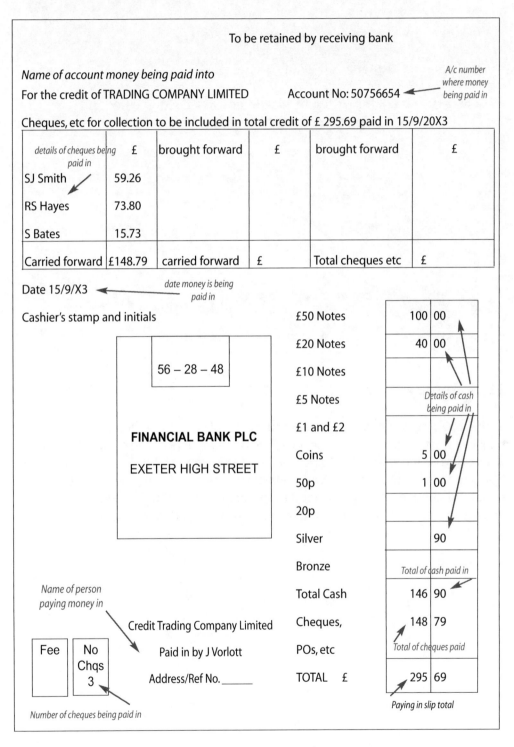

The details of filling in a paying-in slip are covered in more detail in a later chapter.

10 Test your knowledge

1   If a cheque is paid into your bank account on Wednesday when will it normally clear?

2   Who are the three parties to a cheque?

3   When does a cheque become out of date?

4   Today's date is 3 January 20X3 and you receive a cheque dated 11 January 20X3. What type of cheque is this?

5   What is the significance of an account payee crossing on a cheque?

6   What is a standing order?

7   What is the difference between a standing order and a direct debit?

8   What is the BACS system?

9   What is the CHAPS system of payment for?

[Answers on p. 181]

11 Summary

In this chapter you have been introduced to some of the details of the UK banking system. In particular you need to be aware of how the clearing system works, of the different methods of payment through the banking system and how credit and debit cards work. Of particular importance are the details regarding cheques, as you will need to understand what makes a valid cheque and be able to deal with a cheque that you receive that is not valid.

Answers to chapter activities & 'test your knowledge' questions

△ **ACTIVITY 1** △△△△

The funds held are owed by the bank to the company. From the bank's point of view they are therefore a liability, i.e. owed back to the company.

△ **ACTIVITY 2** △△△△

(a)   Barclays Bank pays Lloyds Bank the sum of £2m.
(b)   Adjustment of the banks' balances held at the Bank of England.

△ **ACTIVITY 3** △△△△

The cheque must pass through the clearing system before the Mid-West Bank knows whether or not it has been paid. In the meantime, the bank may be reluctant to allow David to draw out cash against uncleared funds.

△ **ACTIVITY 4** △△△△

(a)   Mary Chang, on behalf of Chang Fashions Limited
(b)   Royal Bank plc
(c)   K Mitchell

△ **ACTIVITY 5** △△△△

(a)   Yes. The cheque is out of date and must be re-issued by the drawer.
(b)   No.

△ **ACTIVITY 6** △△△△

Direct debit. Standing order is not appropriate since the amount of the payment varies from month to month.

Test your knowledge ▷ ▷ ▷

1   Friday

2   The drawer – the person who wrote the cheque
    The payee – the person to whom the cheque is made payable
    The drawee – the bank upon which the cheque is drawn

3   Six months after the date on the cheque.

4   A post-dated cheque.

5   Such a cheque can only be paid into the bank account of the payee

6   An instruction to a customer's bank to pay a third party a fixed amount on a regular date.

7   A direct debit is an instruction to the bank to allow a third party to take a sum from the customer's account (both the date and amount can vary) whereas a standing order is an instruction for the customer's bank to pay a third party a certain amount on a certain date.

8   A system for making payments which are on magnetic tape or disk rather than paper.

9   An electronic clearing system for large sums.

CHECKING RECEIPTS

INTRODUCTION

This chapter deals with the receipt of monies in various forms and, in particular, the checking, accounting for and paying in of such receipts.

KNOWLEDGE & UNDERSTANDING

- Cheques, including crossings and endorsements (Elements 1 and 2)
- Credit card procedures (Elements 1 and 2)

CONTENTS

1 Receiving money in a retail business
2 Receiving monies for credit sales
3 Settlement discounts

PERFORMANCE CRITERIA

- Check receipts against records (Element 30.1)
- Deal with discrepancies (Element 30.1)

KAPLAN PUBLISHING

1 Receiving money in a retail business

1.1 Introduction

Different types of business will receive money in different forms. For example a retail organisation will receive cash, cheques, credit card and debit card payments through the till.

In contrast a totally credit sales based organisation will rarely receive cash and credit/debit card payments but will receive cheques through the post to pay sales invoices which have been sent to customers.

In this section we will start with a look at the checks that should be carried out by a retailer receiving various types of payment through the till.

1.2 Receiving cash

If cash payments are made for goods then the till operator should input the correct price for the goods, check the amount of money offered by the customer, enter this amount in the till or cash register, put the money into the till and pay out to the customer the correct change which will have been calculated by the till.

1.3 Accepting cheques

If a cheque is accepted as payment from an individual rather than a business, then it must be accompanied by a cheque guarantee card.

If a cheque is accepted with a valid cheque guarantee card, this means that the bank will pay the cheque; the cheque is guaranteed.

1.4 Cheque guarantee card

- For a £100 cheque guarantee card, this card guarantees that a cheque for up to £100 will be paid by the bank, regardless of the amount of money in that account.
- Only one £100 cheque for each transaction is allowed.
- The cheque must not exceed £100, or the bank can refuse to pay anything.
- Some cards guarantee cheques for higher amounts than £100.
- The cheque guarantee card is usually the same card as the individual's debit card.

1.5 Checks to carry out on a cheque guarantee card

Look at the following cheque which is supported by a cheque guarantee card, and think of the checks that must be carried out before the cheque is accepted.

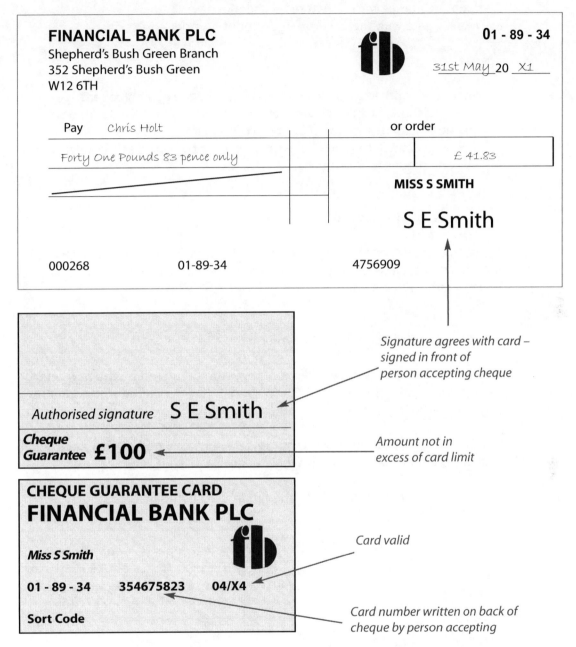

FINANCIAL BANK PLC
Shepherd's Bush Green Branch
352 Shepherd's Bush Green
W12 6TH

01 - 89 - 34

31st May 20 X1

Pay   Chris Holt   or order

Forty One Pounds 83 pence only   £ 41.83

MISS S SMITH

S E Smith

000268   01-89-34   4756909

Signature agrees with card – signed in front of person accepting cheque

Authorised signature S E Smith

Cheque Guarantee £100

Amount not in excess of card limit

CHEQUE GUARANTEE CARD
FINANCIAL BANK PLC

Miss S Smith

01 - 89 - 34   354675823   04/X4

Sort Code

Card valid

Card number written on back of cheque by person accepting

Note: Cheques from companies cannot be guaranteed by a cheque guarantee card.

If the retailer is suspicious in any way he should contact the bank which has issued the card.

1.6 Summary of checks

Card
- Card is valid (start and expiry date)
- Signature agrees with signature on cheque
- Details agree with the cheque (e.g. account number, sort code)

Cheque
- Correct date
- Amount does not exceed the amount on the cheque guarantee card
- Amount is the same in both words and figures
- Cheque signed in presence of person accepting it
- Cheque guarantee card number written on back by person accepting it
- Only one cheque for the purchase

1.7 Payment by credit card

A customer may choose to pay using a credit card. Most retailers today will be linked to the credit card company by computer rather than needing to manually issue a credit card voucher.

1.8 Computerised credit card payments

Many retail businesses have taken the opportunity offered by the new information technology system EFTPOS to simplify the procedure for accepting payment by credit card.

The retailer installs a terminal which is generally attached to the electronic cash register or is part of the cash register itself.

The terminal is linked directly to the credit card company's computer at its operations centre by telephone line.

The exact format of the credit card sales voucher depends upon the equipment used, but it will normally have only two copies. The cardholder signs at least one of the copies which is returned to the retailer for the retailer's records. The other copy is for the cardholder's records. In recent months even the customer's signature is no longer needed as many retailers have introduced the PIN system whereby the customer simply enters their PIN number into the credit card machine rather than having to sign the credit card voucher.

```
1900 2359
CASA ITALIA PIZZERIA
05/07/X1  21:58
Express: 2554006633579400


TOTAL   £15.80


Auth code: 54662
THANK YOU
SIGN BELOW
Please debit my account as shown


_____
```

No banking of the vouchers need be done by the retailer because all transactions are immediately transferred electronically by the terminal via the telephone line.

The terminal automatically performs any authorisation procedures by contacting the computer at the operation centre.

1.9 What is EFTPOS?

Electronic Funds Transfer at Point of Sale (EFTPOS) is a system which uses advanced information technology.

EFTPOS – A national scheme which links terminals in shops and supermarkets with the processing department of banks, building societies and credit card companies.

The system is very flexible because it allows almost any type of credit card or debit card to be accepted by one system.

○ EXAMPLE   ○○○○

- Janet is a 27-year-old nurse from South Wales. She has gone into a petrol filling station on the M3 and filled her car with petrol.
- She wishes to pay by credit card. The filling station is linked up to the EFTPOS system.
- Janet's credit card is a Visa card. The filling station's bank is Lloyds TSB Bank in Gravesend, Kent.

Explain the sequence of transactions.

Solution

- Janet produces her card at the cash desk (point of sale).
- The sales assistant swipes or puts the card into a card reader on a terminal attached to the cash register.
- The sales assistant enters the amount of the purchase into the cash register.
- The information on the magnetic strip on the card is read by the retailer's terminal. A coded message (scrambled for security) is sent by telephone line to the central EFTPOS processing centre. This includes details of the amount. The card details are recorded and the request is sent to Visa for authorisation by telephone line.
- The Visa processing computer checks certain details.
- The customer is asked to enter her PIN number followed by enter which is validated by the credit card company.
- In this case, the Visa processing computer authorises the purchase and updates its records. It notifies the central EFTPOS processing centre of the authorisation.

- The central EFTPOS processing centre transmits the authorisation to the retailer's terminal.
- A two-part credit card sales voucher is printed out and one copy given to Janet.
- The cash register also prints a receipt.
- After authorisation, the central EFTPOS processing centre sends details of the purchase to Lloyds Bank where the money is transferred into the filling station's account.
- The sales assistant gives Janet her card, her copy of the credit card sales voucher and her receipt.

This has all taken a matter of minutes.

1.10 Floor limits

Often credit card companies will set a maximum floor limit on amounts that can be accepted on a credit card for payment e.g. no purchases over £200. However if a customer wishes to use a card for a higher value purchase the company can be contacted for authorisation.

1.11 Checks to be made on the credit card

When accepting payment by credit card, the retailer must check that the card has not reached its expiry date and that the signature on the voucher matches that on the card, or that the PIN number has been accepted. If authorisation is not given for a transaction by the credit card company then the credit card should not be accepted as this will mean that the credit limit has been exceeded or else that the card has been notified as having been stolen.

> **▷ ACTIVITY 1** ▷ ▷ ▷ ▷

(AAT CA D94)

A customer wishes to purchase £320 of clothes from a shop using a credit card for payment. The floor limit set by the credit card company is £100.

(a) Is it possible that the transaction can still go ahead despite the floor limit?

(b) Briefly explain the reason for your answer.

[Answer on p. 205]

Debit cards were introduced in the previous chapter.

- **Debit cards** – The debit card is a method of making payments direct from a bank account without having to write a cheque or produce a cheque guarantee card.

The payments are made by the customer using the EFTPOS technology described above. Payments made appear on the customer's bank statement alongside any other payments made by cheque, standing order, direct debit, etc.

If the payment is not authorised by the bank then the debit card should not be accepted for payment as this may mean that the customer does not have enough funds in their account.

Whatever method is used to pay for retail sales it is vital that the person receiving the payment checks all cheques, guarantee cards and credit/debit cards thoroughly to ensure they are valid. Otherwise the business may not receive payment for the goods sold.

2 Receiving monies for credit sales

2.1 Introduction

When a business makes credit sales then it normally receives money from debtors in the post. This will normally be in the form of cheques and it is important that there is strict control of these cheques.

2.2 Remittance lists

All cash received should be listed on a **remittance list** (sometimes known as a **cheques received list**). The list should give details of:
· the customer;
· the invoice numbers to which the payment relates (if known);
· the amount paid; and
· any discount allowed (see later in this chapter).

The list should be totalled and signed.

2.3 Using remittance advices

When a business issues an invoice to a customer, the invoice will often have a detachable slip. This slip is called a **remittance advice**.

This **remittance advice** is a slip returned by the customer when paying an invoice so as to identify what the payment is for. This makes it much easier for the business receiving the cheque to know which outstanding invoices are actually being paid by this cheque.

REMITTANCE ADVICE

*Name and address of business
the cheque is being sent to*

To:

A. J. Broom & Company Limited
59 Parkway
Manchester
M2 6EG

*Name and address of
business sending cheque*

Company name:	Trail Blazers
Address:	Mount House
	West Street
	Manchester
	M4 7FL

*VAT registration
number of business
sending cheque*

Tel:	0161 484 6490
Fax:	0161 484 6491
VAT Reg no:	32141108
Date:	15 Sept X3

Date	Your ref	Amount £	Discount taken £	Paid £
15 Aug X3	68204	618.40	30.92	587.48
20 Aug X3	68210	426.94	21.34	405.60

*Invoice amounts
being paid*

*Cheque
total*

Total paid

£ 993.08

*Cheque
number*

Cheque no   041261

When receiving cheques from a customer it is vital to ensure that the correct amount has been paid. This can be done by agreeing the amount of the cheque to the details on the remittance advice and to the invoices themselves.

▷ ACTIVITY 2   ▷ ▷ ▷ ▷

(AAT CA D94)

A remittance advice is a document sent by a supplier to a customer to advise the customer that goods ordered have been sent off to the customer.
True/False

[Answer on p. 205]

This morning the following cheques and supporting remittance advices were received in the post by your organisation, A. J. Broom & Company Ltd.

You are required to check the remittance advice and cheque amounts to the invoices given to ensure that the correct amount has been received.

NATIONAL BANK PLC　　　　　　　　　　　　　**19-40-60**

18 Coventry Road
Birmingham
B13 2TU

12 Sept 20 X3

Pay　A. J. Broom & Company　　　　　　　or order

Account payee

Two Thousand two hundred and

£2,204.46

four pounds and 46 pence

F Lloyd

LLOYD CONSTRUCTION

200550　　　　19-14-60　　　　50731247

WESTERN BANK　　　　　　　　　　　　　　**20-16-80**

21 High Street
Bristol
BS1 4TZ

14 Sept 20 X3

Pay　A. J. Broom & Company　　　　　　　or order

Account payee

One thousand nune hundred and

£1,967.19

sixty seven pounds and 19 pence

P Smithson

PATRICK CARPENTERS

046178　　　　20-16-80　　　　41643121

CENTRAL BANK
52 Warwick Road
Birmingham
B13 4XT

40-18-30

15 Sept 20 X3

Pay	A. J. Broom & Company			or order
One thousand two hundred and				£1,228.74
twenty eight pounds and 74 pence				

Account payee

J P Roberts

ROBERTS CONSTRUCTION

020106   40-18-30   31164992

REMITTANCE ADVICE

To:

A. J. Broom & Company Limited
59 Parkway
Manchester
M2 6EG

Company name: Lloyd Construction
Address: Broom Way
Keswick

Tel: 0461 238 9191
Fax: 0461 238 9186
VAT Reg no: 431116208
Date: 12 Sept 20X3

Date	Your ref	Amount £	Discount taken £	Paid £
23 Aug	68226	1,025.78	–	1,025.78
30 Aug	68235	1,178.68	–	1,178.68

Total paid £ 2,204.46

Cheque no 200550

REMITTANCE ADVICE

To:	Company name:	Patrick Carpenters
A. J. Broom & Company Limited 59 Parkway Manchester M2 6EG	Address: Tel: Fax: VAT Reg no: Date:	Simba Industrial Estate Leeds 0714 304 2990 0714 304 2963 318 4861 27 14 Sept 20X3

Date	Your ref	Amount £	Discount taken £	Paid £
23 Aug	68229	1,614.69	–	1,614.69
23 Aug	3217	(352.50)	–	(352.50)
4 Sept	68237	705.00	–	705.00

Total paid   £ 1,967.19

Cheque no   046178

REMITTANCE ADVICE

To:	Company name:	Roberts Construction
A. J. Broom & Company Limited 59 Parkway Manchester M2 6EG	Address: Tel: Fax: VAT Reg no: Date:	Chillian Park Oldham 0201 632 497 0201 632 498 331 4986 91 15 Sept 20X3

Date	Your ref	Amount £	Discount taken £	Paid £
23 Aug	68230	1,288.74	–	1,288.74

Total paid   £ 1,288.74

Cheque no   020106

Invoice   68226

A.J. Broom & Company Limited

59 Parkway
Manchester
M2 6EG
Tel: 0161 560 3392
Fax: 0161 560 5322

**Lloyd Construction
Broom way
Keswick**

Tax Point: 23 August 20X3
VAT reg no: 452 4585 48

Code	Supply	Description	Quantity	VAT rate %	Unit price £	Amount exclusive of VAT £
950 BB3	Sale	Cotswold Bricks	3	17.50	300.00	900.00
Trade discount 3%						27.00
						873.00
VAT at 17.5%						152.78
Total amount payable						**1,025.78**

Invoice 68235

A.J. Broom & Company Limited

59 Parkway
Manchester
M2 6EG
Tel: 0161 560 3392
Fax: 0161 560 5322

**Lloyd Construction
Broom way
Keswick**

Tax Point: 30 August 20X3
VAT reg no: 452 4585 48

Code	Supply	Description	Quantity	VAT rate %	Unit price £	Amount exclusive of VAT £
159 504	Sale	Roof tiles – red	5	17.50	195.50	977.50
874 KL5	Sale	Brick tiles	1	17.50	56.65	56.65
						1,034.15
Trade discount 3%						31.02
						1,003.13
VAT at 17.5%						175.55
Total amount payable						**1,178.68**

Invoice   68229

A.J. Broom & Company Limited

Patrick Carpenters
Simba Industrial
Estate
Leeds

59 Parkway
Manchester
M2 6EG
Tel: 0161 560 3392
Fax: 0161 560 5322
Tax Point: 23 August 20X3
VAT reg no: 452 4585 48

Code	Supply	Description	Quantity	VAT rate %	Unit price £	Amount exclusive of VAT £
336 BTB	Sale	Roof tiles – black	10	17.50	123.00	1,230.00
667 LL5	Sale	Softwood plank – 20cm	14	17.50	10.30	144.20

| | | | | | | 1,374.20 |
| VAT at 17.5% | | | | | | 240.49 |

| Total amount payable | | | | | | **1,614.69** |

Invoice   68237

A.J. Broom & Company Limited

Patrick Carpenters
Simba Industrial
Estate
Leeds

59 Parkway
Manchester
M2 6EG
Tel: 0161 560 3392
Fax: 0161 560 5322
Tax Point: 4 September 20X3
VAT reg no: 452 4585 48

Code	Supply	Description	Quantity	VAT rate %	Unit price £	Amount exclusive of VAT £
630 CC4	Sale	Oak veneer in panels	3	17.50	200.00	600.00

| VAT at 17.5% | | | | | | 105.00 |

| Total amount payable | | | | | | **705.00** |

Credit note   3217

A.J. Broom & Company Limited

**Patrick Carpenters
Simba Industrial
Estate
Leeds**

59 Parkway
Manchester
M2 6EG
Tel: 0161 560 3392
Fax: 0161 560 5322
Tax Point: 23Augusr 20X3
VAT reg no: 452 4585 48

Code	Supply	Description	Quantity	VAT rate %	Unit price £	Amount exclusive of VAT £
950 BB3	Return	Cotswold Bricks	1	17.50	300.00	300.00
VAT at 17.5%						52.50

Total amount credited   **352.50**

Invoice   68230

A.J. Broom & Company Limited

**Roberts Construction
Chillian Park
Oldham**

59 Parkway
Manchester
M2 6EG
Tel: 0161 560 3392
Fax: 0161 560 5322
Tax Point: 23Augusr 20X3
VAT reg no: 452 4585 48

Code	Supply	Description	Quantity	VAT rate %	Unit price £	Amount exclusive of VAT £
160 TT7	Sale	Insulation	5	17.50	95.50	477.50
632 BS4	Sale	Brick tiles	20	17.50	33.25	665.00
						1,142.50
Trade discount 4%						45.70
						1,096.80
VAT at 17.5%						191.94
Total amount payable						**1,288.74**

Solution

From Lloyd Construction

	£
Invoice number 68226	1,025.78
Invoice number 68235	1,178.68
	2,204.46

This agrees with the cheque.

From Patrick Carpenters

	£
Invoice number 68229	1,614.69
Invoice number 68237	705.00
Credit note 3217	(352.50)
	1,967.19

This agrees with the cheque.

From Roberts Construction

Invoice number 68230	£1,288.74

This does not agree with the cheque as the cheque is made out for £1,228.74. This discrepancy should be brought to the attention of the manager responsible for credit control at Roberts Construction and a polite letter should be written to the customer explaining the error that has been made. Request can be made for payment but if this is a regular customer then the additional amount may simply be added to the next cheque that Roberts Construction sends.

2.4 Cheque received with no accompanying remittance advice

If a cheque arrives in the post from a customer with no remittance advice or other confirmation of which invoices are being paid then it will be necessary to examine the details of this customer's transactions in the subsidiary ledger.

The name of the customer should be fairly obvious from the name of the payer on the cheque – this will be printed by the bank as well as signed by the customer. The individual account for this debtor must then be extracted from the subsidiary ledger in an attempt to match the payment received to invoices and credit notes.

O EXAMPLE

A cheque has been received in the post this morning from A J Holland, a credit customer, for £878.00 but it is not supported by any other documentation.

The individual debtor account for A J Holland has been found in the subsidiary ledger.

A J Holland

	£		£
13/05/X2 Invoice 2256	336.67	20/05/X2 Credit 249	54.09
18/05/X2 Invoice 2271	846.23		
20/05/X2 Invoice 2280	447.69		
25/05/X2 Invoice 2288	147.73		

Solution

By a process of trial and error it can be discovered that the invoices that are being paid off are number 2256, 2280 and 2288 less the credit note. It would appear therefore that the cheque is for the correct amount although there might be some concern as to why invoice 2271 has not been paid, maybe there is some dispute over the amount of this invoice which should be investigated.

Always check figures carefully as such errors are often easy to miss.

2.5 Checking cheques

The rules regarding the validity of cheques were covered in the previous chapter. When cheques are received in the post it is important that they are checked for their validity, particularly in respect of:
· the date;
· the words and figures agree;
· the cheque is signed.

O EXAMPLE

The following three cheques were received in the post today, 3 June 20X6, by your organisation, L L Traders.

Check each one carefully to ensure that they are valid.

FINANCIAL BANK PLC
Shepherd's Bush Green Branch
352 Shepherd' Bush Green
W12 6TH

fb

01-89-34

1 June 20 X5

Pay L L Traders   or order

Three hundred pounds only   £300.00

MISS S SMITH

S Smith

000267   01-89-34   47586909

WESTERN BANK PLC
Stevenage Branch
29 High Street
Stevenage SG5 1BJ

WB

23-90-34

22 May 20 X6

Pay L J Traders   or order

Two hundred and forty three pounds and   £243.18

18 pence

J LEONARD

J Leonard

000341   23-90-34   37586261

NORTHERN BANK PLC
Ealing Branch
15 London Road
W5 4DT

NB

23-47-34

30 May 20 X6

Pay L L Traders   or order

One hundred and ninety six pounds   £169.23

23 pence

P BUTLER

P Butler

000476   22-47-34   20586484

Solution

The first cheque is dated 1 June 20X5 whereas today's date is 3 June 20X6. Therefore this cheque is out of date and must be returned to the customer requesting a replacement cheque.

The second cheque is made out to L J Traders instead of L L Traders. Again this must be returned to the customer with a request for a replacement cheque.

The third cheque is made out for £196.23 in words but £169.23 in figures. This cheque must also be returned to the customer with a request for a replacement cheque.

You must always be very thorough in assessments checking carefully each aspect of the cheque – date, words and figures, payee, signature, etc.

▷ ACTIVITY 3 ▷ ▷ ▷ ▷

(AAT CA D93)

(a)   Today is the 15 March 20X3. Would the cheque below be accepted for payment if it were now presented to the National Bank plc?

(b)   Give two reasons for your answer.

NATIONAL BANK PLC 18 Coventry Road Birmingham	(NB)	**19-14-60** _14/8_ 20 _X2_

Pay   Music World Limited   or order

Ten thousand and twenty pounds 42p   £1,020-42

P DUNSTER

200550   19-14-60   50731247

[Answer on p. 205]

3 Settlement discounts

3.1 Introduction

When a settlement discount is offered to a customer, this will normally be offered as a percentage amount. If a customer takes advantage of the discount they will calculate it themselves, therefore it is important to check that this is correct.

3.2 Checks to make

Where a payment is received after deducting a settlement discount then great care should be taken in checking this receipt.

Step 1 Check back to the original invoice to ensure that the discount is valid, ie that the customer has paid within the stated period.
Step 2 Check that the correct percentage discount has been taken and that it has been correctly calculated.

O EXAMPLE OOOO

Cheques have been received from two credit customers. Today's date is 3 October 20X3.

| Garden Supplies Ltd | £2,168.81 |
| Porter & Co | £963.91 |

The invoices that these cheques are paying are given below.

You are required to check that the receipt is for the correct amount.

Invoice 66293

A.J. Broom & Company Limited

59 Parkway
Manchester
M2 6EG
Tel: 0161 560 3392
Fax: 0161 560 5322
Tax Point: 20 September 20X3
VAT reg no: 452 4585 48

**Garden Supplies Ltd
Grange Hill
Chester**

Code	Supply	Description	Quantity	VAT rate %	Unit price £	Amount exclusive of VAT £
950 BB3	Sale	Cotswold bricks	2	17.50	300.00	600.00
159 504	Sale	Roof riles – red	6	17.50	195.50	1,173.00
874 KL5	Sale	Brick tiles	3	17.50	56.65	169.95
						1,942.95
VAT at 17.5%						323.01
Total amount payable						**2,265.96**

5% settlement discount is offered for payments received within 10 days of the invoice date.

Invoice 66299

A.J. Broom & Company Limited

59 Parkway
Manchester
M2 6EG

Porter & Co
Cunard Place
Manchester

Tel: 0161 560 3392
Fax: 0161 560 5322

Tax Point: 26 September 20X3
VAT reg no: 452 4585 48

Code	Supply	Description	Quantity	VAT rate %	Unit price £	Amount exclusive of VAT £
262BPT	Sale	Lined Oak Panels 1m2	6	17.50	145.00	870.00

VAT at 17.5%						144.63

Total amount payable						**1,014.63**

5% settlement discount is offered for payments received within 10 days of the invoice date.

Solution

The invoice to Garden Supplies Ltd is dated 20 September. As today's date is 3 October then the payment has not been received within 10 days of the invoice date which are the stated terms for the settlement discount. Therefore the customer should be politely informed of this fact and a request made for the balance of the invoice to be paid, 5% x £1,942.95 = £97.15.

The invoice to Porter & Co is dated 26 September and therefore is valid in terms of date. However the correct amount of the discount should be £43.50 (5% x £870). The discount that has been taken is £50.73 (5% x £1,014.64). Again the customer must be informed of the error and the balance requested. For such a small amount, £7.23 (£50.73 - £43.50), the credit controller may decide that this amount can be added to the next payment from Porter & Co if they are regular customers.

In assessments you must always check all discount calculations and dates very thoroughly.

Remember that as the VAT has already been calculated on the assumption that the discount has been taken the amount of discount is based on the net of VAT amount.

KAPLAN PUBLISHING

3.3 Recording any settlement discounts taken

When the settlement discounts have been checked and are valid it is important that the amount of the discount is noted. This should be either on the back of the cheque or on the remittance list. This is necessary because when the primary records are written up for these receipts (see next chapter) the amount of the discount must be recorded.

△ **ACTIVITY 4**   △ △ △ △

(AAT CA D92)

Hairdressing Supplies Ltd have recently received payment from a valued new customer, Allied Hairdressers Limited of Chichester, in respect of their first order for supplies.

The conditions of payment applying to the order were Hairdressing Supplies' normal ones of 2.5% cash discount if paid within ten days of the receipt of the invoice, otherwise payment in full must be made by the end of the month following the date of the invoice.

However, the customer had paid five weeks after the date of the invoice but had still deducted the cash discount. Enquiries revealed that they had received the invoice two days after it was posted to them.

Marjorie Thistlewaite, the accountant, agreed that the company should not press for payment of the discount and has asked you to draft a tactful letter to confirm this but to remind the customer of the agreed conditions of payment.

[Answer on p. 205]

3.4 Automated payments

In the previous chapter we have seen how payments can be made directly into and out of bank accounts. It is entirely possible that a customer might pay an amount due with a bank giro credit. This amount would then appear as a credit in the bank statement. Just as with a cheque receipt this automated receipt must be checked back to the original invoices to ensure that it is for the correct amount and to check for items such as settlement discounts deducted.

4   Test your knowledge

1   If a customer offers to pay for goods costing £80 by writing out two cheques both supported by a £50 cheque guarantee card, should the payment be accepted?

2   When a cheque guarantee card is offered in support of a cheque payment, what should be checked on the guarantee card?

3   What is a remittance list?

4   What is a remittance advice?

5   Why are remittance advices useful to the business receiving the cheques?

6   When a cheque is received from a credit customer what checks should be made on the cheque itself?

7   If a customer has taken a settlement discount in making a payment what checks should be carried out?

8   A customer has sent a cheque for payment of an invoice with a net amount of £1,000, VAT of £166.25 and a gross value of £1,166.25. The customer has taken advantage of a 5% settlement discount. How much should the cheque be for?

[Answers on p. 206]

5   Summary

This chapter has concentrated on all of the important checks that must be made when receiving money from customers to ensure that the correct amounts have been paid and that the payment method is valid. Cash, cheques and credit card payments must be carefully checked by a retailer. A supplier on credit terms has to make a number of checks when cheques are received from a customer. Is the cheque for the correct amount given the invoices that are paid? Is any settlement discount valid and correctly calculated? Are the cheques that have been received correctly made out so that they can be paid into the organisation's bank account?

Answers to chapter activities & 'test your knowledge' questions

△ ACTIVITY 1   △ △ △ △

(a)   Yes
(b)   The credit card company can be contacted by phone to authorise use of the card for the purchase.

△ ACTIVITY 2   △ △ △ △

False. A remittance advice is a slip that the customer can send back to the supplier with his payment to identify what the payment is for.

△ ACTIVITY 3   △ △ △ △

(a)   No
(b)   Any two from the following:
    (i)   The cheque has not been signed.
    (ii)   The cheque is out of date.
    (iii)   The words and figures on the cheque are not the same.

△ ACTIVITY 4   △ △ △ △

HAIRDRESSING SUPPLIES Limited
(Head Office)
Station Road, Dorking, Surrey GU10 1ZZ

The Accountant   1 April 20X0
Allied Hairdressers Limited
99 Castle Street
Chichester
Sussex

Dear Sir

Cash discount

Thank you for your cheque for £195 in respect of our invoice dated 10 February 20X0.

We note, however, that you have deducted cash discount of 2.5% before payment, which was made at least two weeks after the date up to which discount was allowed.

You will be aware that our terms of payment are that 2.5% cash discount may be deducted if payment is made within 10 days of the date of receipt of the invoice, otherwise payment must be made in full by the end of the month following the date of the invoice.

We do not intend to press for payment of the balance in this instance, but would ask you to noté our terms of payment in respect of future transactions.

Yours faithfully

Marjorie Thistlewaite

Marjorie Thistlewaite
Company Accountant

Test your knowledge

1   No. A cheque guarantee card only covers one cheque for each transaction.

2   · That the account details on the card relate to the cheque
    · That the card covers the amount of the cheque
    · That the signature on the card is that on the cheque
    · That the card has not expired

3   A remittance list is a list of all of the cheques received each day.

4   A remittance advice is a detachable slip at the bottom of an invoice that a customer can return with the payment made.

5   When a cheque is received with an accompanying remittance advice it is easy for the receiving business to determine which invoice is being paid.

6   · Words and figures agree
    · Valid date
    · Payee name is correct
    · Cheque is signed

7   · That the payment was received within the timescale of the settlement discount terms
    · That the settlement discount has been correctly calculated and deducted

8   Discount should be 5% x £1,000 = £50
    Cheque should be for £1,166.25 – 50 = £1,116.25

BANKING RECEIPTS

INTRODUCTION

Having looked at the checks that must be carried out when money is received into a business, in this chapter we will look at how to pay the monies into the bank.

KNOWLEDGE & UNDERSTANDING

· The function, form and use of banking documentation (Elements 1, 2 and 3)
· Methods of handling and storing money, including the security aspects (Element 2)

CONTENTS

1   Paying monies into the bank

PERFORMANCE CRITERIA
·   Prepare paying-in documents (Element 30.1)

1 Paying monies into the bank

1.1 Introduction

Once the cheques that have been received in the post have been recorded on the remittance list and checked for accuracy then they must be paid into the bank account as soon as possible. The business may also have some cash to pay in to the bank from retail sales and possibly some credit card vouchers. The details of all of these must be entered onto a paying-in slip in order to pay them into the bank account.

1.2 Paying-in slip

A paying-in slip is a summary of details of money paid into a bank account. There is a standard format with a few variations between banks. There will be a space in which to record all of the details of any cheques paid in and a schedule for listing the details of any cash paid into the account.

				To be retained by receiving bank	
For the credit of TRADING COMPANY LIMITED				Account No: 50756654	

Cheques, etc for collection to be included in total credit of £ 295.69 paid in 15/9 20 X3

	£	brought forward	£	brought forward	£
SJ Smith	59.26				
RS Hayes	73.80				
S Bates	15.73				
Carried forward	£148.79	carried forward	£	Total cheques, etc	£

Date 15/9/X3

£50 Notes	100	00
£20 Notes	40	00
£10 Notes		
£5 Notes		
£1 and £2 Coins	5	00
50p	1	00
20p		
Silver		90
Bronze		
Total Cash	146	90
Cheques, POs, etc	148	79
TOTAL £	295	69

56 – 28 – 48

FINANCIAL BANK PLC

EXETER HIGH STREET

Fee	No Chqs
	3

Credit Trading Company Limited

Paid in by J Vorlott

Address/Ref No. _____

1.3 Banking credit card vouchers

In many businesses credit card payments are processed automatically using the EFTPOS system. However, in some businesses where a mechanical imprinter is still used, credit card sales vouchers and refund vouchers are paid into a bank.

These are summarised on a retail voucher summary and the total (only) is included on a normal bank paying-in slip.

Retail voucher summary – Slip completed by a retailer when banking credit card vouchers. It normally has four copies: two for the retailer's records and two for the bank.

1.4 Completing the retail voucher summary

The retailer will complete the back of the summary (given below) first with the total amount of each credit card voucher and any refund vouchers.

	£	p
Please do not pin or staple this voucher as this will affect the machine processing.		
1		
2		
3		
All sales vouchers must be deposited within three banking days of the dates shown on them.		
4		
5		
6		
7		
If you are submitting more than 26 vouchers please enclose a separate listing.		
8		
9		
10		
If a voucher contravenes the terms of the retailer agreement then the amount shown on the voucher may be charged back to your bank account, either direct or via your paying in branch.		
11		
12		
13		
14		
15		
16		
Similarly, if the total amount shown on the Retail Voucher Summary does not balance with our total of vouchers, the difference will be credited (or debited) to your bank account.		
17		
18		
19		
20		
21		
22		
23		
24		
25		
26		

SALES VOUCHERS   TOTAL

	£	p
1		
2		
3		
4		
5		
6		
7		

REFUND VOUCHERS   TOTAL

The total of sales vouchers and refund vouchers is then transferred to the front of the retail voucher summary (given below). The final total on the front of the summary is then entered onto the paying-in slip.

Have you imprinted the summary with your Retailer's Card?

Bank processing copy of Summary with your Vouchers in correct order:

1 Summary
2 Sales Vouchers
3 Refund Vouchers

Keep Retailer's copy and Retailer's Duplicate copy

No more than 200 Vouchers to each Summary

Do not use Staples, Pins, Paper Clips

_____
Retailer's Signature

VISA			
		Items	Amount
Sales vouchers			
Less Refund Vouchers			
Date		Total £	:

MasterCard   EUROCARD

Retailer Summary

Complete this summary for every Deposit of Sales Vouchers and enter the **Total** on your normal Current Account paying-in slip

Retailer's Copy

Retailer Summary

1.5 Credit card vouchers in an electronic system

It was mentioned in an earlier chapter that many retailers now process credit cards electronically by swiping the card through a card reader. In such a system there is no need to pay the credit card vouchers into the bank as they are automatically credited to the business' bank account at the end of each day by each credit card company.

○ EXAMPLE   ○○○○

You are in charge of preparing the paying-in slip for today 3 July 20X6 for your business Thames Traders.

The remittance list for the cheques received from customers today is as follows:

S Jones	£125.40	
Kirby & Co	£53.80	
Holpoint Ltd	£237.50	(cash discount £12.50)
Peterslee Ltd	£126.78	
Johnson & Co	£220.80	(cash discount £9.20)

You are also required to bank the following cash:

£20 notes	6
£10 notes	15
£5 notes	8
£2 coins	4
£1 coins	24
50 pence coins	7
20 pence coins	15
10 pence coins	14
5 pence coins	2
2 pence coins	23
1 pence coins	14

Finally you are required to complete the retail voucher summary for the four credit card vouchers given below and enter the total onto the paying-in slip.

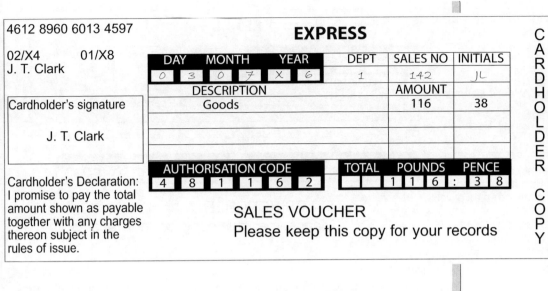

4612 8960 6013 4597

02/X4   01/X8
J. T. Clark

EXPRESS

C A R D H O L D E R   C O P Y

Cardholder's signature

J. T. Clark

DAY	MONTH	YEAR	DEPT	SALES NO	INITIALS
0 3	0 7	X 6	1	142	JL
DESCRIPTION				AMOUNT	
Goods				116	38

AUTHORISATION CODE						TOTAL	POUNDS		PENCE	
4	8	1	1	6	2		1 1 6	:	3 8	

SALES VOUCHER
Please keep this copy for your records

Cardholder's Declaration:
I promise to pay the total amount shown as payable together with any charges thereon subject in the rules of issue.

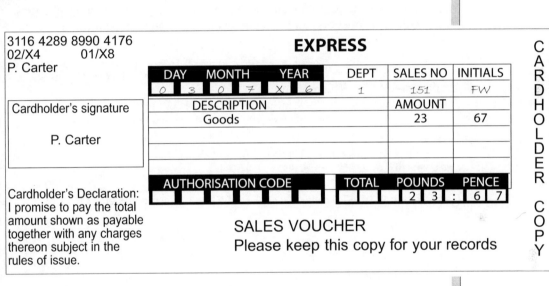

3116 4289 8990 4176
02/X4   01/X8
P. Carter

EXPRESS

C A R D H O L D E R   C O P Y

Cardholder's signature

P. Carter

DAY	MONTH	YEAR	DEPT	SALES NO	INITIALS
0 3	0 7	X 6	1	151	FW
DESCRIPTION				AMOUNT	
Goods				23	67

AUTHORISATION CODE						TOTAL	POUNDS		PENCE	
							2 3	:	6 7	

SALES VOUCHER
Please keep this copy for your records

Cardholder's Declaration:
I promise to pay the total amount shown as payable together with any charges thereon subject in the rules of issue.

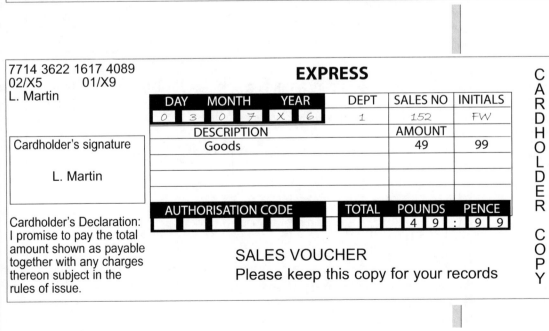

7714 3622 1617 4089
02/X5   01/X9
L. Martin

EXPRESS

C A R D H O L D E R   C O P Y

Cardholder's signature

L. Martin

DAY	MONTH	YEAR	DEPT	SALES NO	INITIALS
0 3	0 7	X 6	1	152	FW
DESCRIPTION				AMOUNT	
Goods				49	99

AUTHORISATION CODE						TOTAL	POUNDS		PENCE	
							4 9	:	9 9	

SALES VOUCHER
Please keep this copy for your records

Cardholder's Declaration:
I promise to pay the total amount shown as payable together with any charges thereon subject in the rules of issue.

0614 4072 7361 4972
02/X5   01/X8
T. P. Berry

EXPRESS

DAY	MONTH	YEAR	DEPT	SALES NO	INITIALS
0 3	0 7	X 6	1	157	FW

DESCRIPTION		AMOUNT	
Goods		67	45

Cardholder's signature

T. P. Berry

AUTHORISATION CODE						TOTAL	POUNDS		PENCE	
							6 7	:	4 5	

Cardholder's Declaration:
I promise to pay the total
amount shown as payable
together with any charges
thereon subject in the
rules of issue.

SALES VOUCHER
Please keep this copy for your records

C
A
R
D
H
O
L
D
E
R

C
O
P
Y

Solution

Work carefully through each element of preparing the paying-in slip – cheques, cash, credit card vouchers – ensuring that you record all of the information accurately.

To be retained by receiving bank

For the credit of   Thames Traders

Cheques, etc for collection to be included in total credit of £1,372.37 paid in 3 July 20X6

	£	brought forward	£416.70	brought forward	£764.28
S Jones	125.40	Peterslee Ltd	126.78	Credit Card	£257.49
Kirby & Co	53.80	Johnson & Co	220.80	vouchers	
Holpoint Ltd	237.50	(£9.20 disc.)			
(£12.50 disc.)					
Carried forward	£416.70	carried forward	£764.28	Total cheques, etc	£1,021.77

Date __3/7/X6_____

Cashier's stamp and initials

56 – 28 – 48

FINANCIAL BANK PLC

EXETER HIGH STREET

Fee	No Chqs		
	5		

Paid in by J Vorlott

Address/Ref No. _____

	£	p
£50 Notes	-	-
£20 Notes	120	00
£10 Notes	150	00
£5 Notes	40	00
£2 Coins	8	00
£1 Coins	24	00
50p	3	50
20p	3	00
Silver	1	50
Bronze	0	60
Total Cash	350	60
Cheques, POs, etc	1,021	77
TOTAL £	1,372	37

Have you imprinted the summary with your Retailer's Card?

Bank processing copy of Summary with your Vouchers in correct order:

1 Summary

2 Sales Vouchers

3 Refund Vouchers

Keep Retailer's copy and Retailer's Duplicate copy

No more than 200 Vouchers to each Summary

Do not use Staples, Pins, Paper Clips

_____

Retailer's Signature

Complete this summary for every Deposit of Sales Voucher and enter the **Total** on your normal Current Account paying-in slip

VISA

	Items	Amount	
Sales vouchers	4	257	49
Less Refund Vouchers	0	–	
Date	Total		
03/07/X6	£	257 : 49	

MasterCard   EUROCARD

Retailer Summary

Retailer's Copy

Retailer Summary

Please do not pin or staple this voucher as this will affect the machine processing.

All sales vouchers must be deposited within three banking days of the dates shown on them.

If you are submitting more than 26 vouchers please enclose a separate listing.

If a voucher contravenes the terms of the retailer agreement then the amount shown on the voucher may be charged back to your bank account, either direct or via your paying in branch.

Similarly, if the total amount shown on the Retail Voucher Summary does not balance with our total of vouchers, the difference will be credited (or debited) to your bank account.

	£	p
1	116	38
2	23	67
3	49	99
4	67	45
5		
6		
7		
8		
9		
10		
11		
12		
13		
14		
15		
16		
17		
18		
19		
20		
21		
22		
23		
24		
25		
26		

SALES VOUCHERS   TOTAL

	257	49
	£	p
1		
2		
3		
4		
5		
6		
7		

REFUND VOUCHERS   TOTAL

Accuracy is of great importance when filling in documents such as the paying-in slip. Therefore, always make sure that you go back and check all of your additions and totals.

1.6 Using the paying-in slip

The paying-in slip will normally be photocopied and then used to write up the cash receipts book. Therefore it is important that the amount of cash discount is noted on the paying-in slip as this will be necessary for writing up the cash book.

▷ ACTIVITY 1   ▷ ▷ ▷ ▷

You are the cashier of Trading Company Ltd and have received the following cash from customers on 29 August 20X4.

£20	notes	–	3
£10	notes	–	2
£5	notes	–	3
£1	coins	–	28
50p	coins	–	15
20p	coins	–	17
10p	coins	–	35
5p	coins	–	12
2p	coins	–	18
1p	coins	–	23

The following cheques also await banking and must be paid into the bank on the paying-in slip.

	£
C Hardy	116.24
I Hampton (discount £4.13)	202.37
Southpoint Ltd	601.23
C Trails	413.23

You must:

(a)   total the cash received; and

(b)   complete the paying-in slip.

There is a paying-in slip for you to complete below.

KAPLAN PUBLISHING

		To be retained by receiving bank	
For the credit of _____			
Cheques, etc for collection to be included in total credit of £		paid in 20	

	£	brought forward	£	brought forward	£
Carried forward	£	carried forward	£	Total cheques, etc	£

Date

Cashier's stamp and initials

56 – 28 – 48

FINANCIAL BANK PLC

EXETER HIGH STREET

Fee	No Chqs

Paid in by_____

Address/Ref No. _____

£50 Notes		
£20 Notes		
£10 Notes		
£5 Notes		
£1 and £2 Coins		
50p		
20p		
Silver		
Bronze		
Total Cash		
Cheques, POs, etc		
TOTAL £		

[Answer on p. 218]

1.7 Paying in cash and cheques

We have already seen the preparation of the paying-in slip.

The individual who is paying in takes the cash, cheques, credit card vouchers and paying in book to the bank and hands them to the cashier behind the counter.

The cashier:
· agrees the items to be paid in against the information on the paying-in slip;
· checks the other details on the paying-in slip (e.g. date, payee);
· stamps both copies;
· removes the bank's copy (the top copy);
· returns the paying-in book.

Cash which is paid into the bank must be bagged up by the customer before taking it to the bank.

Different coins must be put in separate plastic bags (supplied by the bank) up to certain values decided on by the bank (e.g. £5 worth of 50 pence pieces).

This helps speed up the process of paying-in cash at the bank. The bank will then recount the cash, either by weighing it or using a money-counting machine.

Any cash paid in will be credited direct to the business's account when the branch records all of the transactions for the day.

Cheques paid in are sorted and put through the clearing system.

1.8 Using the nightsafe

The nightsafe is a service offered by most of the high street banks. A small annual fee is charged.

The nightsafe is used by shops and businesses who wish to bank their takings after the banks have closed, and do not want to keep takings in their safe overnight. Only cash and cheques can be deposited in this way.

The nightsafe is sited on an outside wall of the branch of the bank.

The bank supplies a leather pouch in which the takings are placed, and a key to open the nightsafe. The nightsafe is opened with the key and the pouch placed in the container inside. The pouch is then released from the container into the nightsafe itself when the nightsafe has been closed again.

Users of the nightsafe are advised to open it again to check that the pouch has dropped out of sight.

Both copies of the paying-in slip are put in the pouch. The customer's copy is stamped and returned with the empty pouch on the next working day.

1.9 Security procedures

We have seen that cash and cheques should be paid into the bank as soon as they are received. This may mean that each day a member of staff takes the cash and cheques to the bank. If the amounts of cash are large then care should be taken. It is advisable for two members of staff to take the cash, to go to the bank at different times of day and not to necessarily use the same route or routine on every occasion.

If the amount of cash is very large then a security firm should be used to transport the cash.

2 Test your knowledge ▷ ▷ ▷

1 What figures should be completed on a paying-in-slip?

2 What is a retail credit card voucher summary used for?

3 What is a night safe and what is its purpose?

[Answers on p. 218]

3 Summary

In this chapter we have seen how to write up a paying-in slip and the details that must be included on this document. This is an important document and therefore it is vital that it is produced accurately. Make sure when you fill out the paying-in slip that all of your additions of the cheques, cash and credit card vouchers are correct. Whenever filling out any such document you should always go back and check that it has been correctly totalled.

Answers to chapter activities & 'test your knowledge' questions

△ ACTIVITY 1 △ △ △ △

To be retained by receiving bank

For the credit of TRADING COMPANY LIMITED
Cheques, etc for collection to be included in total credit of £1,471.66 paid in 29/8 20X4

	£	brought forward	£318.61	brought forward	£
C Hardy	116.24	Southpoint Ltd	601.23		
I Hampton	202.37	C Trails	413.23		
(discount £4.13)					
Carried forward	£318.61	carried forward	£ 1,333.07	Total cheques, etc	£

Date 29/8/X4

Cashier's stamp and initials

56 – 28 – 48

FINANCIAL BANK PLC

EXETER HIGH STREET

Fee	No Chqs
	4

A N Other

Paid in by_____

Address/Ref No. _____

£50 Notes		
£20 Notes	60	00
£10 Notes	20	00
£5 Notes	15	00
£1 and £2 Coins	28	00
50p	7	50
20p	3	40
Silver	4	10
Bronze		59
Total Cash	138	59
Cheques, POs, etc	1,333	07
TOTAL £	1,471	66

Test your knowledge △ △ △

1 · The total of each cheque being paid in
  · The total of each denomination of cash
  · The total of any credit card vouchers
  · The total of vouchers and cheques
  · The cash total
  · The total of all monies being paid in

2 A retail credit card voucher summary is used to list and total any credit card vouchers that are being paid into the bank.

3 A night safe is a facility provided by many high street banks which allows monies to be paid into the bank to be deposited in the night safe after bank closing hours so that it does not have to be kept on the business premises for the night.

DEBTORS' STATEMENTS

INTRODUCTION

In this chapter we consider communication with our debtors. If we are to receive the money owed to us on time it is important to ensure that the customers are fully aware of the amount they owe us and our credit terms.

KNOWLEDGE & UNDERSTANDING

· Relationship between the accounting system and the ledger (Elements 1, 2 and 3)

CONTENTS

1 Accounting for credit sales and receipts from customers
2 Debtors' statements
3 Communication with customers

PERFORMANCE CRITERIA

· Enter receipts into the cash book, subsidiary ledger and main ledger (Element 30.1)
· Produce statements of account for debtors (Element 30.1)
· Write to customers in an appropriate style to request payment of an overdue account (Element 30.1)

1 Accounting for credit sales and receipts from customers

1.1 Introduction

Before we consider the preparation of debtors' statements, we will firstly bring together all of the accounting that has taken place for credit sales and receipts from credit customers in one example so that you can see how it all fits together. It is important that you understand how the amount owed by customers is calculated and recorded.

○ EXAMPLE ○○○○

Given below is the sales day book, sales returns day book and cash receipts book for the first month of trading by Nick Brookes.

SALES DAY BOOK

Date	Invoice No	Customer name	Code	Total	VAT	Net
20X2				£	£	£
03/04	001	Mayer Ltd	SL1	185.65	27.65	158.00
04/04	002	Elizabeth & Co	SL2	257.34	37.34	220.00
07/04	003	Hofen Partners	SL3	129.25	19.25	110.00
10/04	004	Penken Bros	SL4	157.91	22.91	135.00
14/04	005	Mayer Ltd	SL1	206.80	30.80	176.00
18/04	006	Hofen Partners	SL3	122.20	18.20	104.00
21/04	007	Mayer Ltd	SL1	253.80	37.80	216.00
24/04	008	Penken Bros	SL4	167.27	24.27	143.00
26/04	009	Mayer Ltd	SL1	192.70	28.70	164.00
28/04	010	Elizabeth & Co	SL2	233.95	33.95	200.00
28/04	011	Penken Bros	SL4	138.03	20.03	118.00
				2,044.90	300.90	1,744.00

SALES RETURNS DAY BOOK

Date	CN No	Customer name	Code	Total	VAT	Net
20X2				£	£	£
10/04	CN001	Mayer Ltd	SL1	49.35	7.35	42.00
17/04	CN002	Penken Bros	SL4	39.77	5.77	34.00
				89.12	13.12	76.00

CASH RECEIPTS BOOK

Date	Narrative	Total	VAT	Debtors	Cash sales	Discount
		£	£	£	£	£
20X2						
07/04	Cash sales	374.23	55.73		318.50	
15/04	Elizabeth & Co	250.74		250.74		6.60
18/04	Mayer Ltd	136.30		136.30		
21/04	Cash sales	566.93	84.43		482.50	
21/04	Penken Bros	115.11		115.11		3.03
28/04	Hofen Partners	129.25		129.25		
		1,572.56	140.16	631.40	801.00	9.63

Solution

First we must post the totals from each of the books of prime entry to the main ledger accounts. As this is the first month of trading there will of course be no opening balances on any of the ledger accounts.

Sales ledger control account

		£			£
30/04	SBD	2,044.90	30/04	SRDB	89.12
			30/04	CRB	631.40
			30/04	CRB – discount	9.63

VAT account

		£			£
30/04	SRDB	13.12	30/04	SDB	300.90
			30/04	CRB	140.16

Sales account

		£			£
			30/04	SDB	1,744.00
			30/04	CRB	801.00

Sales returns account

		£		£
30/04	SRDB	76.00		

Discounts allowed account

		£		£
30/04	CRB	9.63		

Once the entries have been made in total to the main ledger accounts then each individual invoice, credit note, cash receipt and discount must be entered into the individual debtor accounts in the subsidiary ledger.

Mayer Ltd

		£			£
03/04	001	185.65	10/04	CN001	49.35
14/04	005	206.80	18/04	CRB	136.30
21/04	007	253.80			
26/04	009	192.70			

Elizabeth & Co

		£			£
04/04	002	257.34	15/04	CRB	250.74
28/04	010	233.95	15/04	CRB – discount	6.60

Hofen Partners

		£			£
07/04	003	129.25	28/04	CRB	129.25
18/04	006	122.20			

Penken Bros

		£			£
10/04	004	157.91	17/04	CN002	39.77
24/04	008	167.27	21/04	CRB	115.11
28/04	011	138.03	21/04	CRB – discount	3.03

From this you can see how the full accounting system for credit sales works and the information that is accumulated in each of the individual debtor accounts in the subsidiary ledger.

2 Debtors' statements

2.1 Introduction

The sales ledger clerk prepares monthly statements to send to debtors:
- to remind them that certain invoices are due for payment;
- to reconfirm amounts outstanding where credit notes have been issued.

> **◻ DEFINITION** ◻◻◻◻
>
> A statement is a document issued (normally monthly) by a supplier to a customer showing unpaid sales invoices and the amount due in total.

2.2 Layout of statement

Statements can be prepared in a number of different ways. Some also have remittance advices attached to them in order to encourage early payment.

A remittance advice is a blank document that the customer fills out when making a payment to the supplier. It shows the total payment being made and which invoices (less credit notes) the payment is paying off.

2.3 Preparing a debtors' statement

A debtors' statement will normally be prepared from the information in the debtors' individual account in the subsidiary ledger. Different businesses will use different formats but the basics that must be shown are all invoices, credit notes, payments received and discounts for the period together with usually a running total of the balance.

2.4 Procedure for preparing a debtors' statement

When preparing a statement for a credit customer, it is important that all details are correct therefore a logical and accurate approach is required.

Step 1 Find the customer's account in the filing system for the subsidiary ledger.

Step 2 Work through the account by date order listing each transaction in turn on the statement – invoices as a debit and credit notes, payments and discounts as credits.

Step 3 Return to the start of the statement and calculate the balance at each transaction date to appear in the balance column.

○ EXAMPLE ○○○○

Given below are the subsidiary ledger accounts for two of Nick Brookes' customers. We will start by balancing each account to show the total amount due by each customer.

Mayer Ltd   SL01

		£			£
03/04	001	185.65	10/04	CN001	49.35
14/04	005	206.80	18/04	CRB	136.30
21/04	007	253.80			
26/04	008	192.70	Balance c/d		653.30
		838.95			838.95
Balance b/d		653.30			

Penken Bros   SL04

		£			£
10/04	004	157.91	17/04	CN002	39.77
24/04	008	167.27	21/04	CRB	115.11
28/04	011	138.03	21/04	CRB – discount	3.03
				Balance b/d	305.30
		463.21			463.21
Balance c/d		305.30			

We can now use this information to prepare statements for these two customers as at the end of April 20X2.

Solution

	NICK BROOKES
To: Mayer Ltd	225 School Lane
	Weymouth
	Dorset WE36 5NR
	Tel: 0149 29381
	Fax: 0149 29382
	Date: 30/04/X2

STATEMENT

Date	Transaction	Debit £	Credit £	Balance £
03/04	INV001	185.65		185.65
10/04	CN001		49.35	136.30
14/04	INV005	206.80		343.10
18/04	Payment		136.30	206.80
21/04	INV007	253.80		460.60
26/04	INV008	192.70		653.30

May we remind you that our credit terms are 30 days
With 3% discount for payment within 14 days

	NICK BROOKES
	225 School Lane
	Weymouth
To: Penken Bros	Dorset WE36 5NR
	Tel: 0149 29381
	Fax: 0149 29382
	Date: 30/04/X2

STATEMENT

Date	Transaction	Debit £	Credit £	Balance £
10/04	INV004	157.91		157.91
17/04	CN002		39.77	118.14
21/04	Payment		115.11	
21/04	Discount		3.03	0.00
24/04	INV008	167.27		167.27
28/04	INV011	138.03		305.30

May we remind you that our credit terms are 30 days
With 3% discount for payment within 14 days

These are documents that are being sent to customers, therefore it is extremely important that it is completely accurate. Always check your figures and additions.

You are to prepare a statement to be sent out to one customer, Jack Johnson, for the month of May 20X6. At the start of May this customer did not owe your business, Thames Traders, any money. The subsidiary ledger account for Jack for the month of May is given below.

Jack Johnson

Date		£	Date		£
03 May	Invoice 1848	38.79	08 May	Credit note 446	12.40
07 May	Invoice 1863	50.70	15 May	Cash receipt	77.09
10 May	Invoice 1870	80.52	24 May	Credit note 458	16.50
18 May	Invoice 1881	42.40			
23 May	Invoice 1892	61.20			
30 May	Invoice 1904	27.65			

You are required to prepare a statement for Jack on the blank statement given below.

Thames Traders

To: Date:

	STATEMENT			
Date	Transaction	Debit £	Credit £	Balance £

May we remind you that our credit terms are 30 day

[Answer on p. 228]

3 Communication with customers

If there is a problem with a customer's balance then it will be normal practice to write a polite letter to the customer requesting payment and enquiring if there is any problem with the amounts shown in the statement. If there are no problems or disputed invoices but payment is still not received within a reasonable time then this initial letter should be followed by a letter with a firmer tone requesting payment. This may include a statement that the matter will be put into the hands of your business's solicitors if payment if not received. However, this will be a matter of policy within each business.

○ EXAMPLE ○○○○

You are the credit controller for GoGo Limited, a wholesaler of discount children's clothing. You have been reviewing the aged debtors' listing. The following customer is causing you concern:

	Total £	Current £	30+ days £	60+ days £
Candy Limited	556.78	0	0	556.78

You must write a letter to this customer to ask for payment.

Solution

GoGo Limited
225 Western Road
Anytown
Anyshire AN1 2RN

Creditors' Ledger Clerk   23 August 20X4
Candy Limited
53 High Street
Anytown
Anyshire AN1 6BN

Dear Sir

Outstanding balance

According to our records your company has an outstanding balance of £556.78.

Our normal credit terms are 30 days. As this debt is now over 60 days old we would be very grateful if you could send us your payment immediately.

If you have any queries please do not hesitate to contact me.

Yours faithfully

AN Smith
Credit Controller

Do not be tempted to write a letter that sounds angry or threatening. Polite efficiency is what is required.

4 **Test your knowledge**

1 What is the procedure for preparing a debtor's statement?

2 What is a debtor's statement?

[Answers on p. 228]

5 Summary

In this chapter all of the accounting entries for sales invoices, credit notes and receipts from debtors were brought together. We also saw how to produce a statement to be sent to a customer from the customer's account in the subsidiary ledger.

We have also introduced an aged debt analysis. You do not need to be able to produce one but you do need to be able to use it to determine any customers who appear to be causing problems with debt collection. It is important when communicating with customers that you deal effectively but politely at all times.

Answers to chapter activities & 'test your knowledge' questions

△ **ACTIVITY 1**   △ △ △ △

Thames Traders

To: Jack Johnson

Date: 31 May 20X6

STATEMENT				
Date	Transaction	Debit £	Credit £	Balance £
03 May	Inv 1848	38.79		38.79
07 May	Inv 1863	50.70		89.49
08 May	CN 446		12.40	77.09
10 May	Inv 1870	80.52		157.61
15 May	Payment		77.09	80.52
18 May	Inv 1881	42.40		122.92
23 May	Inv 1892	61.20		184.12
24 May	CN 458		16.50	167.62
30 May	Inv 1904	27.65		195.27

May we remind you that our credit terms are 30 days

Test your knowledge △ △ △

1   · Find the customer's account in the subsidiary ledger
    · List each transaction in turn on the statement
    · Calculate the balance after each transaction

2   A debtor's statement is a document sent to a customer detailing unpaid invoices and the total amount due.

KAPLAN PUBLISHING

ACCOUNTING FOR SALES – SUMMARY

INTRODUCTION

We have studied the double entry bookkeeping for sales and receipts in detail at the start of this book.

At that time we concentrated on the basic entries so that the double entry would be clear. It is now time to 'put some flesh on the bones' and study these transactions again using more realistic simulation-type material.

KNOWLEDGE & UNDERSTANDING

- Business transactions and documents involved (Elements 1, 2 and 3)
- Double entry bookkeeping, including balancing accounts (Elements 1, 2 and 3)
- Accounting for receipts from credit customers and customers without credit accounts (Element 1)
- The use of the cash book and the cash book as part of the double entry system or as books of prime entry (Element 3)

CONTENTS

1 The sales day book
2 The analysed sales day book
3 The sales returns day book
4 The analysed cash book

PERFORMANCE CRITERIA

- Enter sales invoices and credit notes into sales day book and sales returns day book (Element 30.1)
- Post sales invoices and credit notes into the subsidiary (sales) ledger and main (general) ledger (Element 30.1)
- Enter receipts into the cash book, subsidiary ledger and main ledger (Element 30.1)

1 The sales day book

○ EXAMPLE ○○○○

Given below are three invoices that have been sent out by your organisation today. You are required to record them in the sales day book

INVOICE

A.J. Broom & Company Limited

Invoice to:	59 Parkway
T J Builder	Manchester
142/148 Broadway	M2 6EG
Oldham	Tel: 0161 560 3392
OD7 6LZ	Fax: 0161 560 5322

Deliver to:	Invoice no:	69489
As above	Tax point:	28 August 20X3
	VAT reg no:	625 9911 58
	Delivery note no:	68612
	Account no:	SL21

Code	Description	Quantity	VAT rate %	Unit price £	Amount exclusive of VAT £
874 KL7	Brown Brick Roof Tiles	40	17.5	43.95	1,758.00

		1,758.00
Trade discount 5%		87.90
		1,670.10
VAT at 17.5%		283.49
Total amount payable		1,953.59

Deduct discount of 3% if paid within 14 days

INVOICE

A.J. Broom & Company Limited

Invoice to:	59 Parkway
McCarthy & Sons	Manchester M2 6EG
Shepherds Moat	Tel: 0161 560 3392
Manchester M6 9LF	Fax: 0161 560 5322

Deliver to:	Invoice no:	69490
As above	Tax point:	28 August 20X3
	VAT reg no:	625 9911 58
	Delivery note no:	68610
	Account no:	SL08

Code	Description	Quantity	VAT rate %	Unit price £	Amount exclusive of VAT £
617 BB8	Red Wall Bricks	400	17.5	2.10	840.00
294 KT6	Insulation Brick	3	17.5	149.90	449.70

		1,289.70
Trade discount 4%		51.58
		1,238.12
VAT at 17.5%		216.67
Total amount payable		1,454.79

INVOICE

A.J. Broom & Company Limited

Invoice to:
Trevor Partner
Anderson House
Bank Street
Manchester M1 9FP

Deliver to:
As above

59 Parkway
Manchester
M2 6EG
Tel: 0161 560 3392
Fax: 0161 560 5322

Invoice no:	69491
Tax point:	28 August 20X3
VAT reg no:	625 9911 58
Delivery note no:	68613
Account no:	SL10

Code	Description	Quantity	VAT rate %	Unit price £	Amount exclusive of VAT £
611 TB4	Bathroom Tiles	160	17.5	5.65	904.00
					904.00

Trade discount 2%

	18.08
	885.92

VAT at 17.5%

	151.93

Total amount payable

	1,037.85

Deduct discount of 2% if paid within 21 days

Solution

SALES DAY BOOK						
Date	Invoice No	Customer name	Code	Total £	VAT £	Net £
28/08/X3	69489	T J Builder	SL21	1,953.59	283.49	1,670.10
28/08/X3	69490	McCarthy & Sons	SL08	1,454.79	216.67	1,238.12
28/08/X3	69491	Trevor Partner	SL10	1,037.85	151.93	885.92

2 The analysed sales day book

2.1 Introduction

Many organisations analyse their sales into different groups. This may be analysis by different products or by the geographical area in which the sale is made. If the sales are eventually to be analysed in this manner in the accounting records then they must be analysed in the original book of prime entry, the sales day book.

○ EXAMPLE ○○○○

You work for an organisation that makes sales to five different geographical regions. You are in charge of writing up the sales day book and you have listed out the details of the invoices sent out yesterday, 15 August 20X1. They are given below and must be entered into the sales day book and the totals of each column calculated.

The invoice details are as follows:

	£
Invoice number 167 – France	
Worldwide News – (Code W5)	
Net total	2,500.00
VAT	437.50
Gross	2,937.50
Invoice number 168 – Spain	
Local News – (Code L1)	
Net total	200.00
VAT	35.00
Gross	235.00
Invoice number 169 – Germany	
The Press Today – (Code P2)	
Net total	300.00
VAT	52.50
Gross	352.50
Invoice number 170 – Spain	
Home Call – (Code H1)	
Net total	200.00
VAT	35.00
Gross	235.00
Invoice number 171 – France	
Tomorrow – (Code T1)	
Net total	100.00
VAT	17.50
Gross	117.50
Invoice number 172 – Russia	
Worldwide News – (Code W5)	
Net total	3,000.00
VAT	525.00
Gross	3,525.00

KAPLAN PUBLISHING

Solution

SALES DAY BOOK										
Date	Invoice No	Customer name	Code	Total	VAT	Russia	Poland	Spain	Germany	France
				£	£	£	£	£	£	£
15/08/X1	167	Worldwide	W5	2,937.50	437.50					2,500.00
	168	Local News	L1	235.00	35.00			200.00		
	169	The Press Today	P2	352.50	52.50				300.00	
	170	Home Call	H1	235.00	35.00			200.00		
	171	Tomorrow	T1	117.50	17.50					100.00
	172	Worldwide News	W5	3,525.00	525.00	3,000.00				
				7,402.50	1,102.50	3,000.00	-	400.00	300.00	2,600.00

When you have totalled the columns you can check your additions by 'cross-casting'. If you add together the totals of all of the analysis columns and the VAT column, they should total the figure in the 'Total' column.

▷ ACTIVITY 1   ▷ ▷ ▷ ▷

Sweepings Ltd is a wall covering manufacturer. It produces four qualities of wallpaper:

01	–	Anaglypta
02	–	Supaglypta
03	–	Lincrusta
04	–	Blown Vinyl

Francis is a sales ledger clerk and he is required to write up the sales day book each week from the batch of sales invoices he receives from the sales department.

He has just received this batch of sales invoices which show the following details. All sales are standard-rated for VAT.

Invoice no	Date	Customer	Description	Amount (inc VAT) £
1700	06.09.X1	Gates Stores	Anaglypta, 188 rolls	470.00
1701	06.09.X1	Texas	Blown Vinyl, 235 rolls	1,762.50
1702	07.09.X1	Dickens	Blown Vinyl, 188 rolls	1,410.00
1703	07.09.X1	Hintons DIY	Supaglypta, 470 rolls	1,880.00
1704	08.09.X1	Co-op Stores	Anaglypta, 94 rolls	235.00
1705	08.09.X1	B & Q Stores	Lincrusta, 125 rolls	1,175.00
1706	09.09.X1	Ferris Décor	Supaglypta, 235 rolls	940.00
1707	09.09.X1	Ferris Décor	Blown Vinyl, 94 rolls	705.00
1708	10.09.X1	Homestyle	Lincrusta, 25 rolls	235.00
1709	10.09.X1	Quick Style	Anaglypta, 47 rolls	117.50

Show how this information would appear in the sales day book given below, including the totals of the relevant columns.

SALES DAY BOOK									
Date	Invoice	Customer	Code	Total	VAT	Group 01	Group 02	Group 03	Group 04
				£	£	£	£	£	£

[Answer on p. 243]

▷ ACTIVITY 2 ▷▷▷▷

Given below are the totals from the analysed sales day book for an organisation for a week.

Sales day book				
	Gross £	VAT £	Sales Type 1 £	Sales Type 2 £
Totals	8,471.75	1,261.75	4,320.00	2,890.00

You are required to post these totals to the main ledger accounts given below:

SLCA account

£	£

Sales – Type 1 account

£	£

Sales – Type 2 account

£	£

VAT account

£	£

[Answers on p. 243]

3 The sales returns day book

3.1 Introduction

When goods are returned by customers and credit notes sent out then these credit notes are also recorded in their own book of prime entry, the sales returns day book.

3.2 Sales returns day book

The sales returns day book is effectively the reverse of the sales day book but will have the same entries, the total of the credit note, including VAT, the VAT element and the net amount, excluding the VAT.

○ EXAMPLE   ○○○○

Given below are the totals from three credit notes that your organisation has sent out this week, the week ending 21 January 20X4. They are to be recorded in the sales returns day book.

Credit note no:	03556	To: J Slater & Co	Code: SL67
		£	
Goods total		126.45	
VAT		22.12	
Credit note total		148.57	

Credit note no:	03557	To: Paulsons	Code: SL14
		£	
Goods total		58.40	
VAT		10.22	
Credit note total		68.62	

Credit note no:	03558	To: Hudson & Co	Code: SL27
		£	
Goods total		104.57	
VAT		18.29	
Credit note total		122.86	

Solution

Sales returns day book

Date	Credit note no	Customer name	Code	Total	VAT	Net
				£	£	£
21/01/X4	03556	J Slater & Co	SL67	148.57	22.12	126.45
21/01/X4	03557	Paulsons	SL14	68.62	10.22	58.40
21/01/X4	03558	Hudson & Co	SL27	122.86	18.29	104.57

3.3 Analysed sales returns day book

If the business keeps an analysed sales day book then it will also analyse its sales returns day book in exactly the same manner.

○ EXAMPLE ○○○○

In an earlier example we considered the sales day book for an organisation that makes sales to five different geographical regions. The sales returns day book would also be analysed into these geographical regions. The details of two credit notes issued this week are given and are to be written up in the sales returns day book. Today's date is 21 October 20X6.

Credit note no: 0246 – Poland	To: Russell & Sons	Code: R3
	£	
Goods total	85.60	
VAT	14.98	
	100.58	

Credit note no: 0247 – Germany	To: Cleansafe	Code: C7
	£	
Goods total	126.35	
VAT	22.11	
	148.46	

Solution

Sales returns day book

Date	Credit	Customer	Code	Total £	VAT £	Russia £	Poland £	Spain £	Germany £	France £
21/10/X6	0246	Russell & Sons	R03	100.58	14.98		85.60			
21/10/X6	0247	Cleansafe	C07	148.46	22.11				126.35	

▷ ACTIVITY 3

A business analyses its sales into Product 1 sales and Product 2 sales. During the week ending 14 March 20X4 the following credit notes were sent out to customers.

CN3066	£120.00 plus VAT	–	Product 2, Customer K Lilt, Code L04
CN3067	£16.00 plus VAT	–	Product 1, Customer J Davis, Code D07
CN3068	£38.00 plus VAT	–	Product 1, Customer I Oliver, Code O11
CN3069	£80.00 plus VAT	–	Product 2, Customer D Sharp, Code S02

Enter the credit notes in the analysed sales returns day book given below and total the day book for the week.

Sales returns day book

Date	Credit Note No	Customer Name	Code	Total £	VAT £	Product 1 £	Product 2 £

[Answer on p. 243]

▷ ACTIVITY 4

Given below are the totals from the analysed sales returns day book for an organisation for a week:

Date	Customer Name	Credit note no	Code	Total £	VAT £	Sales Type 1 £	Sales Type 2 £
25/09/X2				589.26	87.76	327.00	174.50

Post these totals to the main ledger accounts.

[Answer on p. 244]

3.4 Posting to the subsidiary ledger accounts

As well as posting the totals from the books of prime entry to the main ledger accounts each individual invoice and credit note must also be posted to the individual customer's account in the subsidiary sales ledger.

○ EXAMPLE ○○○○

Here is an account from the subsidiary sales ledger of Frosty Limited, a glass manufacturer which specialises in glassware for the catering trade.

Account name: **Account code:**

	£		£

You have taken over writing up the subsidiary ledger because the ledger clerk has been ill for several months.

You have gathered together the following information about sales. The customer is a new customer whose name is Arthur Pickering. The account code will be SP05.

Sales invoices

Date	Invoice Number	Gross £	VAT £	Net £
02/05/X1	325	585.60	87.21	498.39
03/06/X1	468	238.90	35.58	203.32
15/06/X1	503	113.43	16.89	96.54
16/06/X1	510	48.70	7.25	41.45
24/06/X1	CN048	27.73	4.13	23.60
17/07/X1	604	441.12	65.69	375.43

Solution

Account name: Arthur Pickering   **Account code:** SP05

		£			£
02/05/X1	Inv 325	585.60	24/06/X1	CN048	27.73
03/06/X1	Inv 468	238.90			
15/06/X1	Inv 503	113.43			
16/06/X1	Inv 510	48.70			
17/07/X1	Inv 604	441.12			

Remember that sales invoices are always entered on the debit side of the customer's account and credit notes on the credit side of the account.

4 The analysed cash book

4.1 Introduction

In order to revise the layout of the cash receipts book consider the following example.

Cash receipts book for the week commencing 15 September 20X4

Date	Narrative	Total £	VAT £	Debtors £	Cash/cheque Sales £	Discount allowed £
15 Sept	Paying-in slip 584	653.90		653.90		
16 Sept	Paying-in slip 585	864.60		864.60		
17 Sept	Paying-in slip 586	953.58	9.84	887.54	56.20	
18 Sept	Paying-in slip 587	559.57		559.57		
19 Sept	Paying-in slip 588	234.23	27.74	48.00	158.49	
		3,265.88	37.58	3,013.61	214.69	

The bankings are a mixture of cash sales and cheques from debtors. The VAT is just the VAT on the cash/cheque sales. There are no discounts.

Check that the three analysis column totals add back to the total column total.

O EXAMPLE ○○○○

Returning to the cash receipts book, post the totals to the main ledger accounts.

Cash receipts book

Date	Narrative	Total £	VAT £	Debtors £	Cash/cheque sales £	Discount allowed £
15 Sept	Paying-in slip 584	653.90		653.90		
16 Sept	Paying-in slip 585	864.60		864.60		
17 Sept	Paying-in slip 586	953.58	9.84	887.54	56.20	
18 Sept	Paying-in slip 587	559.57		559.57		
19 Sept	Paying-in slip 588	234.23	27.74	48.00	158.49	
		3,265.88	37.58	3,013.61	214.69	

Solution

The double entry for posting the cash receipts book totals is:

		£	£
DR	Bank account	3,265.88	
CR	VAT account		37.58
	Sales ledger control account		3,013.61
	Sales account		214.69

Bank account

	£		£
Cash receipts book (CRB)	3,265.88		

VAT account

	£		£
		CRB	37.58

Sales ledger control account

	£		£
		CRB	3,013.61

Sales account

	£		£
		CRB	214.69

Note that the description of each transaction is the primary record that it came from, the cash receipts book, shortened to CRB.

▷ ACTIVITY 5   ▷ ▷ ▷ ▷

The cheques received from customers of Passiflora Products Ltd, a small company which produces herbal remedies and cosmetics and supplies them to shops and beauty parlours, for a week are given below:

Cheques received

	Paying-in slip/customer	Amount £	Discount allowed £
01/5/X6	Paying-in slip 609		
	Natural Beauty	11,797.05	176.95
	Grapeseed	417.30	6.26
	New Age Remedies	6,379.65	95.69
	The Aromatherapy Shop	9,130.65	136.96
03/5/X6	Paying-in slip 610		
	Comfrey Group	5,689.20	85.34
	Natural Elegance	2,056.89	30.85
08/5/X6	Paying-in slip 611		
	The Herbalist	8,663.45	129.95
12/5/X6	Paying-in slip 612		
	Edwards Pharmacy	106.42	
	Healthworks	17,213.94	258.21
19/5/X6	Paying-in slip 613		
	The Beauty Box	11,195.85	167.94
	Crystals	54.19	
25/5/X6	Paying-in slip 614		
	The Village Chemist	7,662.55	114.94
29/5/X6	Paying-in slip 615		
	Brewer Brothers	2,504.61	37.57
30/5/X6	Paying-in slip 616		
	Lapis Lazuli	112.58	
31/5/X6	Paying-in slip 617		
	Lorelei	5,618.40	84.27
	Spain & Co, Chemists	197.93	

Required:

(a) Enter the totals for each paying-in slip (including discounts) into the cash receipts book given below.

(b) Total the cash receipts book and post the totals for the month to the main ledger accounts given.

(a)   Cash receipts book

Date	Narrative	Total £	VAT £	Debtors £	Other £	Discount £

(b)   Main ledger

Sales ledger control account

£		£

Discount allowed account

£		£

[Answer on p. 244]

▷ ACTIVITY 6   ▷ ▷ ▷ ▷

Given below are the details of paying-in slip 609 from the previous activity, Passiflora Products Ltd. You are required to enter the details in the subsidiary ledger accounts given.

Paying-in slip 609

	Amount £	Discount allowed £
Natural Beauty	11,797.05	176.95
Grapeseed	417.30	6.26
New Age Remedies	6,379.65	95.69
The Aromatherapy Shop	9,130.65	136.96

Natural Beauty

	£		£
Opening balance	17,335.24		

The Aromatherapy Shop

	£		£
Opening balance	12,663.42		

New Age Remedies

	£		£
Opening balance	6,475.34		

Grapeseed

	£		£
Opening balance	423.56		

[Answer on p. 245]

5 Test your knowledge ▷ ▷ ▷

1 Why is there no discount allowed column in the analysed sales day book?

2 Calculate the VAT on a credit sale for £1,000 where a 5% settlement discount is offered to the customer.

3 A customer takes a settlement discount of £57 when paying his invoice. What is the double entry for this £57 in the books of the seller?

4 A customer returns goods which were invoiced to him for £400 plus VAT and which have been paid for. What is the double entry in the main ledger of the books of the seller to record the original sale and payment and the raising of the credit note?

5 When customer X pays £500 including VAT for a sale made on credit to the seller Y, what entries does Y make in his analysed cash received book?

Date	Narrative	Total	VAT	Debtors	Cash/cheque sales	Discount allowed
		£	£	£	£	£

6 When customer Z pays £500 including VAT to the seller Y for a cash sale, what entries does Y make in his analysed cash received book?

Date	Narrative	Total	VAT	Debtors	Cash/cheque sales	Discount allowed
		£	£	£	£	£

[Answers on p. 245]

6 Summary

In this chapter we have pulled together into one place all the main documents and double entry for the sales cycle. If you have had any trouble with any of these points, you should refer again to the earlier chapters of the textbook where the double entry is explained in basic terms.

KAPLAN PUBLISHING

Answers to chapter activities & 'test your knowledge' questions

△ ACTIVITY 1   △ △ △ △

SALES DAY BOOK

Date	Invoice	Customer	Code	Total	VAT	Group 01	Group 02	Group 03	Group 04
				£	£	£	£	£	£
06/09/X1	1700	Gates Stores		470.00	70.00	400.00			
06/09/X1	1701	Texas		1,762.50	262.50				1,500.00
07/09/X1	1702	Dickens		1,410.00	210.00				1,200.00
07/09/X1	1703	Hintons DIY		1,880.00	280.00		1,600.00		
08/09/X1	1704	Co-op Stores		235.00	35.00	200.00			
08/09/X1	1705	B & Q Stores		1,175.00	175.00			1,000.00	
09/09/X1	1706	Ferris Décor		940.00	140.00		800.00		
09/09/X1	1707	Ferris Décor		705.00	105.00				600.00
10/09/X1	1708	Homestyle		235.00	35.00			200.00	
10/09/X1	1709	Quick Style		117.50	17.50	100.00			
				8,930.00	1,330.00	700.00	2,400.00	1,200.00	3,300.00

△ ACTIVITY 2   △ △ △ △

SLCA

	£		£
SDB	8,471.75		

Sales – Type 1 account

	£		£
		SDB	4,320.00

Sales – Type 2 account

	£		£
		SDB	2,890.00

VAT account

	£		£
		SDB	1,261.75

△ ACTIVITY 3   △ △ △ △

SALES RETURNS DAY BOOK

Date	Credit note no	Customer name	Code	Total £	VAT £	Product 1 £	Product 2 £
14/3	3066	K Lilt	L04	141.00	21.00		120.00
14/3	3067	J Davis	D07	18.80	2.80	16.00	
14/3	3068	I Oliver	O11	44.65	6.65	38.00	
14/3	3069	D Sharp	S02	94.00	14.00		80.00
				298.45	44.45	54.00	200.00

△ ACTIVITY 4 △△△△

Sales ledger control account

	£			£
			SRDB	589.26

Sales returns – Type 1

	£			£
SRDB	327.00			

Sales returns – Type 2

	£			£
SRDB	174.50			

VAT account

	£			£
SRDB	87.76			

△ ACTIVITY 5 △△△△

(a)   Cash receipts book

Date	Narrative	Total £	VAT £	Debtors £	Others £	Discount £
01/05/X6	Cheques – 609	27,724.65		27,724.65		415.86
03/05/X6	Cheques – 610	7,746.09		7,746.09		116.19
08/05/X6	Cheques – 611	8,663.45		8,663.45		129.95
12/05/X6	Cheques – 612	17,320.36		17,320.36		258.21
19/05/X6	Cheques – 613	11,250.04		11,250.04		167.94
25/05/X6	Cheques – 614	7,662.55		7,662.55		114.94
29/05/X6	Cheques – 615	2,504.61		2,504.61		37.57
30/05/X6	Cheques – 616	112.58		112.58		
31/05/X6	Cheques – 617	5,816.33		5,816.33		84.27
		88,800.66	–	88,800.66	–	1,324.93

(b)   Main ledger

Sales ledger control account

	£			£
			CRB	88,800.66
			CRB – discount allowed	1,324.93

Discount allowed account

	£			£
CRB	1,324.93			

△ ACTIVITY 6   △△△△

Natural Beauty

	£			£
Opening balance	17,335.24		CRB	11,797.05
			CRB – discount	176.95

The Aromatherapy Shop

	£			£
Opening balance	12,663.42		CRB	9,130.65
			CRB – discount	136.96

New Age Remedies

	£			£
Opening balance	6,475.34		CRB	6,379.65
			CRB – discount	95.69

Grapeseed

	£			£
Opening balance	423.56		CRB	417.30
			CRB – discount	6.26

Test your knowledge ▷ ▷ ▷

1 There is no discount allowed column because the value of an invoice entered in the sales day book is always the amount before the discount as you do not know whether or not the customer will take the discount.

2 $(£1,000 – (5\% \times £1,000)) \times 17.5\% = £166.25$

3 Debit discount allowed £57; credit SLCA £57
(Note that £57 will also be entered on the credit side of the individual debtors account in the subsidiary sales ledger.)

4

Sales

	£				£
			SLCA	(1)	400

Sales returns

		£		£
SLCA	(3)	400		

VAT

		£			£
SLCA	(3)	70	SLCA	(1)	70

SLCA

		£			£
Sales plus VAT	(1)	470	Bank	(2)	470
			Sales returns plus VAT	(3)	470

Bank

		£		£
SLCA	(2)	470		

5

Date	Narrative	Total £	VAT £	Debtors £	Cash/cheque £	Discount £
	X	500		500		

6

Date	Narrative	Total £	VAT £	Debtors £	Cash/cheque £	Discount £
	Z	500	74.46		425.54	

CREDIT PURCHASES: DOCUMENTS

INTRODUCTION

You will be required to deal with many aspects of the purchases that a business makes. This will involve the procedure for making the purchase and the procedures for paying for the purchase.

In this chapter we will study the documents required when making a purchase.

KNOWLEDGE & UNDERSTANDING

- Business transactions and documents involved (Element 1, 2 and 3)
- Credit limits (Element 1)
- Documentation for payments (Element 2)
- Different ordering systems: Internet, verbal and written (Element 2)
- Discrepancies arising from supplier invoices (Element 3)

CONTENTS

1 Summary of a credit purchase
2 Ordering goods and services
3 Receipt of the goods
4 The purchase invoice
5 Credit notes

PERFORMANCE CRITERIA

- Check suppliers' invoices for accuracy and against source documents (Element 30.2)
- Check calculations, including discounts, on suppliers' invoices and credit notes (Element 30.2)
- Check suppliers' credit notes against correspondence or other relevant source documents (Element 30.2)
- Write to suppliers to resolve discrepancies in invoices (Element 30.2)

1 Summary of a credit purchase

The main document flows for a credit purchase are illustrated below. The various documents are described in the paragraphs that follow.

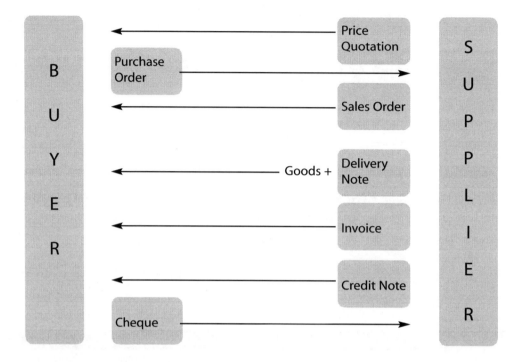

2 Ordering goods and services

2.1 Introduction

There are a variety of different methods of placing an order with a supplier.

(a) **Telephone**
If an order is made by telephone then it is important that the details are confirmed with the supplier in writing. This may be by the supplier sending your organisation an order confirmation or alternatively by you following up the telephone order with a written confirmation of the details.

(b) **In writing**
If an order is to be made in writing then again you would expect an order confirmation to be sent back to you by the supplier confirming all of the details of the order, for example, price, discounts and delivery details.

(c) **Fax**
An order could be made with a supplier by sending a fax. This is similar to sending an order in writing, only that it is received sooner by the supplier. However again you would expect to receive an order confirmation from the supplier.

(d)   **Internet**

These days it is also possible to order many goods over the internet as there are many websites that allow you to purchase goods directly online. This should only be considered if it is a procedure that is allowed by your organisation's policy manual and this course of action should be authorised by the appropriate person before any order is placed. It is advisable to only order goods from reputable, well-known organisations but if the organisation is unknown then try to find one that at least has a telephone number that will allow you to verify their authenticity. A copy of the order placed over the internet should be printed out to act as a purchase order and be filed accordingly.

In all instances of ordering, a copy of the order or order confirmation should be filed so that it can be compared with the actual goods when they arrive and eventually with the purchase invoice.

2.2 An internal purchasing system

When a department needs goods and services from outside suppliers it may make an internal request using a **purchase requisition.**

A purchase requisition is an internal document by which a department requests purchases from an outside supplier.

When the purchasing department of a business receives a purchase requisition then it will start the procedures of the purchasing system.

This will normally start with price enquiries being made of a number of different suppliers in order to identify the supplier who will provide the goods at the best price and with the best terms. The suppliers will then send a price quotation in order for the purchasing department to be able to compare prices and terms.

A typical quotation is shown below. Note that this is exactly the same as the quotation received in the examples in Chapter 10 where we studied the sales order systems. The purchasing system is the 'mirror image' of the sales system and the documents are the same. We are simply looking at these systems from the point of view of the customer rather than the supplier.

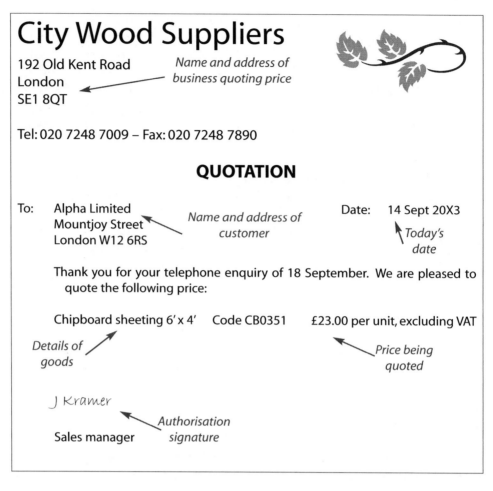

When the supplier has been chosen then a purchase order will be sent out to that supplier.

2.3 Purchase order

☐ **DEFINITION**

A purchase order is a document sent to a supplier confirming an order for goods or services.

Each purchase order must be authorised by the relevant department head or supervisor before being sent to the supplier. Each department head has an **authorisation limit**. Orders above that value must be authorised by a director, eg managing director.

Only approved suppliers (shown on an official list) should be used.

Purchase orders should be sequentially numbered and carefully controlled and filed in numerical order for later use.

An example purchase order is shown overleaf:

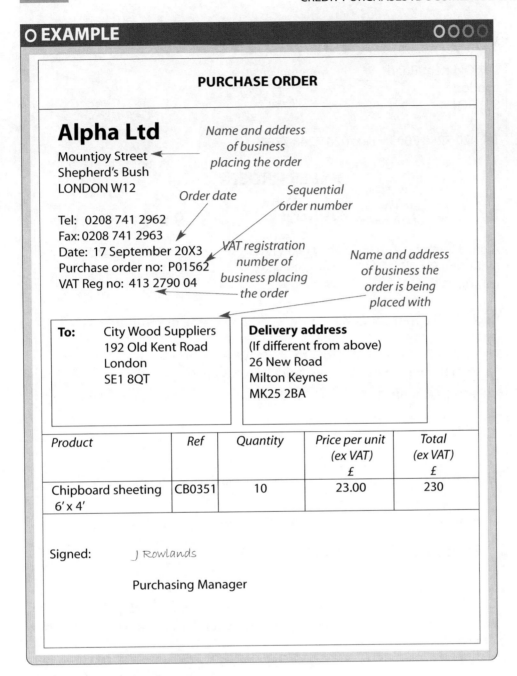

PURCHASE ORDER

Alpha Ltd — *Name and address of business placing the order*

Mountjoy Street
Shepherd's Bush
LONDON W12

Order date   *Sequential order number*

Tel: 0208 741 2962
Fax: 0208 741 2963
Date: 17 September 20X3
Purchase order no: P01562   *VAT registration number of business placing the order*
VAT Reg no: 413 2790 04

Name and address of business the order is being placed with

To:	City Wood Suppliers 192 Old Kent Road London SE1 8QT	**Delivery address** (If different from above) 26 New Road Milton Keynes MK25 2BA

Product	Ref	Quantity	Price per unit (ex VAT) £	Total (ex VAT) £
Chipboard sheeting 6' x 4'	CB0351	10	23.00	230

Signed: *J Rowlands*

Purchasing Manager

2.4 Confirming sales orders

To avoid misunderstandings, a supplier will normally confirm a customer's order by completing a sales order, even if the customer has already sent a written **purchase order**.

A sales order is a document confirming:
· quantity/type of goods or service;
· date of supply;
· location of supply;
· price and terms.

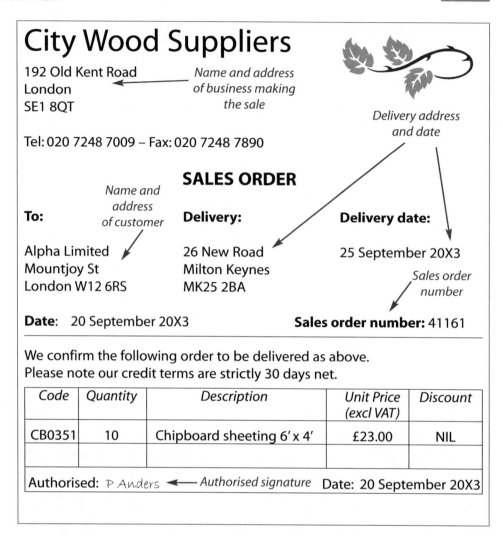

City Wood Suppliers

192 Old Kent Road
London
SE1 8QT

*Name and address
of business making
the sale*

Tel: 020 7248 7009 – Fax: 020 7248 7890

SALES ORDER

*Delivery address
and date*

To:

*Name and
address
of customer*

Alpha Limited
Mountjoy St
London W12 6RS

Delivery:

26 New Road
Milton Keynes
MK25 2BA

Delivery date:

25 September 20X3

*Sales order
number*

Date: 20 September 20X3

Sales order number: 41161

We confirm the following order to be delivered as above.
Please note our credit terms are strictly 30 days net.

Code	Quantity	Description	Unit Price (excl VAT)	Discount
CB0351	10	Chipboard sheeting 6' x 4'	£23.00	NIL

Authorised: *P Anders* ← *Authorised signature* **Date:** 20 September 20X3

3 Receipt of the goods

3.1 Introduction

Once the order has been placed with the supplier then the next stage will be for the goods to be received.

3.2 Delivery note

When the supplier sends the goods they will normally be accompanied by a delivery note.

□ DEFINITION   □□□□

A delivery note is a document that accompanies the goods when they are delivered by the supplier.

The delivery note details the goods that have been delivered to your organisation. When the goods are received by the business they must be checked by the stores or warehouse to ensure that the goods that are detailed on the delivery note are indeed the goods that have been delivered. The goods must also be checked to ensure that they are in good condition. The person in your organisation who has checked the goods will then sign the delivery note.

There will normally be three parts to a delivery note:

Part one – This is kept by your organisation in order to compare to the purchase order to ensure that the goods that have been delivered were ordered and then to the purchase invoice when it is received.

Part two – Returned to the supplier as evidence that you have received the goods detailed on the delivery note.

Part three – Kept by the delivery organisation as evidence that they have delivered the goods and that your organisation has received them.

City Wood Suppliers

192 Old Kent Road
London
SE1 8QT
Tel: 020 7248 7009 – Fax: 020 7248 7890

DN 005673

DELIVERY NOTE

To:	**Delivery:**	**Delivery date:**
Alpha Limited	26 New Road	25 September 20X3
Mountjoy St	Milton Keynes	
London W12 6RS	MK25 2BA	

Date: 21 September 20X3   **Sales order number:** 41161

We confirm the following order to be delivered as above.

Product	Code	Quantity
Chipboard 6' x 4'	CB0351	10

Received in good condition: A Patel

4   The purchase invoice

4.1 Introduction

The final stage in the purchasing system will normally be the receipt of the purchase invoice from the supplier detailing the cost of the goods purchased and the payment terms.

A typical invoice is shown below.

City Wood Suppliers

192 Old Kent Road
London
SE1 8QT

Tel: 020 7248 7009 – Fax: 020 7248 7890

Invoice no:	I005673
Tax point:	21 September 20X3
VAT reg no:	618 2201 63
Delivery note:	DN005673
Account no:	AL6215

INVOICE

To:

Alpha Limited
Mountjoy St
London W12 6RS

Delivery:

26 New Road
Milton Keynes
MK25 2BA

Delivery date:

25 September 20X3

Date: 21 September 20X3

Sales order number: 41161

Product	Code	Quantity	Price per unit £	Total £
Chipboard 6' x 4'	CB0351	10	23.00	230.00
			VAT	40.25
				270.25

4.2 Checks on purchase invoices

Once the purchase invoice arrives then a number of checks need to be made on it before it can be passed for payment.

4.3 Order and receipt of goods

Firstly the purchase invoice must be checked to the purchase order and to the delivery note. This is to ensure that not only is this an invoice for goods that were ordered but also for goods that were received. In particular check the description and the quantity of the goods.

For example suppose that the purchase order for goods shows that 100 packs were ordered and the delivery note shows that 100 packs were received. If when the invoice arrives it is for 120 packs then the supplier should be politely informed of the error and a credit note requested.

4.4 Calculations

All of the calculations on the invoice should also be checked to ensure that they are correct. This will include the following:
·   all pricing calculations;
·   any trade discount or bulk discount calculations;
·   the VAT calculations remembering any cash discounts that may be offered;
·   the total addition of the invoice.

4.5 Trade discounts

Remember that trade discounts are a definite amount that is deducted from the list price of the goods for the supplies to some customers. As well as checking the actual calculation of the trade discount on the face of the invoice, the supplier's file or the price quotation should be checked to ensure that the correct percentage of trade discount has been deducted.

Even if no trade discount appears on the purchase invoice, the supplier's file or price quotation must still be checked as it may be that a trade discount should have been deducted but has been inadvertently forgotten by the supplier.

4.6 Bulk discounts

A bulk discount is similar to a trade discount in that it is deducted from the list price on the invoice. However, a bulk discount is given by a supplier for orders above a certain size. As with a trade discount the calculation of any bulk discount must be checked to the supplier's file to ensure that the correct discount has been given.

4.7 Settlement or cash discounts

Settlement or cash discounts are offered to customers in order to encourage early payment of invoices. The details of the settlement discount will normally be shown at the bottom of the purchase invoice and it is up to the customer to decide whether to pay the invoice early enough to benefit from the settlement discount or whether to delay payment and ignore the settlement discount.

Again the supplier's file should be checked to ensure that the correct percentage of settlement discount according to the correct terms has been offered.

If there is no settlement discount offered the supplier's details must still be checked to ensure that the settlement discount has not been forgotten by the supplier.

A trade discount or a bulk discount is a definite reduction in price from the list price whereas a cash or settlement discount is only a reduction in price if the organisation decides to take advantage of it by paying earlier.

4.8 VAT calculations and cash discounts

You will remember from an earlier chapter that when a cash or settlement discount is offered then the VAT calculation is based upon the assumption that the customer will take the settlement discount and pay the discounted price for the goods.

○ EXAMPLE ○○○○

An invoice has a list price of goods of £400.00 with a trade discount of 10% then deducted. A settlement discount of 5% is also offered for payment within 10 days. The goods are charged to VAT at a rate of 17.5%.

How much should the VAT charge on the invoice be and what would be the invoice total?

Solution

	£
List price	400.00
Less: Trade discount 10%	40.00
	360.00
VAT (17.5% x (360 x 95%))	59.85
Invoice total	419.85

▷ ACTIVITY 1 ▷▷▷▷

A business receives an invoice for £2,400 (exclusive of VAT) from a supplier offering a 5% cash discount. What should be the total of the invoice inclusive of VAT at 17.5%

[Answer on p. 263]

Given below are two invoices; they must be thoroughly checked to ensure that they are correct.

Invoice **7761B**

Barrett & Company

Ewe House, Parkside, Oldham.

J Hardy Construction,
Poplar Works,
Poplar Street,
Oldham OL4 6QB

Tel: 0161 338 4444
Fax: 0161 338 5555
Tax Point: 28 August 20X3
VAT Reg No: 268 9104 07

Code	Supply	Description	Quantity	VAT rate	Unit price £	Amount (£) exclusive of VAT
734 226	Sale	Insular Bricks	40	17.50%	16.25	650.00
874 KL5	Sale	Brick Tiles	15	17.50%	43.12	664.80
Total						1,296.80
VAT at 17.5%						226.94
Total amount payable						1,523.74

A settlement discount of 5% is offered for payment within 20 days of the invoice date.

Invoice **68553**

A.J. Broom & Company Limited.
59 Parkway, Manchester M2 6EG

J Hardy Construction,
Poplar Works,
Poplar Street,
Oldham OL4 6QB

Tel: 0161 560 3392
Fax: 0161 560 5322
Tax Point: 23 August 20X3
VAT Reg No: 417 1066 22

Code	Supply	Description	Quantity	VAT rate	Unit price £	Amount (£) exclusive of VAT
950 BB3	Sale	Cotswold Bricks	3	17.50%	300.00	900.00
159 504	Sale	Roof Tiles – Red	5	17.50%	195.50	977.50
874 KL5	Sale	Brick Tiles	1	17.50%	56.65	56.65
Total						1,934.15
Less: trade discount 2%						28.68
						1,905.47
VAT at 17.5%						333.46
Total amount payable						**2,238.93**

Solution

Invoice from Barrett & Co
· the calculation of the brick tiles total is incorrect – it should be 15 x £43.12 = £646.80;
· the VAT has been incorrectly calculated as it has been taken on the invoice total instead of on the figure that would be due if the cash discount were taken. The VAT should be 95% x 17.5% x £1,296.80 = £215.59.

Invoice from A J Broom & Co
· the trade discount of 2% has been incorrectly calculated and this means that the VAT is also incorrect. The supplier should be notified of these errors and a credit note requested.

In assessments you should thoroughly check every figure and every calculation on a purchase invoice just as you would in practice.

▷ ACTIVITY 2 ▷▷▷▷

(AAT CA D92)
When passing a purchase invoice for payment, what two aspects need to be checked, other than calculations?

[Answer on p. 263]

4.9 Invoices for services

Invoices or bills can also be received for services such as rent, electricity, cleaning, etc. There will be no delivery note, however the accuracy of the invoice can be checked and it should be sent to the appropriate person to be authorised. This person should be able to assess whether the service has in fact been received and was required.

5 Credit notes

5.1 Introduction

A credit note is simply the reverse of an invoice. It is sent by a supplier to a customer either to correct an error on a previous invoice or because the customer has returned some goods that do not therefore need to be paid for. Exactly the same checks should be made on credit notes as on invoices. The reason for the credit note and the amount that has been credited should be checked, so should all of the calculations and the VAT.

If Alpha Ltd returned two panels of wood, the credit note would be as follows.

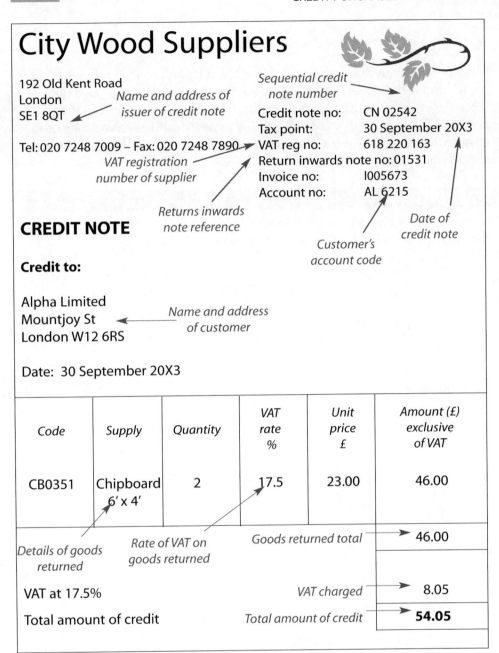

City Wood Suppliers

192 Old Kent Road
London
SE1 8QT

Name and address of issuer of credit note

Tel: 020 7248 7009 – Fax: 020 7248 7890

VAT registration number of supplier

Returns inwards note reference

CREDIT NOTE

Credit to:

Alpha Limited
Mountjoy St
London W12 6RS

Name and address of customer

Date: 30 September 20X3

Sequential credit note number

Credit note no:	CN 02542
Tax point:	30 September 20X3
VAT reg no:	618 220 163
Return inwards note no:	01531
Invoice no:	I005673
Account no:	AL 6215

Customer's account code

Date of credit note

Code	Supply	Quantity	VAT rate %	Unit price £	Amount (£) exclusive of VAT
CB0351	Chipboard 6' x 4'	2	17.5	23.00	46.00

Details of goods returned

Rate of VAT on goods returned

Goods returned total	46.00
VAT at 17.5% — *VAT charged*	8.05
Total amount of credit — *Total amount of credit*	**54.05**

▷ **ACTIVITY 3**   ▷ ▷ ▷ ▷

(AAT CA D92)
State the document appropriate to each of the following stages for purchasing and paying for goods.

(a)   Notification to purchasing manager of need to order.

(b)   Request to supplier to supply goods.

(c)   Form accompanying goods sent by supplier.

[Answer on p. 263]

5.2 The importance of checking documents

Every purchase invoice or credit note received by an organisation, whether it is for goods or services, must be thoroughly checked and approved before it is entered into the accounting records. The checks must ensure that the invoice is for goods or services actually ordered and received, and also ensure that the invoice or credit note is accurately made up, including checks on all calculations and VAT.

▷ ACTIVITY 4   ▷ ▷ ▷ ▷

Given below is a purchase invoice and associated documentation. Check the invoice carefully and decide what action should be taken.

DELIVERY NOTE   94511

Town Suppliers
111 City Road
London SE21 2TG
Tel: 020 7248 7123
Fax: 020 7248 7234

To: Delivery address:
Omega Ltd   (if different):
27 Holly Road
Birmingham
B27 4XL

Date: 19 October 20X1

Code	Quantity	Description
PP0292	90	4" x 2" Piranha pine 6′

Received by:................................. Date: ....

PURCHASE ORDER 263

Omega Ltd

27 Holly Road

Birmingham

B27 4XL

To: Town Suppliers

111 City Road

London SE21 2TG

Date: 6 October 20X1

PLEASE SUPPLY TO THE ABOVE ADDRESS

Code	Quantity	Description	Unit price (exclusive of VAT) £
PP0292	100	6' Piranha pine (4" x 2")	3.50

INVOICE 94511

Town Suppliers

111 City Road
London SE21 2TG
Tel: 020 7248 7123
Fax: 020 7248 7234

To:
Omega Ltd
27 Holly Road
Birmingham
B27 4XL

Tax point: 19 October 20X1

VAT Reg No: 234 4610 23

Code	Quantity	Amount exclusive of VAT £	VAT rate %	VAT net £
PP0292	100	350.00	17.5	61.25
	Total	350.00		
	VAT	61.25		
		411.25		

[Answer on p. 263]

6 Test your knowledge

1   When your business wishes to purchase goods from a supplier what document will normally be sent to the supplier?

2   When goods are received from a supplier what document will normally accompany the goods?

3   If goods are returned to a supplier what document would you expect to receive from the supplier?

4   What are the main checks that should be made when a purchase invoice is received?

5   If a bulk discount has been agreed with a supplier how should this be treated on the purchase invoice?

6   A purchase invoice is received for goods with a list price of £1,000 net of VAT. The supplier has agreed a trade discount of 10% and a settlement discount of 2% has been offered. What is the amount of VAT that should be charged on the invoice?

[Answers on p. 263]

7   Summary

In this chapter the documentation that is used in the purchases system is firstly considered. The different methods of ordering goods and services are covered, as well as the documents that are required when goods are received: the delivery note, the purchase invoice and possibly any credit notes. The most important aspect of the chapter, however, are the thorough and accurate checks that must be made on all purchase invoices and credit notes received from suppliers. The invoices and credit notes must be checked to supporting documentation such as the delivery note, purchase order, returns note, etc. All of the calculations on the invoice or credit note should be checked as well as the percentage of trade, bulk and settlement discounts that have been stated on the invoice or credit note.

Answers to chapter activities & 'test your knowledge' questions

△ ACTIVITY 1   △△△△

£2,799

Note: This answer is arrived at as follows:

	£
Goods/services	2,400
VAT @ 17.5% x 2,400 x 95%	399
	——
	2,799
	——

△ ACTIVITY 2   △△△△

(i)   That the goods or services invoiced are as ordered.
(ii) That the goods or services invoiced have been received in good condition or carried out properly.

△ ACTIVITY 3   △△△△

(a)   Purchase requisition
(b)   Purchase order
(c)   Delivery note

△ ACTIVITY 4   △△△△

The delivery note shows that only 90 units were delivered, not the 100 units that were ordered and invoiced.
You should write to the supplier requesting a credit note for the 10 missing units. Once the supplier has agreed the situation, the invoice can then be passed for payment.

Test your knowledge △ △ △

1   Purchase order.

2   Delivery note.

3   Credit note.

4   · Check to the purchase order and delivery note
    · Check all prices and price extensions
    · Check calculations of trade/bulk discounts and that the correct percentage has been used
    · Check VAT calculations
    · Check total addition of the invoice

5   A bulk discount should be deducted from the list price.

6   £1,000 – 100 = £900
    VAT = £900 x 98% x 17.5% = £154.35

MAKING PAYMENTS

INTRODUCTION

Once the invoice for purchases has been received then payment must be made for the goods or services. In this chapter we will consider the different methods of payment, the most appropriate methods of payment, the timing of payments and how the payment procedure works.

KNOWLEDGE & UNDERSTANDING

- Cheques, including crossings and endorsements (Elements 1 and 2)
- Automated receipts and payments (Elements 1 and 2)
- Discrepancies arising from supplier invoices (Element 3)
- Capital and revenue expenditure (Elements 2 and 3)

CONTENTS

1 Payments by cheque
2 Transferring money by different methods
3 Payments to credit suppliers
4 Payment by invoice
5 Payment of suppliers' statements
6 Payment on a set date
7 Authorisation of invoices
8 Cheque requisitions
9 Capital and revenue expenditure

PERFORMANCE CRITERIA

- Calculate suppliers payments from source documentation (Element 30.2)
- Schedule payments, and types of payment, as per company policy (Element 30.2)
- Write to suppliers to resolve discrepancies in invoices (Element 30.2)

1 Payments by cheque

1.1 Introduction

Most of the payments that a business will make will be by cheque. This may be by writing a cheque for cash purchases or sending a cheque to a credit supplier. The detailed legal requirements relating to cheques were covered in Chapter 11 and therefore in this chapter we will only cover these requirements briefly.

1.2 Writing a cheque

When a cheque is written out by a business it is important that it is correctly drawn up. The main factors to consider are:

·   The cheque must be dated with today's date – a cheque is only valid for six months after the date on the cheque and most suppliers would not accept a post-dated cheque so care should be taken when writing the date onto the cheque.

·   The payee's name must be correct – the supplier's name will be on the purchase invoice and this should be correctly reproduced on the cheque otherwise the supplier will not be able to pay the cheque into his bank account.

·   The amount of the cheque in words and figures must agree with each other – if there is a difference then the cheque cannot be paid into the supplier's account and will be returned by the bank to your business.

·   The cheque must be signed by the appropriate cheque signatory within the business – in many businesses it will be the organisation's policy that cheques, particularly if they exceed a certain limit, must be signed by more than one cheque signatory.

·   If any alterations are made to the cheque then these must be initialled by the cheque signatory.

1.3 Stopped cheques

If a cheque is written by your business and sent out to a supplier it can be stopped at any point in time right up until the bank pays it. In order to stop a cheque your business must write to the bank and give clear details of the payee's name, the cheque's number and the amount payable.

> **▷ ACTIVITY 1**   ▷ ▷ ▷ ▷

You are writing out a cheque for £374 as payment for goods. As you write out the cheque you do not notice that you have dated it 1 June 20X1. Today's date is 1 June 20X2.

Will payment of the cheque by the drawer's bank be affected by the incorrect date? Yes/No

Having noticed the error, is it acceptable for you to alter the cheque to the correct date? Yes/No

[Answer on p. 280]

2 Transferring money by different methods

2.1 Introduction

A bank customer can transfer money from his account to another person's account by a number of other methods which do not involve writing cheques.

These methods were covered in Chapter 11 on the banking system.

2.2 The appropriate method of payment

As we have seen in an earlier chapter there are a number of methods available to businesses of making payments – by cheque, standing order, direct debit, bank giro credit, BACS, CHAPS. The organisation will normally have policies regarding which method of payment is to be used for different types of payment.

Most credit suppliers are likely to require payment by cheque or by direct bank giro credit.

Many organisations such as gas, telephone and electricity providers will encourage customers to pay by direct debit. This means that once the direct debit has been set up then this will automatically be taken from your bank account on the agreed day with no action necessary for your business.

Any fixed periodic payments however might be more appropriately made by standing order as a standing order is for a fixed amount on a fixed periodic date.

Often the wages and salaries payments of a business will be one of the largest and most regular of payments that must be made (see Chapter 19). The most common method of making the regular wages and salaries payments to employees is using the BACS system.

3 Payments to credit suppliers

3.1 Authorised documentation

A business must make a payment only if there is authorised documentation to show that the payment is genuine. Authorised documentation might include:
· an invoice which has been signed or stamped by a responsible official;
· a cheque requisition form;
· a memo from a responsible official.

Cheques are normally prepared by the cashier. The cashier should ensure that the amount of the cheque agrees to the authorised documentation.

3.2 Methods of scheduling payments

Different businesses will have different policies for determining the timing of payments to credit suppliers. Some of the most common methods are:

· to pay each invoice that arrives at the latest possible date according to the credit terms;

· to pay a number of invoices at the same time when the supplier's statement is received;

· to make payments on a set day, such as every Friday, and to pay all of those invoices that will have exceeded their credit terms by the following Friday.

4 Payment by invoice

4.1 Introduction

When each invoice is received it is looked at and the latest date on which it can be paid according to the credit terms of the supplier will be determined. The invoice will then be scheduled for payment on this date.

4.2 Invoices and cash discounts

When the cashier is dealing with writing a cheque for payment of an invoice, then the invoice should already be marked as authorised by the appropriate person in the organisation, having checked it against appropriate documentation such as the purchase order and delivery note . The only remaining task is to deal with any cash or settlement discounts.

Firstly it must be checked that it is company policy to take cash discounts. If this is the case then it must be determined whether there is time to make the payment on time and claim the discount. Finally the amount of the cash discount and the net amount that is to be paid should be calculated.

○ EXAMPLE   ○○○○

An invoice shows the following details:

Date: 3 June 20X6

	£
List price of goods	4,000.00
Trade discount 5%	200.00
	3,800.00
VAT	638.40
Invoice total	4,438.40

A settlement discount of 4% is offered for payment received within 10 days of the invoice date.

Suppose that today's date is 7 June.

Solution

Today is 7 June and in order to claim the settlement discount the payment must arrive with the supplier by 13 June. Provided that the payment is made in the next few days and posted to the supplier immediately then the settlement discount can be claimed.

The amount of the discount should then be calculated and deducted from the invoice total. This final amount is the amount for which the cheque should be drawn.

	£
Net of VAT amount	3,800.00
Settlement discount (3,800 x 4%)	(152.00)
	3,648.00
Add: VAT	638.40
Cheque amount	4,286.40

You should always check that the VAT has been correctly calculated on the basis of the assumption that the settlement discount will in fact be taken.

The settlement discount is calculated as the stated percentage of the net invoice amount. The VAT per the invoice is then added to find the final total payment.

▷ ACTIVITY 2

(AAT CA D92)

A company has recently purchased supplies from International Toiletries Ltd for £250, less 20% trade discount, plus 17.5% VAT. International allow 2.5% cash discount for payment within seven days of the receipt of their invoice.

(a) State which of the following total amounts is due for payment by the company if they take advantage of the cash discount.

    A   £237.66
    B   £227.65
    C   £229.12

(b) What would be the VAT inclusive total shown on the original invoice?

[Answer on p. 280]

▷ ACTIVITY 3   ▷ ▷ ▷ ▷

You have received the following invoices from suppliers who offer settlement discounts. You must calculate the discount offered and decide whether or not you can take the discount if you send a cheque today. Today is 21 June 20X9.

	Supplier	Invoice date	Net invoice amount	Discount terms	
(a)	ABC Fencing	20 May 20X9	£239.50	2.5%	30 days
(b)	Brown & Black	15 June 20X9	£458.63	1.5%	28 days
(c)	Peter's Wood Products	10 June 20X9	£168.00	2.0%	14 days
(d)	S J Lever	15 May 20X9	£391.48	2.0%	30 days
(e)	A J Bennett	1 June 20X9	£56.91	2.5%	14 days

[Answer on p.280]

5   Payment of suppliers' statements

5.1 Introduction

Another document that could be used as a document for requisitioning a payment to a supplier is a supplier's statement. A supplier's statement will have the same form as the customer's statement that we considered in an earlier chapter. The supplier's statement could be used when the intention is to pay a number of invoices to this supplier with just one cheque.

5.2 Checking suppliers' statements

Before any payments are made it is important to check that the supplier's statement is correct. Each invoice and credit note should be checked either to the original documentation or to the supplier's account in the subsidiary ledger.

When the accuracy of the statement has been ascertained then it must be determined exactly which invoices from the statement are to be paid.

O **EXAMPLE**   O O O O

Given below is a statement from a supplier together with that supplier's account from the subsidiary ledger.

	Nemo Limited
	23 Park Road
	Oldham
	OL1 1VR

To: Scott Brothers   Date: 31 August 20X3
         34 Festival Way
         Oldham
         OL2 3BD

STATEMENT

Date	Transaction	Total £	Current £	30+ £	60+ £
12 May 20X3	Invoice 2569	92.35			92.35
13 June 20X3	CN 2659	(23.60)			(23.60)
09 July 20X3	Invoice 2701	102.69		102.69	
18 July 20X3	Invoice 2753	133.81		133.81	
02 Aug 20X3	Invoice 2889	56.50	56.50		
10 Aug 20X3	Invoice 2901	230.20	230.20		
28 Aug 20X3	Invoice 3114	243.24	243.24		
	TOTALS	835.19	529.94	236.50	68.75

May we remind you our credit terms are 30 days

Nemo Ltd

		£			£
13 June	CN 2659	23.60	12 May	Invoice 2569	92.35
			09 July	Invoice 2701	102.69
			18 July	Invoice 2753	133.81
			02 Aug	Invoice 2889	56.50
			10 Aug	Invoice 2901	203.20
			28 Aug	Invoice 3114	243.24

To check that the supplier's statement is correct prior to paying any amounts, the statement should be carefully checked to the supplier's account in the subsidiary ledger.

Solution

The invoice dated 10 August is in the subsidiary ledger at a total of £203.20 whereas it appears on the supplier's statement as £230.20.

The purchase invoice itself should be accessed from the filing system to determine whether the amount is £203.20 or £230.20. If the supplier's statement is incorrect then a polite telephone call should be made or letter sent to the supplier, Nemo Ltd, explaining the problem.

5.3 Which invoices to pay

Once the supplier's statement has been checked for accuracy then it has to be decided which invoices shall be paid. Most organisations will have a policy regarding the payment of supplier's invoices or, alternatively, a fairly senior figure in the business will decide each month which invoices are to be paid.

○ **EXAMPLE**   ○○○○

Using the supplier's statement shown above suppose that payment has been authorised for all amounts that have been outstanding for 30 days or more. What amount should the cheque be made out for?

Solution

	£
60+ days total	68.75
30+ days total	236.50
	————
Cheque amount	305.25

5.4 Remittance advices

Some suppliers will attach a remittance advice to the bottom of their statement so that the customer can indicate which invoices less credit notes are being paid with this cheque.

○ **EXAMPLE**   ○○○○

Given below is a supplier's statement from Bart & Partners. Attached to it is the remittance advice. The policy of the business is to pay all of the January and February invoices less credit notes.

Complete the remittance advice on the basis that the payment was made by cheque number 047732 on 4 April 20X2.

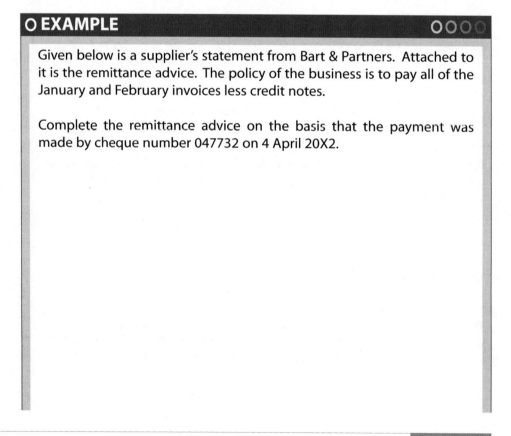

Bart & Partners
Spring House
Park Estate
Oldham OL2 3CF

To: Fells Brothers   Date: 31 March 20X2
     Simpfield House
     Oldham
     OL1 3XJ

STATEMENT

Date	Transaction	Total £	Current £	30+ £	60+ £
15 Jan 20X2	INV 12611	308.50			308.50
01 Feb 20X2	CN 04779	(112.60)		(112.60)	
20 Feb 20X2	INV 12683	419.80		419.80	
02 Mar 20X2	INV 12710	384.20	384.20		
14 Mar 20X2	INV 12748	116.88	116.88		
	TOTALS	1,116.78	501.08	307.20	308.50

May we remind you our credit terms are 30 days

REMITTANCE ADVICE

To:

Company name:

Address:

Date:

Date	Our ref	Amount £	Discount taken £	Paid £
15 Jan 20X2	INV 12611	308.50		
01 Feb 20X2	CN 04779	(112.60)		
20 Feb 20X2	INV 12683	419.80		
02 Mar 20X2	INV 12710	384.20		
14 Mar 20X2	INV 12748	116.88		

Total paid

Cheque no

Solution

REMITTANCE ADVICE

To: Bart & Partners
Spring House
Park Estate
Oldham OL2 3CF

Company name: Fells Brothers

Address: Simpfield House
Oldham OL1 3XJ

Date: 4 April 20X2

Date	Our ref	Amount £	Discount taken £	Paid £
15 Jan 20X2	INV 12611	308.50		308.50
01 Feb 20X2	CN 04779	(112.60)		(112.60)
20 Feb 20X2	INV 12683	419.80		419.80
02 Mar 20X2	INV 12710	384.20		
14 Mar 20X2	INV 12748	116.88		

Total paid £ 615.70

Cheque no 047732

6 Payment on a set date

6.1 Introduction

The problem with paying each invoice on the last possible date that it can be paid is that this means that someone in the organisation is tied up with invoice payments every day. However, the other alternative of paying when the supplier's statement is received means that in many cases the opportunity to take advantage of any settlement discount offered is lost.

6.2 Alternative method

Therefore an alternative method is to set a day each week/fortnight for payment of invoices. On that day all invoices that would have exceeded their credit limit or lost the chance of the settlement discount by the next payment date would be paid.

O EXAMPLE O O O O

Your business has the policy of paying invoices each Friday and on that day to pay all invoices that would either exceed their settlement discount period or that would be exceeding their credit period by the following Friday.

Today is Friday 7 May. The following invoices are in the pile of unpaid invoices. Indicate which invoices would be paid today and why.

KAPLAN PUBLISHING

Supplier	Date	Amount £	Settlement terms
K Fielden	30 Apr	376.90	2% discount for payment within 14 days
Giles Associates	12 Apr	269.46	Net 30 days
Penfold Ltd	05 May	316.58	3% discount for payment within 14 days
Yalders Partners	06 May	146.37	4% discount for payment within 10 days

Solution

K Fielden	30 Apr	376.90	2% discount for payment within 14 days

– in order to take the discount the payment must be received by the supplier by 14 May. As next Friday will be 14 May it is too late to make the payment then so, if the discount is to be taken, payment must be made today.

Giles Associates	12 Apr	269.46	Net 30 days

– as April has 30 days the payment must be received by 12 May. Therefore payment must be made today in order to remain within the stated credit terms.

Penfold Ltd	5 May	316.58	3% discount for payment within 14 days

– in order to take the discount the payment must be received by the supplier by 19 May. Next Friday will be 14 May which should give enough time for the cheque to be drawn and sent to the supplier to arrive by 19 May.

Yalders Partners	6 May	146.37	4% discount for payment within 10 days

– in order to take the discount the payment must be received by the supplier by 16 May. As next Friday is the 14 May, making 16 May the Sunday, it would seem unlikely that if payment were put off until next week, it would reach the supplier in time. Therefore if the discount is to be taken it should be paid today.

7 Authorisation of invoices

7.1 Introduction

In an earlier chapter we saw how all purchase invoices should be thoroughly checked to ensure that they are for goods or services that have been received by the business, that the goods and services have been charged at the correct rate and that all discounts and calculations are correct.

7.2 Authorisation stamp

At this point in the checking process the invoice was stamped with an authorisation stamp or grid stamp which showed that the invoice had been checked and also coded the invoice for the information required for entering it into the accounting records. A typical authorisation stamp at this stage in the process is shown below.

Purchase order no	436129
Invoice no	388649
Cheque no	
Account code	PL70
Checked	J Wilmber
Date	03/05/X4
ML account	006

7.3 Authorisation for payment

As we have seen, different organisations will have different methods of determining precisely when invoices will be paid. The only invoices that will be paid are ones that have already been checked and the authorisation stamp completed. The next stage, however, is for today's list of invoices to be paid to be authorised by the appropriate person within the organisation.

In a small organisation the appropriate person may be the cashier who will write out the cheques. Provided the cashier knows that the invoice has been checked and coded then he/she will determine which invoices need paying and will write out the cheque. At this stage the cheque number is the final entry on the authorisation stamp to show that the cheque has been paid and to ensure that it is not paid a second time in error.

In a larger organisation it may be that a more senior member of the management team must review the invoices due for payment before they are paid. In this case there may be an additional entry on the authorisation stamp for the signature of the manager or he may just initial the stamp itself to indicate to the cashier that payment is to be made.

8   Cheque requisitions

8.1 Introduction

In some instances a payment will need to be made but there is no invoice or bill as yet. Such payments can be made but must be requested by a completed and authorised cheque requisition form.

8.2 Cheque requisition

> **☐ DEFINITION**　　　　　　　　　　　　　　　　　☐☐☐☐
>
> A cheque requisition is a request for a cheque for payment to a third party where there is no invoice or bill to support this payment.
>
> The cheque requisition is a request for a cheque for a certain amount for a payment that does not work its way naturally through the purchase invoice system.

Once a cheque requisition has been completed it must be authorised by an appropriate senior person within the organisation and then the cheque can be issued.

○ EXAMPLE   ○○○○

The managing director's company car is in the garage for a service. At 4 o'clock the garage telephones to say that the car is ready to be collected and the cost of the service has been £342.60. It is necessary to give the garage a cheque for this amount upon collection of the car.

A cheque requisition form must be completed.

Solution

CHEQUE REQUISITION FORM

CHEQUE DETAILS

Date	3 June 20X6
Payee	Ricky's Garage
Amount £	342.60
Reason	Service of MD's car Account code ML03
Invoice no. (attached/to follow)	
Receipt (attached/to follow)	
Required by (Print)	M PLUMMER
(Signature)	M Plummer
Authorised by:	J Swain

---

9   Capital and revenue expenditure

9.1 Introduction

Most payments that are made by a business are for day-to day-expenses. These may be for:

· goods for resale;
· materials to be used in production;
· general expenses.

9.2 Revenue expenditure

These types of everyday expenses for the general running of the business are known as revenue expenditure. The other type of expenditure that a business might incur is capital expenditure.

9.3 Capital expenditure

Capital expenditure is payments for fixed assets. Fixed assets are long term assets for use in the business rather than for items that are either to be sold or to be used in the short term within the business. Typical items of capital expenditure are land and buildings, plant and machinery, office equipment, salesmen's cars, delivery vehicles or fixtures and fittings.

9.4 Payments for capital expenditure

In most cases the appropriate method of payment for a fixed asset will be by payment of a cheque. The procedure is exactly the same as for payments to credit suppliers for goods. The payment must be authorised and the cheque must be correctly prepared.

10 Test your knowledge

1   When writing out a cheque, which entries on the cheque should be checked carefully?

2   An invoice has been received for goods with a list price of £540.00 exclusive of VAT. A 10% trade discount is allowed by the supplier and a 4% settlement discount has been offered. If the discount is to be taken and VAT is payable at 17.5%, for what amount should the cheque be made out?

3   What is a supplier's statement?

4   What is a cheque requisition?

5   Explain the distinction between capital and revenue expenditure.

[Answers on p. 280]

11 Summary

In this chapter we considered the authorisation of the actual payments to be made to suppliers and for services and expenses. Remember that the invoices have already been checked for their accuracy and therefore the key to authorisation of payments is which invoices are to be paid. This will often depend upon the method of payment of invoices that it is the policy of the organisation to use. In some businesses all invoices are checked upon arrival to determine the latest date on which they can be paid in order to either validly claim a settlement discount or stay within the supplier's stated credit terms.

An alternative is to wait until the statement is received from the supplier at the end of the month. Once the statement has been checked to ensure that it is correct, it will be determined which invoices minus credit notes are to be paid.

The statement may be accompanied by a remittance advice which should be completed in order to show which invoices less credit notes are being paid.

The problem with waiting until the supplier's statement is received is that many settlement discounts that are offered are lost due to the payment only being made every month. Therefore an alternative is for the business to set a day each week or possibly every two weeks on which invoices are paid in order either to take advantage of the settlement discount or to ensure that the payment does not exceed the stated credit terms.

Prior to the payment of the invoice it must be authorised. In many small organisations the process of checking the invoice to ensure that the goods or services have been received and the checking of all of the details of the invoice for accuracy is all that is required for authorisation. In other organisations more senior managers might be required to authorise the invoices due to be paid today.

In some instances a cheque will be required although there is no invoice or bill to support it. In this case a cheque requisition form must be completed and authorised by an appropriate senior person within the organisation before the cheque is issued.

Payments may not only be made for revenue expenditure items but also for capital expenditure on fixed assets.

KAPLAN PUBLISHING

Answers to chapter activities & 'test your knowledge' questions

△ ACTIVITY 1   △△△△
(a)   Yes (since the cheque is more than six months old).
(b)   Yes, provided that you initial the date change.

△ ACTIVITY 2   △△△△
(a)   Option C
        (£250 x 80% x 97.5% x 1.175) = £229.12
(b)
                                                            £
        Supplies (£250 less 20% discount)   200.00
        VAT (£200 x 17.5% x 0.975)   34.12
                                                        ———————
        Total   234.12
                                                        ———————

△ ACTIVITY 3   △△△△

	Discount	*Can take discount?*
(a)	£5.99	No
(b)	£6.88	Yes
(c)	£3.36	Yes
(d)	£7.83	No
(e)	£1.42	No

Test your knowledge △ △ △

1 · Date
  · Payee's name
  · Words and figures agree
  · Signed by an authorised signatory
  · Any alterations initialled by the signatory

2
                                                £
        £540 x 90% x 96%   =   466.56
        VAT £466.56 x 17.5%   =   81.64
                                            ———————
                                            548.20
                                            ———————

3   A document received from a credit supplier detailing the invoices currently outstanding.

4   An internal document requesting a cheque where there is no supporting invoice.

5   Capital expenditure is expenditure on fixed assets for long-term use in the business. Revenue expenditure is all other expenditure of the business.

PAYROLL PROCEDURES

INTRODUCTION

We have seen how payments by cheque and other methods are made from the bank account for purchases and expenses and also how small payments are made in cash from the petty cash box. In this chapter we will consider one of the most significant payments that most businesses will make either weekly or monthly – wages and salaries.

KNOWLEDGE & UNDERSTANDING

· Payroll accounting procedures: accounting for gross pay and statutory and non-statutory deductions through the wages and salaries control account; payments to external agencies; security and control; simple gross pay to net calculations but excluding the use of tax and NI tables (Element 2)

CONTENTS

1 Overview of the payroll function
2 Gross pay
3 Income tax
4 National Insurance contributions
5 Other deductions
6 Making payments to employees
7 Payroll accounting procedures

PERFORMANCE CRITERIA

· Make payments to employees and record those payments (Element 30.2)

1 Overview of the payroll function

1.1 Introduction

The payroll system in a business is one of the most important. The payroll staff not only have a responsibility to calculate correctly the amount of pay due to each employee but they must also ensure that each employee is paid on time with the correct amount and that amounts due to external parties such as HM Revenue and Customs are correctly determined and paid on time.

There are many facets to the payroll function and each will be briefly covered as an introduction in this section and then considered in more detail in later sections of the chapter.

1.2 Calculation of gross pay

The initial calculation that must be carried out for each employee is the calculation of the employee's gross pay. Gross pay is the wage or salary due to the employee for the amount of work done in the period which may be a week or a month depending upon how frequently the employees are paid.

Gross pay may depend upon a number of factors:
· basic hours worked;
· overtime hours worked;
· bonus;
· commission;
· holiday pay;
· sick pay.

1.3 Deductions

Once the gross pay for each employee has been determined then a number of deductions from this amount will be made to arrive at the net pay for the employee. Net pay is the amount that the employee will actually receive.

Some deductions are compulsory or statutory:
· Income tax in the form of PAYE;
· National Insurance Contributions (NIC).

Other deductions are at the choice of the employer or employee and are therefore non-statutory:
· Save as you earn;
· Give as you earn;
· Pension contributions.

1.4 Payment of wages or salaries

Once the net pay has been determined then each employee must be paid the correct amount, by the most appropriate method at the correct time.

1.5 Payments to external agencies

As you will see later in the chapter employers deduct income tax and NIC from each employee's wages or salaries and the employer must also pay its own NIC contribution for each employee. This is done by making payment to HM Revenue and Customs on a regular basis and this is therefore another responsibility of the payroll function.

1.6 Accounting for wages and salaries

Finally once the wages and salaries for the period have been paid then the amounts involved must be correctly entered into the ledger accounts.

1.7 Accuracy and confidentiality

Whilst carrying out all of these calculations and functions it is obviously important that the calculations are made with total accuracy. Not only is the amount that each individual will be paid dependent upon these calculations but there is a statutory duty to make the correct deductions from gross pay and to pay these over to HM Revenue and Customs.

Payroll staff deal with confidential and sensitive information about individuals such as the rate of pay for an individual. It is of the utmost importance that such details are kept confidential and are not made public nor allowed to be accessed by unauthorised personnel.

2 Gross pay

2.1 Introduction

Gross pay is the total amount payable to the employee before any deductions have been made. Gross pay can be made up of many different elements, e.g.
· normal wages or salary;
· overtime;
· shift payments;
· bonus;
· commission;
· holiday pay;
· statutory sick pay (or SSP); and
· statutory maternity pay (or SMP).

2.2 Wages and salaries

These are fairly straightforward. Employees will have an agreed monthly, weekly or hourly rate.

The monthly and weekly rates will not need any further calculations.

However, for hourly paid employees calculations will be needed for the total earnings. The source of this information might be clock cards.

> □ **DEFINITION** □□□□
>
> A clock card is a card which records the hours worked by an employee.

As the employee arrives or leaves they put their card in the slot of a special clock. The mechanism inside the clock stamps the time on the card.

The payroll clerk would transfer the number of hours worked onto special calculation sheets.

2.3 Overtime and shift payments

These need to be identified so that the payroll clerk can calculate the amount payable.

Overtime is hours worked which are over and above the agreed number of weekly or monthly hours for that employee. For example, it may be agreed that an employee has a standard working week of 38 hours. If he works for 42 hours in a week then he has worked 4 hours of overtime.

Overtime or shifts worked might be recorded on:
·   clock cards;
·   timesheets; or
·   authorisation forms (signed by the employee's supervisor).

Some employees are paid at a higher rate for overtime. They might be paid at one and a half times the normal rate. This is called time and a half.

Twice the normal rate is double time.

Some employees might be paid premium rates or bonuses for working certain shifts.

2.4 Bonus and commission payments

The business may pay certain employees a bonus. This bonus may be for achieving a particular target.

Company directors often receive a bonus if the company achieves certain profits.

Companies with a large number of sales representatives may pay their sales representatives a commission as part of their salary. This commission is based on the value of the sales they make.

For instance, a salesman might be paid a basic salary of £10,000 a year plus a 1% commission on sales that he makes.

2.5 Holiday pay

Most employers pay their employees even while they are on holiday.

If the employee is paid monthly, then there is no problem. The employee is paid the usual amount at the normal time.

If the employee is paid weekly, they would prefer to be paid for the holiday period in advance. This means that if the employee is taking two weeks' holiday they will have to be paid three weeks' wages at once.

2.6 Statutory sick pay (SSP) and statutory maternity pay (SMP)

For Unit 2 you will really only need to be concerned about basic wages and salaries, overtime and bonus payments.

If there is a reference to SSP or SMP you will be told how to deal with it.

3   Income tax

3.1 Introduction

Everybody in the UK has a potential liability to pay tax on their income!

Individuals pay **income tax**. The rate of tax depends on the size of their income.

> ☐ **DEFINITION**   ☐☐☐☐
>
> Income tax is a tax on individuals' income.

3.2 Tax-free income

Everybody is entitled to some tax-free income.

This tax-free sum is known as the personal allowance.

> **□ DEFINITION**
>
> The personal allowance is an amount which an individual is allowed to earn tax-free.

3.3 How income tax is paid

Employees pay their income tax through the **PAYE** (or Pay As You Earn) **scheme**.

> **□ DEFINITION**
>
> The PAYE scheme is a national scheme whereby employers withhold tax and other deductions from their employees' wages and salaries when they are paid. The deductions are then paid over monthly to HM Revenue and Customs by the employer.

Looking at tax alone, the main advantages of this scheme are:
- employees pay the tax as they earn the income;
- most people do not have to complete a tax return unless they have several different sources of income;
- employers act as unpaid tax collectors (this is a serious responsibility and they can be fined for mistakes); and
- the government receives a steady stream of revenue throughout the year.

3.4 Which personal allowance?

An employer needs to know the personal allowances of their employees. These are calculated by HM Revenue and Customs. HM Revenue and Customs then sends a P6: Notice of Coding to the employer.

> **□ DEFINITION**
>
> The P6: Notice of Coding is a form sent to employers by the tax office showing the tax coding for employees.

> **▷ ACTIVITY 1**
>
> What are the advantages of the PAYE scheme?
>
> [Answer on p. 300]

3.5 Making the calculations easier

The method of spreading the personal allowance across the year can cause rounding errors and differences. To help with this problem, and to make the calculations easier, the Inland Revenue have produced standard tables.

Table A of the pay adjustment tables shows the amount of tax-free pay to date. **Tables SR** and **B** in the taxable pay tables are ready reckoners to calculate the amount of tax payable.

To make the employer's records of the calculations clearer, HM Revenue and Customs issue **standard forms.**

You need to be aware of the existence of these tax tables but you do not need to be able to use them.

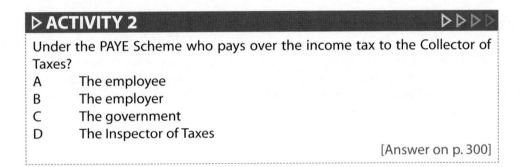

▷ **ACTIVITY 2** ▷ ▷ ▷ ▷

Under the PAYE Scheme who pays over the income tax to the Collector of Taxes?

A   The employee
B   The employer
C   The government
D   The Inspector of Taxes

[Answer on p. 300]

4   National Insurance contributions

4.1 What is National Insurance?

National Insurance is a state scheme which pays certain benefits including:
·   retirement pensions;
·   widow's allowances and pensions;
·   jobseeker's allowance;
·   incapacity benefit; and
·   maternity allowance.

The scheme is run by HM Revenue and Customs.

The scheme is funded by people who are currently in employment.

Most people in employment (including partners in partnerships, and sole traders) who have earnings above a certain level must pay National Insurance contributions.

4.2 Types of National Insurance contributions

Both the employer and the employee pay National Insurance contributions.

(a)   **Employees' National Insurance contributions**

The employer deducts National Insurance contributions from an employee's weekly wage or monthly salary, and pays these to HM Revenue and Customs. Income tax and National Insurance contributions are both taxes on income, but they have different historical origins and are calculated in different ways. Employees' National Insurance is now, however, similar to income tax in many respects, and is really a form of income tax with another name.

Like income tax, employees' NI contributions are deducted from pay. The amount of the contributions an employee pays is linked to his or her earnings, and is obtained by reference to National Insurance tables supplied by HM Revenue and Customs.

You are not required to know how to use NI tables.

(b)   **Employer's National Insurance contributions**

In addition to deducting employees' National Insurance contributions from each employee's wages or salary, an employer is required to pay the employer's National Insurance contributions for each employee. The amount payable for each employee is linked to the size of his or her earnings.

Employer's National Insurance contributions are therefore an employment tax. They are not deducted from the employee's gross pay. They are an additional cost of payroll to the employer, paid for by the employer rather than the employee.

5   Other deductions

5.1 Statutory deductions

So far we have looked at two types of deductions which the employer has to make from their employee's gross pay **by law**. These are **income tax** and **National Insurance** contributions. These are statutory deductions.

5.2 Non-statutory deductions

The employee may also choose to have further deductions made from their gross pay. These include:
- superannuation (pension) payments;
- payments under the **save as you earn scheme**;
- payments under the **give as you earn scheme**; and
- other payments, e.g. subscriptions to sports and social clubs and trade unions.

5.3 Save as you earn

Certain companies may offer their employees the chance to save a regular amount each pay day. These amounts are then used at an agreed date to buy shares in the company. This is an SAYE scheme.

The rules for setting-up and running such a scheme are very strict and the scheme must be approved by HM Revenue and Customs.

5.4 Give as you earn scheme

Employers can choose whether or not to operate this scheme.

The employee chooses a charity and completes a form.

The employer withholds the agreed payments from the employee's wages or salary and pays them over to a charitable trust.

5.5 Other deductions

The employee must agree in writing to any other amounts which are withheld by the employer. This agreement may be part of the employee's contract of service. These deductions may be items such as subscriptions to sports and social clubs and trade unions.

5.6 Summary of deductions and payments

It is time to summarise what deductions the employer makes from the employee's gross salary, and to whom the employer makes the various payments.

To process the payroll an employer must, **for each employee**:
· calculate the gross wage or salary for the period;
· calculate the income tax payable out of these earnings;
· calculate the employee's National Insurance contributions that are deductible;
· calculate any non-statutory deductions;
· calculate the employer's National Insurance contributions.

The employer must then:
· make the payment of net pay to each employee;
· make the payments of all the non-statutory deductions from pay to the appropriate other organisations;
· pay the employee's PAYE, the employee's NIC and the employer's NIC to HM Revenue and Customs for all employees.

○ **EXAMPLE**   ○○○○

John earns £12,000 per annum. His PAYE, NIC and other deductions and the employer's NIC for the month of May 20X4 are:

	£
PAYE	125
Employee's NIC	80
Contribution to personal pension scheme	50
Employer's NIC	85

Calculate:

(a)   John's net pay;

(b)   the cost to the employer of employing John;

(c)   the amounts to be paid to the various organisations involved.

Solution

			Paid by employer to:
Gross pay per month		1,000	
Less: PAYE	125		HMRC
Employee's NIC	80		HMRC
Personal pension	50		Pension company
		(255)	
Net pay		745	John
Employer's NIC	85		HMRC

(a)   John's net pay is £745.

(b)   The cost of employing John is (1,000 + 85) = £1,085.

(c)   The pension company is paid £50 by the employer.
       HM Revenue and Customs is paid £290 by the employer:

	£
PAYE	125
Employee's NIC	80
Employer's NIC	85
	290

Where there are many employees, the employer will pay the amounts calculated per (c) above for all employees to HM Revenue and Customs with one cheque.

6 Making payments to employees

6.1 Introduction

Most employers will have a set day on which employees should be paid, and it is the payroll department's responsibility to ensure that wages are paid on the correct due days.

Weekly paid employees will be paid once a week, normally on the same day each week. Usually the pay day will be either Thursday or Friday.

Monthly paid employees will be paid once a month, and there will be a formula for determining the pay day. For example, this may be:
· the last day of the calendar month;
· the last Thursday or Friday of the calendar month;
· the same date each month, such as the 26th;

Employees may be paid their wages in several ways:
· in cash (but this is now very rare);
· by cheque;
· by bank giro transfer;
· through the Banks Automated Clearing System (BACS).

6.2 The employee's payslip

An employer is obliged by law to prepare a payslip for each employee. The payslip is the documentary evidence that is required of the payment being made to the employee for wages or salary. It sets out the details of the employee's pay for the current period (week or month just ended) and cumulative figures for the tax year to date.

Getting a payslip means that even if the employee receives wages or salary payments directly into his bank account, he is notified of the payment and how much it is by receiving the payslips. Payslips might be distributed to employees at work, or posted to their home address.

A payslip must show details of:
· gross pay;
· deductions (itemised separately);
· net pay.

However, there is not a standard layout for a payslip and so payslips of different employers can look very different.

An example is shown below.

Dickson Engineering					
Employee:	Thomas Cardew			Employee no:	2456
NI No:	TY 45 67 78 L		Tax code: 473L	Date: 11/01/X8	Tax period: Wk 40
PAY FOR WEEK ENDING: 11/01/X8		Hours	Rate £	AMOUNT £	YEAR TO DATE £
Basic		40.0	7.50	300.00	
Overtime		5.0	15.00	75.00	
Shift allowance		2.0	10.00	20.00	
GROSS PAY				**395.00**	
Pension (Employer's pension contribution £25.00)				15.00	
Trade union subscription				10.00	
TOTAL PAY				**370.00**	**16,605.00**
PAYE				57.92	2,711.32
Employee's NI (Employer's NI £36.71)				30.85	
NET PAY				**281.23**	

6.3 Content of the payslip

A payslip must show certain items, by law. Compulsory items are:
· the employer's name;
· the employee's name;
· the date;
· the total gross pay, showing the calculation where it comprises different elements such as bonuses, overtime, etc;
· the employee's pension contribution (if there is any);
· other deductions from, or adjustments to, pay. If a set amount is deducted each pay day the breakdown need not be shown, provided the employee was given the details earlier;
· total gross pay to date for PAYE purposes;
· total tax paid to date in the current tax year and tax due this pay day;
· National Insurance contributions due this pay day;
· net pay.

The payslip may also show additional information (and often does), such as:
· the employee's payroll number;
· the employee's NI number;
· the employee's PAYE code;
· the total National Insurance contributions paid by the employee in the tax year to date;
· the method of payment, such as 'Paid via BACS';
· employer's NIC for the current period;

- employer's NICs for the tax year to date;
- the name of the employee's HM Revenue and Customs tax district and tax reference number for HM Revenue and Customs purposes.

6.4 Another type of payslip

Here is another example of a completed payslip:

EMPLOYER Ltd – Pay Advice					
Employee – John Doe			**Date** 30 September 20X7		
Payments		**Deductions**		**Cumulatives**	
£:p		**£:p**		**£:p**	
Basic pay:	2,000.00	Income tax:	373.55	Gross pay:	13,241.00
Overtime:	172.00	NIC:	196.57	Pay for tax purposes:	13,241.00
Bonus:		Pension:		Tax:	2,287.22
SMP/SPP/SAP:		AVC:		Employees NIC:	1,203.18
SSP:		Charitable Giving :		Employers NIC:	1,400.04
Arrears:		Loan repayment:	50.00	Pension:	
				AVC:	
Total gross pay: 2,172.00		**Total deductions 620.12**		**Net pay**	**1,551.88**
NI number AB 12 34 56 C		Tax Code	480L		

6.5 Generation and distribution of payslips

Where the payroll is processed by computer, the payslip will normally be generated by the computer as one of the output documents.

Otherwise the payslip must be prepared manually.

The number of payslips generated should always equal the number of employees on the payroll.

Payslips are confidential documents and should always be distributed in sealed envelopes. Most computer systems use specially prepared stationery where the payslip is automatically sealed.

Your employer will have set procedures for distributing payslips, and this must always be followed. It may involve handing payslips to employees individually or posting them to the employee's home address. The procedure will vary with the size and type of the organisation.

It is important to ensure that payslips are always distributed within the timescale set by the organisation.

6.6 Reconciling net pay

For each employee, and for the payroll in total, the gross pay must be reconciled with the net pay and deductions made. If the amounts do not reconcile, you have made a mistake. You must correct the mistake before you go any further.

The reconciliation may be made using some form of control sheet often called the wages analysis sheet or the company payroll.

Here is an example of a company payroll.

EMPLOYER Ltd							
COMPANY PAYROLL							
12 June 20X7							
Employee	Gross pay	Tax	Employee's NIC	Employee's pension	Total deductions	Net pay	Employer's NIC
A Jones	228.28	24.27	15.34	18.41	58.02	170.26	17.21
B Smith	256.41	35.27	20.07		55.34	201.07	21.00
C Brown	56.18	2.10	1.59		3.69	52.49	2.63
D Edwards	137.64	17.57	5.33	8.88	31.78	105.86	6.25
E Davies	254.13	37.87	18.20		56.07	198.06	19.15
	932.64	117.08	60.53	27.29	204.90	727.74	66.24

6.7 Payroll checks

Every payday you must reconcile the actual payroll totals with the authorised totals.

All discrepancies must be explained. You should refer to your manager if you are unable to perform the reconciliation.

A further check that you should always make is between the number of employees who are paid on any payday, the number of employees not entitled to pay (if, for example, they are on unpaid leave) and the number of employees on the payroll.

6.8 Paying wages in cash

There are several different methods of paying employees.

Employees no longer have the right to expect payment in cash unless it is included in their contract of employment. Paying employees with cash is very time-consuming.

KAPLAN PUBLISHING

First the total cash required must be calculated. Then the number of notes and coins of each type. (The pay packets must be made up with the exact money.) Then the pay packets are distributed to the employees. Employees must sign to show that they have received their pay packet.

As you can see, **security** and **control** are very important, particularly over:

· cash withdrawals at the bank (these may be delivered by a security firm, e.g. Securicor);
· keeping money in the office (a safe must be used);
· handing out pay packets; and
· keeping pay packets for employees who are absent.

6.9 Paying wages by cheque

Some employers pay their employees by cheque. This is also time-consuming. It is only really practical for a small number of employees.

Cheques must be crossed for security. This means the employees must have bank accounts.

If they are paid by cash or cheque, employees must come to the wages office in person to collect their wages. Employees should also be asked to sign a list as evidence that they have received the money.

6.10 Paying wages by bank giro credit

This is the easiest method of payment. Employees must have bank accounts. Payment is made by transfer into the employees' accounts.

Payment can also be made by BACS, the Bankers Automated Clearing System (see earlier chapter).

6.11 Preparing payslips

Whether they are paid in cash, by cheque or by credit transfer, employees will expect to receive a payslip. This shows how gross pay was calculated and which deductions were made. The information to show was described earlier in this section.

The payroll must be authorised by the senior payroll management before payment is made by any method.

6.12 Paying over tax and NICs collected

The employer must pay over the tax and National Insurance collected to HM Revenue and Customs.

One payment is made to cover all the amounts due. The payment is made using a bank giro credit slip.

HM Revenue and Customs provides a book of pre-printed bank giro credit slips. There is one slip for each month.

7 Payroll accounting procedures

7.1 Introduction

The accounting for wages and salaries is based upon two fundamental principles:
· the accounts must reflect the full cost to the employer of employing someone (which is their gross pay plus the employer's NI contribution);
· the accounts must show the creditor for PAYE and NIC that must be paid over to HM Revenue and Customs on a regular basis, usually monthly.

We therefore need two accounts, plus a third control account.
(a) The wages expense account which shows the full cost of employing the staff.
(b) The PAYE/NIC account which shows the amount to be paid to HM Revenue and Customs.
(c) The wages and salaries control account which acts as a control over the entries in the accounts. There are different ways of writing up this control account, but the way used by AAT is to use this account to control the gross pay and deductions from the employees, plus employers' NIC.

7.2 Double entry

The double entry reflects these two fundamentals and uses three main accounts – the wages and salaries control account, the wages expense account and the PAYE/NIC account.

1   Dr Wages expense account
       Cr   Wages and salaries control account
       with the gross wages of the employees.

2   Dr Wages and salaries control account
       Cr   Bank account
       with the net wages paid to the employees

3   Dr Wages and salaries control account
       Cr   PAYE/NIC account
       with those deductions made from the employees which are payable to the Inland Revenue

4   Dr Wages expense account
       Cr   Wages and salaries control account
       Dr Wages and salaries control account
       Cr   PAYE/NIC account
       with the employer's NI contributions

○ **EXAMPLE**   ○ ○ ○ ○

The wages and salaries information for an organisation for a week is given as follows:

	£
Gross wages	34,000
PAYE deducted	7,400
NIC deducted	5,600
Net pay	21,000
Employer's NIC	7,800

Write up the relevant ledger accounts in the main ledger to reflect this.

Solution

Wages and salaries control account

		£			£
2	Bank account	21,000	1	Wages expense account	34,000
			4	Wages expense account	
				(ers NIC)	7,800
3	PAYE/NIC account (PAYE)	7,400			
3	PAYE/NIC account (ees NIC)	5,600			
4	PAYE/NIC account (ers NIC)	7,800			
		41,800			41,800

Wages expense account

		£			£
1	Wages and salaries control	34,000			
4	Wages and salaries control				
	(ers NIC)	7,800		Bal c/d	41,800
		41,800			41,800
	Bal b/d	41,800			

PAYE/NIC account

		£			£
			3	Wages and salaries control	7,400
			3	Wages and salaries control	5,600
	Bal c/d	20,800	4	Wages and salaries control	7,800
		20,800			20,800
				Bal b/d	20,800

7.3 Commentary on the solution

(a) The wages and salaries control account controls the total gross wages plus the employer's NIC and the amounts paid to the employees, and other organisations (e.g. HM Revenue and Customs for PAYE and NIC). The total gross pay is taken from the company payroll as are the deductions. Assuming that the company payroll schedule reconciles and no errors are made when posting the payroll totals to the account, the account should have a nil balance.

(b) The wages expense account shows the total cost to the employer of employing the workforce (£41,800). This is the gross wages cost plus the employer's own NIC cost.

(c) The PAYE/NIC account shows the amount due to be paid over to HM Revenue and Customs, i.e. PAYE, employee's NIC plus the employer's NIC.

▷ ACTIVITY 3 ▷▷▷▷

Given below is a summary of an organisation's payroll details for a week. You are required to enter the figures in the relevant main ledger accounts.

	£
Gross wages	54,440
PAYE	11,840
Employee's NIC	8,960
Employer's NIC	12,480

[Answer on p. 300]

8 Test your knowledge ▷ ▷ ▷

1   What are the statutory deductions from an employee's pay?

2   What is gross pay?

3   What is net pay?

4   What is the meaning of a personal allowance for income tax purposes?

5   What is the PAYE scheme?

6   Who pays National Insurance Contributions, the employee or the employer?

7   What is overtime?

8   The gross pay for a business for month 1 was £100,000 and the net pay was £67,000 The employer's NIC were £14,000 for the month. What is the total wages and salaries cost for the business for month 1?

9   Who must the employer pay any statutory deductions to?

[Answers on p. 301]

9 Summary

This chapter has introduced the fairly complex taxation elements that affect the payment of wages and salaries. You need to understand in principle how PAYE and NI works and be able to calculate the net pay to employees given the PAYE and NI deductions. However, you do not need to be able to use HM Revenue and Customs tables. Most importantly you do need to understand how wages and salaries are accounted for in the main ledger.

Answers to chapter activities & 'test your knowledge' questions

△ ACTIVITY 1 △△△△

Employees pay tax on their income as they earn it, so do not have to find a large lump sum of cash to pay at the end of the year.

Most people do not have to complete a tax return unless they have several different sources of income.

Employers act as unpaid tax collectors.

The government receives a steady stream of revenue throughout the year.

△ ACTIVITY 2 △△△△

B   The employer

△ ACTIVITY 3 △△△△

Wages and salaries control account

	£		£
Bank account (54,440 – 11,840 – 8,960)	33,640	Wages expense account	54,440
		Wages expense account	12,480
PAYE/NIC account (11,840 + 8,960)	20,800		
PAYE/NIC account	12,480		

Wages expense account

	£		£
Wages and salaries control account	54,440		
Wages and salaries control account	12,480		

PAYE/NIC account

	£		£
		Wages and salaries control account	20,800
		Wages and salaries control account	12,480

KAPLAN PUBLISHING

Test your knowledge △ △ △

1   PAYE and NIC ('pay as you earn' income tax and National Insurance contributions)

2   Gross pay is the total amount due to an employee for the work done in the period

3   Net pay is the gross pay less all deductions

4   An amount that can be earned before any income tax must be paid

5   The Pay As You Earn scheme is a method of paying income tax involving the employer deducting the employee's income tax due for the period from the gross pay and paying it over to HM Revenue and Customs

6   Both the employer and the employee must pay NICs. The employer calculates the total enployee and employer NIC payable each month and pays it to HM Revenue and Customs.

7   Hours that are worked over and above the agreed basic number of hours.

8   £114,000

9   HM Revenue and Customs.

ACCOUNTING FOR PURCHASES – SUMMARY

INTRODUCTION

We have studied the double entry bookkeeping for purchases and payments in detail at the start of this book.

At that time we concentrated on the basic entries so that the double entry would be clear. It is now time to 'put some flesh on the bones' and study these transactions again using more realistic simulation-type material.

KNOWLEDGE & UNDERSTANDING

- Accounting for payments to credit suppliers, and to suppliers where a credit account is not available (Element 2)
- Business transactions and documents involved (Elements 1, 2 and 3)
- Double entry bookkeeping, including balancing accounts (Elements 1, 2 and 3)
- Methods of coding data (Elements 1, 2 and 3)
- Relationship between the accounting system and the ledger (Elements 1, 2 and 3)

CONTENTS

1 Coding of purchase invoices
2 Returns of goods
3 Accounting entries in the main ledger
4 Accounting entries in the subsidiary (purchases) ledger
5 The impact of value added tax
6 Cash (settlement) discounts

PERFORMANCE CRITERIA

- Code purchase invoices and credit notes (Element 30.2)
- Enter purchase invoices and credit notes into the purchases day book and purchases returns day book (Element 30.2)
- Post invoices and credit notes into the subsidiary (purchases) ledger and main (general) ledger (Element 30.2)
- Enter payments in cash book and ledgers (Element 30.2)

1 Coding of purchase invoices

1.1 Introduction

In the purchases day book the purchase invoices are normally given an internal invoice number and are also recorded under the supplier's purchase ledger code and possibly the type of purchase.

1.2 Authorisation stamp

This is often done by stamping an authorisation stamp or grid stamp onto the invoice once it has been thoroughly checked and the relevant details entered onto the authorisation stamp. A typical example of an authorisation stamp is shown below:

Purchase order no	04618
Invoice no	04821
Cheque no	
Account code	PL06
Checked	L Finn
Date	23/02/X2
ML account	07

1.3 Entries on the authorisation stamp

At this stage of entering the invoice in the purchases day book it has been checked to the purchase order and the delivery note, therefore the purchase order number is entered onto the authorisation stamp.

The purchase invoice will then be allocated an internal code number which will be sequential and therefore the next number after the last invoice entered into the purchases day book.

At this stage the invoice will not necessarily have been authorised for payment (see earlier chapter), therefore the cheque number will not yet be entered onto the authorisation stamp.

The purchase invoice details such as trade and settlement discounts should have been checked to the supplier's file to ensure that the correct percentages have been used and at this point the supplier's subsidiary ledger code can be entered onto the authorisation stamp.

The person checking the invoice should then sign and date the authorisation stamp to show that all details have been checked.

Finally, the main ledger account code should be entered. We have seen that in some businesses a simple three column purchases day book will be used with a total, VAT and net column. In such cases all of the invoices will be classified as 'purchases' and will have the main ledger code for the purchases account.

However, if an analysed purchases day book is used then each analysis column will be for a different type of expense and will have a different main ledger code.

If your organisation does have an authorisation stamp procedure then it is extremely important that the authorisation is correctly filled out when the invoice has been checked. Not only is this evidence that the invoice is correct and is for goods or services that have been received, it also provides vital information for the accurate accounting for this invoice.

○ EXAMPLE   ○○○○

Given below are three purchase invoices received and the authorisation stamp for each one. They are to be entered into the purchases day book. Today's date is 25 April 20X1.

INVOICE

Invoice to:
Keller Bros
Field House
Winstead
M16 4PT

Deliver to:
above address

Anderson Wholesale
Westlife Park
Gripton
M7 1ZK
Tel: 0161 439 2020
Fax: 0161 439 2121
Invoice no: 06447
Tax point: 20 April 20X1
VAT reg no: 432 1679 28
Account no: SL14

Code	Description	Quantity	VAT rate	Unit price	Amount exclusive of VAT £
PT417	Grade A Compost	7 tonnes	17.5	15.80	110.60
					110.60
Trade discount 5%					5.53
					105.07
VAT at 17.5%					18.38
Total amount payable					123.45

Purchase order no	34611
Invoice no	37240
Cheque no	
Account code	PL14
Checked	C Long
Date	25/04/X1
ML account	020

INVOICE

Invoice to:	**Better Gardens Ltd**
Keller Bros	Broom Nursery
Field House	West Lane
Winstead	Farforth M23 4LL
M16 4PT	Tel: 0161 380 4444
	Fax: 0161 380 6128

Deliver to:	Invoice no:	46114
above address	Tax point:	21 April 20X1
	VAT reg no:	611 4947 26
	Account no:	K03

Code	Description	Quantity	VAT rate %	Unit price £	Amount exclusive of VAT £
B4188	Tulip bulbs	28 dozen	17.5	1.38	38.64
B3682	Daffodil bulbs	50 dozen	17.5	1.26	63.00
					101.64
VAT at 17.5%					17.25
Total amount payable					118.89

Deduct discount of 3% if paid within 14 days

Purchase order no	34608
Invoice no	37241
Cheque no	
Account code	PL06
Checked	C Long
Date	25/04/X1
ML account	020

INVOICE

Invoice to:
Keller Bros
Field House
Winstead
M16 4PT

Winterton Partners
28/32 Coleman Road
Forest Dene
M17 3AT
Tel: 0161 224 6760
Fax: 0161 224 6761

Deliver to:
above address

Invoice no: I21167
Tax point: 22 April 20X1
VAT reg no: 980 3012 74
Account no: SL44

Code	Description	Quantity	VAT rate %	Unit price £	Amount exclusive of VAT £
A47BT	Seedlings	120	17.5	0.76	91.20

	91.20
Trade discount 7%	6.38
	84.82
VAT at 17.5%	14.55
Total amount payable	99.37

Deduct discount of 2% if paid within 14 days

Purchase order no	34615
Invoice no	37242
Cheque no	
Account code	PL23
Checked	C Long
Date	25/04/X1
ML account	020

Solution

Purchases day book

Date	Invoice no	Code	Supplier	Total £	VAT £	Net £
25/04/X1	37240	PL14	Anderson Wholesale	123.45	18.38	105.07
25/04/X1	37241	PL06	Better Gardens Ltd	118.89	17.25	101.64
25/04/X1	37242	PL23	Winterton Partners	99.37	14.55	84.82

Note that the net total is the invoice amount after deducting any trade discount as the trade discount is a definite reduction in the list price of the goods. At this stage any settlement discount is ignored as it will not necessarily have been decided whether or not to take advantage of the settlement discount.

▷ ACTIVITY 1

You are a purchases clerk for Robins, a soft drink manufacturer. Here is part of the layout of the purchases day book.

Purchases day book

Date	Invoice no	Code	Supplier	Total £	VAT £	01 £	02 £	03 £	04 £

01   represents purchases of parts or raw materials for manufacture
02   represents advertising expenditure
03   represents entertaining expenditure
04   represents purchases of fixed assets

Here are five documents that are to be written up in the purchases day book on 10.11.X2 as necessary.

Document 1

No: 511 X				
	SALES INVOICE		*Drip Farm* **Lover's Lane Norwich NO56 2EZ**	
To: Robins Ltd Softdrink House Wembley London NW16 7SJ			**Tax point: 7.11.X2 VAT Reg No: 566 0122 10**	

Quantity	Description	VAT rate	Price/unit	Total
50 litre drum	Apple juice (inferior)	17½%	£2/litre	100.00
			VAT	17.50
				117.50

Grid stamp on reverse of invoice.

Invoice no	4221
Account code	DF2
Checked	R Robins
Date	9.11.X2
ML account	01

Document 2

Sales Invoice   Inv No: 5177

DAILY NEWS PLC

Europe Way
Southampton
SO3 3BZ

Tax point 5.11.X2
VAT Reg No: 177 0255 01

To: Robins Ltd
           Softdrink House
           Wembley
           LONDON
           NW16 7SJ

Sale details:

4 line advertisement   £
3 weeks   04.10.X2 @ £100/week
               11.10.X2   Net price   300.00
               18.10.X2   VAT 17½%   52.50
                                               ‾‾‾‾‾‾‾‾
                                                352.50
                                               ‾‾‾‾‾‾‾‾

Grid stamp on reverse of invoice.

Invoice no	4222
Account code	DN1
Checked	R Robins
Date	9.11.X2
ML account	02

KAPLAN PUBLISHING

Document 3

RECEIPT

9/11/X2

Received with thanks the sum of
£17.50.

T W Wang

Document 4

SALES ORDER 562		

	Robins Ltd
	Softdrink House
	Wembley
BTEB Stores	LONDON
Gateshead	NW16 7SJ

Quantity	**Description**	**Price**
20 cases	0.75 bottles of Norfolk apple juice	£2/bottle

Document 5

SALES INVOICE P261

STANDARD MACHINES

Starlight Boulevard, Milton Keynes MK51 7LY

To: Robins Ltd
Softdrink House
Wembley
LONDON
NW16 7SJ

Tax point: 6.11.X2
VAT Reg No: 127 0356 02

Quantity	Description	VAT	Price (£)/unit
1	Bottling machine	$17\frac{1}{2}$% VAT	2,000 350
			2,350

Grid stamp on reverse of invoice.

Invoice no.	4223
Account code	SM4
Checked	R Robins
Date	9.11.X2
ML account	04

Answer on p. 326]

2 Returns of goods

2.1 Introduction

Returns may be made for various reasons, e.g.
· faulty goods;
· excess goods delivered by supplier;
· unauthorised goods delivered.

All returned goods must be recorded on a returns outwards note.

2.2 Credit notes

The return should not be recorded until the business receives a **credit note** from the supplier. This confirms that there is no longer a liability for these goods. A credit note from a supplier is sometimes requested by the organisation issuing a debit note.

The credit note should be checked for accuracy against the **returns outwards** note. The calculations and extensions on the credit note should also be checked in just the same way as with an invoice.

2.3 Purchases returns day book

When credit notes are received from suppliers they are normally recorded in their own primary record, the purchases returns day book. This has a similar layout to a purchases day book. If the purchases day book is analysed into the different types of purchase that the organisation makes then the purchases returns day book will also be analysed in the same manner.

2.4 Coding of credit notes

In just the same way as with purchase invoices, credit notes must also be thoroughly checked for accuracy and then coded on an authorisation stamp or grid stamp. This will then provide all of the details that are necessary in order to enter the credit note into the purchases returns day book.

O EXAMPLE   O O O O

Today, 5 February 20X5, three credit notes have been passed as being checked. The details of each credit note and the authorisation stamp are given below. The credit note details are to be entered into the purchases returns day book.

From Calderwood & Co	£
Goods total	16.80
VAT	2.94
Credit note total	19.74

Purchase order no	41120
Credit note	C461
Cheque no	–
Account code	053
Checked	J Garry
Date	05/02/X5
ML account	02

From Mellor & Cross	£
Goods total	104.50
Less: Trade discount 10%	10.45
	94.05
VAT	16.45
Credit note total	110.50

Purchase order no	41096
Credit note	C462
Cheque no	–
Account code	259
Checked	J Garry
Date	05/02/X5
ML account	02

From Thompson Bros Ltd	£
Goods total	37.60
Less: Trade discount 5%	1.88
	35.72
VAT	6.25
Credit note total	41.97

Purchase order no	41103
Credit note	C463
Cheque no	–
Account code	360
Checked	J Garry
Date	05/02/X5
ML account	01

Solution

Purchases returns day book

Date	Credit note no	Code	Supplier	Total £	VAT £	01 £	02 £	03 £	04 £
05/02/X5	C461	053	Calderwood & Co	19.74	2.94		16.80		
05/02/X5	C462	259	Mellor & Cross	110.50	16.45		94.05		
05/02/X5	C463	360	Thompson Bros Ltd	41.97	6.25	35.72			

Note that it is the credit note total which is entered into the total column and the VAT amount into the VAT column. The amount entered into the analysis columns is the goods total less the trade discount. The analysis column is taken from the main ledger code on the authorisation stamp.

▷ ACTIVITY 2 ▷▷▷▷

A newsagents shop has received the following invoices. Write them up in the purchases day book using the format provided. The last internal invoice number to be allocated to purchase invoices was 114.

1.1.X1	Northern Electric – invoice	£235 including VAT at 17.5%
	Northern Gas – invoice	£235.00 (no VAT)
2.1.X1	Post Office Counters – invoice	£117.50 (no VAT)
	Northern Country – invoice	£58.75 including VAT at 17.5%
3.1.X1	South Gazette – invoice	£352.50 including VAT at 17.5%

The supplier codes are as follows:

Northern Country (a newspaper)	N1
Northern Electric	N2
Northern Gas	N3
Post Office Counters	P1
South Gazette (a newspaper)	S1

Purchases day book

Date	Invoice no	Code	Supplier	Total £	VAT £	Goods for resale £	Heat and light £	Postage and stationery £

[Answer on p. 326]

3 Accounting entries in the main ledger

3.1 Introduction

In an earlier chapter we have already come across the main ledger which is the collection of ledger accounts for all of the assets, liabilities, income and expenses of the business. The accounting entries that are to be made in the main ledger are the same as those that have been considered in previous chapters and are made from the totals of the columns in the purchases day book and purchases returns day book.

3.2 Analysed purchases day book

If an analysed purchases day book is being used then there will be a debit entry in an individual purchases or expense account for each of the analysis column totals.

Remember that these totals are the net of VAT purchases/expenses totals.

○ EXAMPLE ○○○○

Reproduced below is a purchases day book for the first week of February 20X5. Each column has been totalled and it must be checked that the totals of the analysis columns agree to the 'Total' column. Therefore you should check the following sum:

	£
01	744.37
02	661.23
03	250.45
04	153.72
VAT	296.15
	_____
	2,105.92
	_____

Purchases day book

Date	Invoice no	Code	Supplier	Total £	VAT £	01 £	02 £	03 £	04 £
20X5									
1 Feb	3569	265	Norweb	148.29	22.09	126.20			
2 Feb	3570	053	Calderwood & Co	98.60			98.60		
3 Feb	3571	259	Mellor & Cross	661.09	98.46		562.63		
4 Feb	3572	360	Thompson Bros Ltd	260.18	38.75	221.43			
5 Feb	3573	023	Cooplin Associates	18.90				18.90	
	3574	056	Heywood Suppliers	272.07	40.52			231.55	
	3575	395	William Leggett	45.37	6.76				38.61
	3576	271	Melville Products	366.49	54.58	311.91			
	3577	301	Quick-Bake	99.68	14.85	84.83			
	3578	311	Roger & Roebuck	135.25	20.14				115.11
				2,105.92	296.15	744.37	661.23	250.45	153.72

The totals of the purchases day book will now be posted to the main ledger accounts.

Solution

Purchase ledger control account

	£			£
			PDB	2,105.92

VAT account

	£		£
PDB	296.15		

Purchases – 01 account

	£		£
PDB	744.37		

Purchases – 02 account

	£		£
PDB	661.23		

Purchases – 03 account

	£		£
PDB	250.45		

Purchases – 04 account

	£		£
PDB	153.72		

3.3 Purchases returns day book

The purchases returns day book is kept in order to record credit notes received by the business. The totals of this must also be posted to the main ledger.

O EXAMPLE   OOOO

Given below is a purchases returns day book for the week. The totals are to be posted to the main ledger accounts.

Purchases day book

Date	Credit note no	Code	Supplier	Total £	VAT £	01 £	02 £	03 £	04 £
20X3									
4 May	CN 152	PL21	Julian R Partners	129.25	19.25		110.00		
6 May	CN 153	PL07	S T Trader	79.90	11.90			68.00	
8 May	CN 154	PL10	Ed Associates	68.85	10.25		58.60		
8 May	CN 155	PL03	Warren & Co	105.28	15.68	89.60			
				383.28	57.08	89.60	168.60	68.00	–

Solution

First, check that each of the column totals add back to the total column total:

	£
VAT	57.08
01	89.60
02	168.60
03	68.00
04	–
	383.28

Then post the totals to the main ledger accounts:

Purchases ledger control account

	£		£
Purchases return day book (PRDB)	383.28		

VAT account

	£		£
		PRDB	57.08

Purchases returns – 01

	£		£
		PRDB	89.60

Purchases returns – 02

£			£
		PRDB	168.60

Purchases returns – 03

£			£
		PRDB	68.00

If the purchases returns day book is analysed then there will be an account in the main ledger for each different category of purchases returns.

▷ ACTIVITY 3 ▷▷▷▷

Given below is the purchases day book. You are required to check the total of each analysis column and that the total of each analysis column agrees to the total column, and then to enter the totals in the correct main ledger accounts.

Purchases day book								
Date	Invoice	Code	Supplier	Total	VAT	Goods for sale	Heat and light	Postage and stationery
no				£	£	£	£	£
01.01.X1	115	N2	Northern Electric	235.00	35.00		200.00	
	116	N3	Northern Gas	235.00			235.00	
02.01.X1	117	P1	Post Office	117.50				117.50
	118	N1	Northern Country	58.75	8.75	50.00		
03.01.X1	119	S1	South Gazette	352.50	52.50	300.00		
				998.75	96.25	350.00	435.00	117.50

[Answer on p. 326]

4 Accounting entries in the subsidiary (purchases) ledger

4.1 Subsidiary ledger

So that a business knows how much it owes to each credit supplier, it maintains a subsidiary ledger which consists of records of amounts owed to each supplier (or creditor). Each supplier has their own page or card (or account) in the ledger.

4.2 Typical supplier's account

Purchase invoices are recorded on the right hand side (credit side) just as they are in the purchases ledger control account in the main ledger. Individual transactions are transferred from the purchases day book.

Note that the amount recorded for each purchase invoice is the total including VAT, as this is what is owed to each supplier.

Account name: Robert Jones   **Code:** J53

Date	Transaction	£	Date	Transaction	£
			01.8.X3	Invoice 0992	236.93
			03.8.X3	Invoice 0996	92.58
			10.8.X3	Invoice 1032	69.53

○ EXAMPLE   ○○○○

Here is an account from the subsidiary (purchases) ledger of Frosty Limited.

Account name: **Code:**

Date	Transaction	£	Date	Transaction	£

We will write up the account for Jones Brothers, account number PJ06. This is a new supplier.

Frosty Limited has only been trading for a short time and is not yet registered for VAT.

Purchase invoices and credit notes

02.5.X1	9268	£638.26
06.6.X1	9369	£594.27
15.6.X1	9402	£368.24
17.6.X1	C Note 413	£58.62
19.6.X1	9568	£268.54

Solution

Account name: Jones Brothers   **Account number:** PJ06

Date	Transaction	£	Date	Transaction	£
17.6.X1	Credit note 413	58.62	02.5.X1	Invoice 9268	638.26
			06.6.X1	Invoice 9369	594.27
			15.6.X1	Invoice 9402	368.24
			19.6.X1	Invoice 9568	268.54

Each purchase invoice from the Purchases Day Book must be entered on the credit side of that individual suppliers account in the subsidiary ledger. Any credit notes recorded in the Purchases Returns Day Book must be recorded on the debit side of the supplier's account. Where there is VAT involved the amount to be recorded for an invoice or credit note is the gross amount or VAT inclusive amount.

5 The impact of value added tax

5.1 Introduction

Having looked at the accounting for purchase invoices and credit notes, we will now move on to consider the accounting for payments to suppliers. First we will consider the impact of VAT in this area.

When writing up the payments side of the cash book VAT must be considered.

Any payments to suppliers or creditors included in the Purchases ledger column need have no analysis for VAT as the VAT on the purchase was recorded in the purchases day book when the invoice was initially received.

However any other payments on which there is VAT must show the gross amount in the Total column, the VAT in the VAT column and the net amount in the relevant expense column.

○ EXAMPLE   ○○○○

Peter Craddock is the cashier for a business which manufactures paper from recycled paper. The payments that were made for one week in September are as follows:

15 September	Cheque no 1151 to K Humphrey (credit supplier)	£1,034.67
	Cheque no 1152 to Y Ellis (credit supplier)	£736.45
	Cheque no 1153 to R Phipps (credit supplier)	£354.45
	Standing order for rent	£168.15
	Direct debit to the electricity company	£130.98 (including VAT of £22.92)
16 September	Cheque no 1154 to L Silton (credit supplier)	£1,092.75
	Cheque no 1155 to the insurance company	£103.18
17 September	Cheque no 1156 to F Grange (credit supplier)	£742.60
	Cheque no 1157 to Hettler Ltd for cash purchases	£420.00 plus VAT
18 September	Cheque no 1158 to J Kettle (credit supplier)	£131.89
	BACS payment of wages	£4,150.09
19 September	Cheque no 1159 to Krane Associates for cash purchases	£186.00 plus VAT

Enter these transactions into the cash payments book, total the columns and post the totals to the main ledger.

Solution

Date	Details	Cheque no	Total £	VAT £	Purchases ledger £	Cash purchases £	Rent £	Electricity £	Wages £	Insurance £
15/9	K Humphrey	1151	1,034.67		1,034.67					
	Y Ellis	1152	736.45		736.45					
	R Phipps	1153	354.45		354.45					
	Rent	SO	168.15				168.15			
	Electricity	DD	130.98	22.92				108.06		
16/9	L Silton	1154	1,092.75		1,092.75					
	Insurance	1155	103.18							103.18
17/9	F Grange	1156	742.60		742.60					
	Hettler Ltd	1157	493.50	73.50		420.00				
18/9	J Kettle	1158	131.89		131.89					
	Wages	BACS	4,150.09						4,150.09	
19/9	Krane Ass	1159	218.55	32.55		186.00				
			9,357.26	128.97	4,092.81	606.00	168.15	108.06	4,150.09	103.18

The analysis column totals should add back to the Total column – this must always be done to check the accuracy of your totalling.

	£
VAT	128.97
Purchases ledger	4,092.81
Cash purchases	606.00
Rent	168.15
Electricity	108.06
Wages	4,150.09
Insurance	103.18
	9,357.26

Purchase ledger control account

		£		£
19/9	CPB	4,092.81		

VAT account

		£		£
19/9	CPB	128.97		

Purchases account

		£		£
19/9	CPB	606.00		

Electricity account

		£		£
19/9	CPB	108.06		

Salaries account

	£		£
19/9 CPB	4,150.09		

Rent account

	£		£
19/9 CPB	168.15		

Insurance account

	£		£
19/9 CPB	103.18		

All of the entries in the main ledger accounts are debit entries. The credit entry is the total column of the cash payments book and these individual debit entries form the double entry.

6   Cash (settlement) discounts

6.1 Introduction

If a business takes advantage of cash discounts on items purchased, the discount is treated as **income** as it is a benefit to the business i.e. although the invoice is paid earlier, the amount paid is less than the invoice net amount due to the discount.

Cash or settlement discounts are recorded in a memorandum column in the cash book. The memorandum column does not form part of the double entry. It requires an entire piece of double entry itself (see below).

The business must record these settlement discounts. Trade discounts are not recorded in the cash book.

An extra column is included in the analysed cash payments book. This should be the final right hand column.

○ EXAMPLE   ○○○○

The following four payments have been made today, 12 June 20X6:

Cheque number 22711 B Caro	Purchases ledger code CL13
	£342.80 after taking a settlement discount of £14.20
Cheque number 22712 S Wills	Cash purchases of £235.00 inclusive of VAT
Cheque number 22713 P P & Co	Purchases ledger code CL22 £116.40
Cheque number 22714 W Potts	Purchases ledger code CL18 £162.84

The relevant subsidiary (purchases) ledger accounts are shown over the page.

B Caro (CL 13)

	£		£
		PDB Invoice	357.00

W Potts (CL 18)

	£		£
PRDB Credit note	10.00	PDB Invoice	172.84

P P & Co (CL 22)

	£		£
		PDB Invoice	116.40
		PDB Invoice	121.27

In this example we will:
- write up the cash payments book for the day;
- total the columns to check that they add back to the total of the Total column;
- enter the totals in the main ledger;
- write up each individual entry in the subsidiary ledger.

Solution

Date	Details	Cheque	Code	Total £	VAT £	Purchases ledger £	Cash purchases £	Other £	Discounts £
12 Jun	B Caro	22711	CL13	342.80		342.80			14.20
	S Wills	22712		235.00	35.00		200.00		
	PP&Co	22713	CL22	116.40		116.40			
	W Potts	22714	CL18	162.84		162.84			
				857.04	35.00	622.04	200.00	–	14.20

Total Check

	£
Purchases ledger	622.04
Cash purchases	200.00
VAT	35.00
	857.04

Note that the discount received column is not included in the total check as this is simply a memorandum column.

Main ledger

Purchase ledger control account

	£		£
CPB	622.04		
CPB – discount	14.20		

Purchases account

	£		£
CPB	200.00		

VAT account

	£		£
CPB	35.00		

Discounts received account

	£		£
		CPB	14.20

When posting the cash payments book to the main ledger there are two distinct processes. Firstly enter the totals of each of the analysis columns as debits in their relevant accounts in the main ledger. Then do the double entry for the discounts received – debit the purchase ledger control account and credit the discounts received account.

Subsidiary ledger

B Caro (CL 13)

		£			£
CPB	Payment	342.80	PDB	Invoice	357.00
CPB	Discount	14.20			

Note that the discount is entered here as well as the cash payment.

W Potts (CL 18)

		£			£
PRDB	Credit note	10.00	PDB	Invoice	172.84
CPB	Payment	162.84			

P P & Co (CL 22)

		£			£
CPB	Payment	116.40	PDB	Invoice	116.40
			PDB	Invoice	121.27

▷ **ACTIVITY 4**

Given below is a completed cash payments book.

You are required to:

(a) Total each of the columns and check that the totals add across to the total column.
(b) Post the totals to the main ledger accounts given.
(c) Post the individual creditor entries to the creditors' accounts in the subsidiary ledger, also given.

Date	Details	Cheque no	Code	Total £	VAT £	Purchases ledger £	Cash purchases £	Wages £
1/7	G Hobbs	34	PL14	325.46		325.46		
1/7	Purchases	35	ML03	66.98	9.98		57.00	
2/7	Purchases	36	ML03	49.53	7.37		42.16	
3/7	P Taylor	37	PL21	157.83		157.83		
3/7	S Dent	38	PL06	163.58		163.58		
4/7	K Smith	39	ML07	24.56				24.56

[Answer on p. 327]

7 **Test your knowledge**

1 Why is there no discount received column in the purchases day book?

2 When cross-casting the analysed cash payments book, do you include the discount received column in your calculations?

3 What is the double entry for a settlement discount received of £100?

4 In the subsidiary purchases ledger, would a settlement discount received of £75 be entered on the debit or credit side of the individual creditor account?

5 In the subsidiary purchases ledger, why is there no corresponding double entry in a discount received account corresponding to the entry in the individual creditor account?

[Answers on p.328]

8 **Summary**

In this chapter we have pulled together into one place all the main documents and double entry for the purchases cycle. If you have had any trouble with any of these points, you should refer again to the earlier chapters of the textbook where the double entry is explained.

Answers to chapter activities & 'test your knowledge' questions

△ **ACTIVITY 1**   △△△△

Purchases day book

Date	Invoice no	Code	Supplier	Total £	VAT £	01 £	02 £	03 £	04 £
10/11/X2	4221	DF2	Drip Farm	117.50	17.50	100.00			
10/11/X2	4222	DN1	Daily News plc	352.50	52.50		300.00		
10/11/X2	4223	SM4	Standard Machines	2,350.00	350.00				2,000.00
				2,820.00	420.00	100.00	300.00	–	2,000.00

Document 3 receipt is not a purchase invoice, it is a receipt for cash paid.

Document 4 is a sales order to supply 20 cases of bottled juice. It is not a purchase invoice so would not appear in the purchases day book.

△ **ACTIVITY 2**   △△△△

Purchases day book

Date	Invoice no	Code	Supplier	Total £	VAT £	Goods for resale £	Heat and light £	Postage and stationery £
01.01.X1	115	N2	Northern Electric	235.00	35.00		200.00	
	116	N3	Northern Gas	235.00	–		235.00	
02.01.X1	117	P1	Post Office Counters	117.50	–			117.50
	118	N1	Northern Country	58.75	8.75	50.00		
03.01.X1	119	S1	South Gazette	352.50	52.50	300.00		
				998.75	96.25	350.00	435.00	117.50

△ **ACTIVITY 3**   △△△△

	£
Goods for resale	350.00
Heat and light	435.00
Postage and stationery	117.50
VAT	96.25
Total	998.75

Purchases (goods for resale)

	£		£
PDB	350.00		

Heat and light

	£		£
PDB	435.00		

Postage and stationery

	£		£
PDB	117.50		

VAT

	£		£
PDB	96.25		

Purchases ledger control account

	£		£
		PDB	998.75

△ ACTIVITY 4 △△△△

(a)   Cash payments book

Date	Details	Cheque no	Code	Total £	VAT £	Purchases ledger £	Cash purchases £	Wages £
1/7	G Hobbs	34	PL14	325.46		325.46		
1/7	Purchases	35	ML03	66.98	9.98		57.00	
2/7	Purchases	36	ML03	49.53	7.37		42.16	
3/7	P Taylor	37	PL21	157.83		157.83		
3/7	S Dent	38	PL06	163.58		163.58		
4/7	K Smith	39	ML07	24.56				24.56
				787.94	17.35	646.87	99.16	24.56

Check that totals add across:

	£
VAT	17.35
Purchases ledger	646.87
Cash purchases	99.16
Wages	24.56
	787.94

(b)   **Main ledger accounts**

Purchases ledger control account

	£		£
CPB	646.87		

Cash purchases account

	£		£
CPB	99.16		

Wages account

	£		£
CPB	24.56		

VAT account

	£		£
CPB	17.35		

(c)   **Subsidiary ledger**

G Hobbs   **PL14**

	£		£
CPB	325.46		

P Taylor   **PL21**

	£		£
CPB	157.83		

S Dent   **PL06**

	£		£
CPB	163.58		

Test your knowledge

1   The purchases day book lists the value of the invoice sent by the supplier. This value is not affected by the settlement discount and so there is no column for the discount.

2   No. The discount received column is a memorandum column to remind the bookkeeper to make the double entry in the main ledger.

3   Debit purchases ledger control account £100; credit discount received account £100.

4   The £75 would be entered on the debit side of the individual creditor account. The discount received represents a reduction in the creditor – hence a debit entry.

5 The purpose of the subsidiary (purchases) ledger is to provide the detailed entries in each individual creditor account that goes to make up the total entries in the PLCA. The discounts received are therefore entered as debits in the individual creditor accounts just as they are in the PLCA. There is no need to make the corresponding entries in a discount received account because this has already been done as part of the double entry with the PLCA.

PETTY CASH SYSTEMS

INTRODUCTION

As well as making payments from the business bank account by cheque or other methods considered in the previous chapter, most businesses will also carry a certain amount of cash on the premises known as petty cash. The purpose of this cash is in order to make small business payments for which writing a cheque would not be appropriate, such as payment in the local shop for tea, coffee and milk for the staff kitchen. In this chapter we will consider how a petty cash system will work, the documentation required and how petty cash payments are accounted for.

KNOWLEDGE & UNDERSTANDING

- Methods of handling and storing money including the security aspects (Element 2)
- Petty cash procedures (Element 3)
- The use of the petty cash book and cash book as part of the double entry system or as books of prime entry (Element 3)
- Importance of reconciling bank statements, control accounts and petty cash records (Element 3)

CONTENTS

1 Petty cash systems
2 Petty cash vouchers
3 Maintaining petty cash records
4 Posting the petty cash book
5 Petty cash control account
6 Reconciling petty cash

PERFORMANCE CRITERIA

- Operate a petty cash system, including imprest system (Element 30.3)
- Reconcile petty cash control account with cash in hand and petty cash book (Element 30.3)

1 Petty cash systems

1.1 Introduction

We have seen in the previous chapters how most business payments are made out of the business bank account by cheque, standing order, direct debit or other automated payment mechanisms. However, most businesses will require small amounts of cash for payment for items such as stamps, coffee, tea, taxi fares, train fares, etc. The cash that is held is known as petty cash.

□ DEFINITION

Petty cash is the small amount of cash that most businesses will hold in order to make small cash payments.

1.2 Petty cash box

Cash being held on business premises is obviously a security risk. Therefore it is important that the petty cash is secure. It will normally be kept in a locked petty cash box and usually this itself will be held in the safe. Only the person responsible for the petty cash should have access to the petty cash box.

1.3 Payment of petty cash

Petty cash will usually be paid out to employees who have already incurred a small cash expense on behalf of the business, such as buying coffee and milk in the local shop or paying for a train fare that the business is to reimburse. It is obviously important that payments are only made out of the petty cash box for valid business expenses that have been incurred. For this reason petty cash should only ever be given to an employee on receipt by the petty cashier of an authorised petty cash voucher and, where appropriate, VAT receipt.

□ DEFINITION

A petty cash voucher is an internal document that details the business expenditure that an employee has incurred out of his own money.

This voucher must be authorised before any amounts can be paid to that employee out of the petty cash box.

A typical petty cash voucher is shown below:

	PETTY CASH VOUCHER		*Sequential voucher number*	
Authorised by F R Clarke	*Received by* L Kent	*Signature of claimant*	No	4173
Date	*Description*		*Amount*	
4 April 20X1	Train Fare		12	50
	Total		12	50

Signature of person authorising voucher

Details of expenditure

Total paid to employee

> ## ▷ ACTIVITY 1   ▷ ▷ ▷ ▷

(AAT CA J92)

Give two ways in which the company might attempt to maintain security over the petty cash.

[Answer on p. 356]

1.4 The imprest system

Many businesses use the imprest system for petty cash. Using an imprest system makes petty cash easier to control and therefore reduces the possibility of error and fraud.

The business decides on a fixed amount of petty cash (the imprest) which is just large enough to cover normal petty cash requirements for a period (usually a week). This amount of petty cash is withdrawn from the bank.

Claims are paid out of petty cash by a voucher being completed for each amount of petty cash paid out. The vouchers are kept in the petty cash box so that the amount of cash held decreases and is replaced by vouchers.

At any given time, the total contents of the box (i.e. petty cash plus amounts withdrawn represented by vouchers) should equal the amount of the imprest.

At the end of the period, a cheque is drawn for the total of the vouchers which restores the petty cash float to the amount of the imprest. The vouchers are removed from the petty cash box and filed.

○ **EXAMPLE** ○○○○

The imprest amount for a petty cash system is £150, which is the amount paid into the petty cash box on 1 November. At the end of the week the total of the vouchers in the petty cash box is £125.05. How much cash is required in order to replenish the petty cash box to the imprest amount?

Solution

£125.05, the amount paid out on the basis of the petty cash vouchers.

▷ **ACTIVITY 2** ▷▷▷▷

(AAT CA J92)
Allsports Limited maintains an imprest amount for the petty cash of £250. During the current period, the sum of £180 is paid out, supported by petty cash vouchers. At the end of the period, what amount should be drawn out of the bank?

[Answer on p. 356]

1.5 Non-imprest petty cash system

An imprest petty cash system as in the previous example is the most common method of dealing with and controlling petty cash. However some businesses may use a non-imprest system. This might be where a set amount of cash is withdrawn each week and paid into the petty cash box no matter what the level of expenditure in that week.

For example it may be an organisation's policy to cash a cheque for £50 each Monday morning for use as petty cash for the week. The danger here is either that petty cash requirements are more than £50 in the week in which case the petty cash box will run out of money. Alternatively week after week expenditure is significantly less than £50 each week, leading to a large amount of cash building up in the petty cash box.

▷ **ACTIVITY 3**   ▷▷▷▷

(AAT CA D92)

You receive the following memorandum:

HAIRDRESSING SUPPLIES LIMITED

MEMORANDUM

To:	Chris	Date: 29 March 20X2
From:	Phyllis Cranborne	
Subject:	Petty cash	

Marjorie Thistlethwaite mentioned to me yesterday that she wanted me to take responsibility for petty cash commencing on 1 June.

Could you please let me have a brief summary of how the petty cash imprest system works?

Thanks.

Phyllis

Draft a suitable reply.

[Answer on p. 356]

2   Petty cash vouchers

2.1 Introduction

We have already seen the importance of petty cash vouchers as any payment of petty cash should not be made unless supported by a properly completed petty cash voucher which has been authorised.

2.2 Completing a petty cash voucher

If an employee wishes to be reimbursed for a business expense that he has incurred himself then he must complete a petty cash voucher. Different businesses will have different policies regarding amounts that can be paid out as petty cash but most organisations will require that petty cash vouchers are supported by documentation to show that the expenditure has occurred.

Most businesses will require petty cash vouchers to be supported by a receipt or other evidence of the payment such as a train ticket for a train fare.

O **EXAMPLE**   OOOO

The petty cashier for your organisation is on holiday and you have been asked to act as petty cashier in her absence. You have been given the policy documents relating to petty cash and have discovered the following:

- a petty cash imprest system is operated with an imprest amount of £300 per week;
- no single petty cash voucher for more than £30 can be paid out of petty cash; any claims for amounts greater than £30 must be made using a cheque requisition;
- all petty cash claims other than taxi fares (see below) must include a valid receipt or evidence of payment;
- taxi fares of less than £5 can be paid without a receipt; all others must be supported by a receipt from the taxi;
- other transport expenses such as rail or underground fares exceeding £3 must be supported by a ticket showing the price of the fare or evidence of payment of the fare;
- other transport expenses of less than £3 do not need evidence of payment;
- no single employee can make claims of more than £30 on any one day.

On your first day of acting as petty cashier you have to deal with the following petty cash vouchers.

PETTY CASH VOUCHER			
Authorised by	Received by P Mallins	No	3562
Date	Description	Amount	
12 June X6	Tea and biscuits for office	12	73
	Total	12	73

Receipt attached

PETTY CASH VOUCHER			
Authorised by	Received by N Nixon	No	3563
Date	Description	Amount	
12 June X6	Taxi	3	80
	Total	3	80

PETTY CASH VOUCHER			
Authorised by	Received by J KARL	No	3564
Date	Description	Amount	
12 June X6	Bus fare	2	50
	Total	2	50

PETTY CASH VOUCHER			
Authorised by	Received by G Hull	No	3565
Date	Description	Amount	
12 June X6	Taxi	6	00
	Total	6	00

PETTY CASH VOUCHER			
Authorised by	Received by F Trent	No	3566
Date	Description	Amount	
12 June X6	Train fare	12	80
	Total	12	80

Ticket attached

PETTY CASH VOUCHER			
Authorised by	Received by P Phillips	No	3567
Date	Description	Amount	
12 June X6	Entertaining	35	00
	Total	35	00

Restaurant bill attached

PETTY CASH VOUCHER			
Authorised by	*Received by* V Close	*No*	3568
Date	*Description*	*Amount*	
12 June X6	Underground ticket	3	60
	Total	3	60

PETTY CASH VOUCHER			
Authorised by	*Received by* P Mallins	*No*	3569
Date	*Description*	*Amount*	
12 June X6	Entertaining	20	00
	Total	20	00

Restaurant bill attached

For each voucher explain whether you would be able to authorise it for payment from petty cash.

You must check each petty cash voucher carefully, together with any supporting documentation, to ensure that a valid payment can be made.

Solution

Voucher 3562 – Amount is less than £30 and supported by receipt – authorise for payment.

Voucher 3563 – Taxi fare of less than £5 therefore no receipt required – authorise for payment.

Voucher 3564 – Bus fare of less than £3 therefore no receipt required – authorise for payment.

Voucher 3565 – Taxi fare of more than £5 but no receipt – cannot authorise for payment.

Voucher 3566 – Train fare with ticket attached – authorise for payment.

Voucher 3567 – Claim for more than £30 – cannot authorise for payment – cheque requisition required.

Voucher 3568 – Underground ticket for more than £3 but no evidence of payment – cannot authorise for payment.

Voucher 3569 – Claim made by P Mallins who has already claimed £12.73 today (voucher no 3562) making a total of £32.73 – cannot authorise for payment.

2.3 VAT and petty cash vouchers

If an expense includes an amount of VAT, then the amounts recorded on the petty cash vouchers should be the net amount, the amount of VAT and the total payment.

▷ ACTIVITY 4

You are the petty cashier for your organisation. During your lunch break five receipts have appeared on your desk from employees making petty cash claims.

The receipts are as follows:

£2.99	Chocolate biscuits
£5.58	Stationery (includes VAT)
£20.00	Computer disks (includes VAT)
£8.90	Train fare
£3.95	Coffee and milk

The last petty cash voucher to be used was number 158. You are required to fill out and authorise petty cash vouchers for each of these receipts ready for payment of the petty cash to the employees concerned. Use the blank petty cash vouchers given.

Today's date is 7 September 20X1.

PETTY CASH VOUCHER

Authorised by	Received by	No
Date	Description	Amount
	Total	

PETTY CASH VOUCHER

Authorised by	Received by	No
Date	Description	Amount
	Total	

PETTY CASH VOUCHER

Authorised by	Received by	No
Date	Description	Amount
	Total	

PETTY CASH VOUCHER		
Authorised by	*Received by*	*No*
Date	*Description*	*Amount*
	Total	

PETTY CASH VOUCHER		
Authorised by	*Received by*	*No*
Date	*Description*	*Amount*
	Total	

[Answer on p. 357]

3   Maintaining petty cash records

3.1 Introduction

The petty cash vouchers are recorded in their own book of prime entry which is known as the petty cash book. The petty cash book, similar to the cash receipts book and the cash payments book, is not only a primary record but is normally also kept as part of the main ledger double entry system.

The petty cash book is a primary record and is also part of the main ledger.

3.2 Layout of the petty cash book

The petty cash book is normally set out as a large ledger account with a small receipts side and a larger analysed payments side. A typical petty cash book is set out below.

Receipts			Payments								
Date	Narrative	Total £	Date	Narrative	Voucher no	Total £	Postage £	Cleaning £	Tea & coffee £	Sundry £	VAT £
1 Nov	Bal b/f	35.50									
1 Nov	Cheque 394	114.50	1 Nov	ASDA	58	23.50			23.50		
			2 Nov	Post Office Ltd	59	29.50	29.50				
			2 Nov	Cleaning materials	60	14.76		12.56			2.20
			3 Nov	Postage	61	16.19	16.19				
			3 Nov	ASDA	62	10.35		8.81			1.54
			4 Nov	Newspapers	63	18.90				18.90	
			5 Nov	ASDA	64	11.85				10.09	1.76

3.3 Receipts side of the petty cash book

The receipts side of the petty cash book only requires one column, as the only receipt into the petty cash box is the regular payment into the petty cash box of cash drawn out of the bank account.

The only receipt into the petty cash box is the cash regularly paid into the petty cash box from the bank account.

3.4 Payments side of the petty cash book

Payments out of the petty cash box will be for a variety of different types of expense and an analysis column is required for each type of expense in the same way as the cash payments book is analysed. Note that a column is also required for VAT, as if a petty cash expense includes VAT this must also be analysed out. Remember that any VAT included in a petty cash expense must be shown separately on the petty cash voucher.

Any VAT shown on the petty cash voucher must be analysed out into the VAT column and the net amount shown in the expense analysis column.

3.5 Writing up the petty cash book

When cash is originally paid into the petty cash book then this will be recorded on the receipts side (debit side) of the petty cash book.

Each petty cash voucher will then in turn be written up in the petty cash book on the payments side.

Petty cash vouchers are pre-numbered to ensure that none are mislaid and they will be written into the petty cash book in number order with each item of expenditure being recorded in the correct analysis column.

⊙ EXAMPLE ○○○○

A business has just started to run an imprest petty cash system with an imprest amount of £100. £100 is withdrawn from the bank account and paid into the petty cash box on 3 April 20X1.

During the first week the following authorised petty cash vouchers were paid.

These transactions will now be recorded in the petty cash book.

PETTY CASH VOUCHER			
Authorised by T Smedley	Received by P Lannall	No	0001
Date	Description	Amount	
3 April 20X1	Tea/coffee/milk	4	73
	Total	4	73

PETTY CASH VOUCHER			
Authorised by T Smedley	Received by R Sellers	No	0002
Date	Description	Amount	
3 April 20X1	Train fare	14	90
	Total	14	90

PETTY CASH VOUCHER			
Authorised by T Smedley	Received by F Dorne	No	0003
Date	Description	Amount	
4 April 20X1	Stationery	4	00
	VAT	0	70
	Total	4	70

PETTY CASH VOUCHER

Authorised by T Smedley	Received by P Dent	No	0004
Date	Description	Amount	
5 April 20X1	Postage costs	16	35
	Total	16	35

PETTY CASH VOUCHER

Authorised by T Smedley	Received by H Polly	No	0005
Date	Description	Amount	
7 April 20X1	Train fare	15	30
	Total	15	30

PETTY CASH VOUCHER

Authorised by T Smedley	Received by P Lannall	No	0006
Date	Description	Amount	
8 April 20X1	Milk/biscuits	3	85
	Total	3	85

Solution

Petty cash book

Receipts			Payments								
Date	Narrative	Total £	Date	Narrative	Voucher no	Total £	Postage £	Travel £	Tea & coffee £	Sundry £	VAT £
20X1 03/04	Cash	100.00	20X1 03/04	Tea/coffee	0001	4.73			4.73		
			03/04	Train fare	0002	14.90		14.90			
			04/04	Stationery	0003	4.70				4.00	0.70
			05/04	Postage	0004	16.35	16.35				
			07/04	Train fare	0005	15.30		15.30			
			08/04	Milk/biscuits	0006	3.85			3.85		

4 Posting the petty cash book

4.1 Introduction

Now that we have seen how the petty cash book is written up we must next post the totals of the petty cash book to the main ledger accounts.

Remember that the petty cash book is part of the main ledger double entry system. Therefore the receipt of cash is the debit entry in the petty cash account and only the related credit entry is the cash coming out of the bank account and therefore recorded in the cash payments book .

The total of the payments is effectively the credit entry in the petty cash account and therefore the only postings that are required are the related debit entries to the relevant expense accounts.

4.2 Posting the petty cash receipt

The receipt into the petty cash box has come from cash being withdrawn from the bank account. This will have been done by writing out a cheque for cash and withdrawing this from the bank. Therefore the cheque should be recorded in the cash payments book as a payment when the cash payments book is written up.

The receipt of the cash into the petty cash box is recorded in the receipts side of the petty cash book, debit side.

As both the petty cash book and the cash payments book are normally part of the main ledger double entry system, the double entry has been completed. The debit is the entry into the petty cash book and the credit entry is the entry in the cash payments book.

4.3 Posting the petty cash payments

The petty cash book is part of the main ledger double entry system so the total column in the petty cash payments side is the credit entry to the petty cash account.

All that is required is therefore the debit entries to match this. These debit entries are taken from the totals of each of the analysis columns.

The total from each analysis column is debited to the relevant main ledger account.

KAPLAN PUBLISHING

O EXAMPLE ○○○○

The petty cash book written up in an earlier example is given again below. This is to be posted to the main ledger accounts.

Petty cash book

Receipts			Payments								
Date	Narrative	Total £	Date	Narrative	Voucher no	Total £	Postage £	Travel £	Tea & coffee £	Sundry £	VAT £
20X1 03/04	Cash	100.00	20X1 03/04	Tea/coffee	0001	4.73			4.73		
			03/04	Train fare	0002	14.90		14.90			
			04/04	Stationery	0003	4.70				4.00	0.70
			05/04	Postage	0004	16.35	16.35				
			07/04	Train fare	0005	15.30		15.30			
			08/04	Milk/biscuits	0006	3.85			3.85		

Solution

Step 1 Each of the columns in the petty cash payments side must be totalled.

The accuracy of your totalling should be checked by ensuring that all of the analysis column totals add back to the total of the 'total' column in the petty cash book payments side.

Petty cash book

Receipts			Payments								
Date	Narrative	Total £	Date	Narrative	Voucher no	Total £	Postage £	Travel £	Tea & coffee £	Sundry £	VAT £
20X1 03/04	Cash	100.00	20X1 03/04	Tea/coffee	0001	4.73			4.73		
			03/04	Train fare	0002	14.90		14.90			
			04/04	Stationery	0003	4.70				4.00	0.70
			05/04	Postage	0004	16.35	16.35				
			07/04	Train fare	0005	15.30		15.30			
			08/04	Milk/biscuits	0006	3.85			3.85		
						59.83	16.35	30.20	8.58	4.00	0.70

Check the totals:

	£
Postage	16.35
Travel	30.20
Tea and coffee	8.58
Sundry	4.00
VAT	0.70
	59.83

Step 2 Each of the analysis column totals must now be entered into the main ledger accounts as debit entries.

VAT account

	£		£
Petty cash book (PCB)	0.70		

The entry has come from the petty cash book and this is the reference – this is now shortened to PCB.

Postage account

	£		£
PCB	16.35		

Travel account

	£		£
PCB	30.20		

Tea and coffee account

	£		£
PCB	8.58		

Sundry expenses account

	£		£
PCB	4.00		

▷ ACTIVITY 5 ▷▷▷▷

Summary of petty cash vouchers in hand at 31 October 20X7

Date	Description	Total £	VAT included £
1/10	Envelopes (Administration)	19.72	2.93
4/10	Cleaner (Administration)	8.75	
6/10	Food for staff lunch (Marketing)	17.13	
6/10	Taxi fares (Marketing)	16.23	
6/10	Rail fares (Marketing)	43.75	
10/10	Postage (Administration)	4.60	
15/10	Tea and coffee (Production)	4.39	
17/10	Light bulbs and refuse sacks (Distribution)	8.47	1.26
20/10	Flowers for reception (Administration)	21.23	
26/10	Cleaner (Administration)	8.75	

(a) Write up the payments side of the petty cash book for October 20X7 from the information given.

KAPLAN PUBLISHING

You should allocate a sequential voucher number to each entry in the petty cash book. The last voucher number to be allocated in September was 6578.

Use the blank petty cash book provided.

(b)   Total each of the columns in the petty cash book and cross-cast them.

(c)   Post the totals to the main ledger accounts given.

PETTY CASH BOOK – PAYMENTS

Date	Voucher no	Total £		Production £		Distribution £		Marketing £		Administration £		VAT £	

Production expenses account

£	£

Distribution expenses account

£	£

Marketing expenses account

£	£

Administration expenses account

£	£

VAT account

£	£

[Answer on p. 358]

5 Petty cash control account

5.1 Introduction

In most cases the petty cash book is not only a book of prime entry but also part of the main ledger. However in other businesses the petty cash book will be simply a book of prime entry and a petty cash control account will be maintained in the main ledger.

5.2 Petty cash control account

The petty cash control account summarises the information in the petty cash book and is posted from the petty cash book. When cash is put into the petty cash box the petty cash control account will be debited and the total of the petty cash payments for the period will be credited to the petty cash control account.

○ EXAMPLE ○○○○

A business runs a petty cash imprest system with an imprest amount of £100. At 1 May there was £32.56 remaining in the petty cash box and £67.44 of cash was withdrawn from the bank and put into the petty cash box to restore the imprest amount. During the month of May the total payments from the petty cash book were £82.16.

Write up the petty cash control account.

Solution

Petty cash control account

	£		£
Balance b/f	32.56	Payments	82.16
Receipt	67.44	Balance b/f	17.84
	————		————
	100.00		100.00
Balance c/f	17.84		

5.3 Reconciliation of the petty cash with the petty cash control account

The balance on the petty cash control account at the end of each period should be equal to the amount of cash remaining in the petty cash box. If there is a difference then this must be investigated.

5.4 Possible causes of difference

If there is more cash in the petty cash box than the balance on the petty cash control account this could be due to an error in writing up the petty cash book as more has been recorded in payments than has actually been paid out. In this case the entries in the petty cash book should be checked to the underlying petty cash vouchers to discover the error.

If there is less cash in the petty cash box than the balance on the petty cash control account this could also be due to an error in writing up the petty cash book as this time less payments have been recorded in the petty cash control account than were actually made. This may be due to a petty cash voucher having been omitted from the petty cash book and therefore again the under-lying petty cash vouchers should all be checked to their entries in the petty cash book.

If no accounting errors or posting errors can be found then the cause is likely to be one of the following:

·   an error has been made in paying a petty cash voucher and more money was handed out than was recorded on the voucher;
·   cash has been paid out of the petty cash box without a supporting voucher;
·   cash could have been stolen from the petty cash box.

In such cases the matter should be investigated and security of the petty cash and petty cash procedures improved.

○ EXAMPLE   ○○○○

The petty cash control account from the previous example is repro-duced.

Petty cash control account

	£		£
Balance b/f	32.56	Payments	82.16
Receipt	67.44	Balance b/f	17.84
	100.00		100.00
Balance b/f	17.84		

What action should be taken if when the petty cash was counted at 31 May the amount held in the box was:

(a) £27.84

(b) £7.84

Solution

(a) If the amount of cash in the box was £27.84 then this is £10 more than expected. The following checks should be made:
  · Has the balance on the petty cash control account been correctly calculated?
  · Have the receipt and payments totals been correctly posted to the petty cash control account?
  · Have the payments in the petty cash book been correctly totalled?
  · Has each individual petty cash voucher been correctly recorded in the petty cash book?

(b) If the amount of cash in the box is only £7.84 then this is £10 less than expected. All of the above checks should be carried out and if no accounting errors can be found then it will have to be assumed that either £10 too much has been paid out on a petty cash voucher, £10 has been paid out of the petty cash box without a supporting voucher or that £10 has been stolen from the petty cash box.

6   Reconciling the petty cash

6.1 Introduction

We saw earlier in the chapter that when an imprest system is being used for petty cash then at any point in time the amount of cash in the petty cash box plus the total of the vouchers in the petty cash box should equal the imprest amount.

At regular intervals, usually at the end of each week, this check will be carried out.

6.2 Procedure for reconciling the petty cash box

The total amount of cash in the petty cash box will be counted. The vouchers that have been paid during the week are also in the petty cash box and they must also be totalled.

When the amount of cash is added to the total of the vouchers in the box they should equal the imprest amount.

The petty cash vouchers for the week will then be removed from the box and filed.

○ **EXAMPLE**　　　　　　　　　　　　　　　　　○○○○

The amount of cash remaining in a petty cash box at the end of a week is as follows:

Notes/coins	Quantity
£10	1
£5	2
£2	3
£1	7
50p	9
20p	11
10p	15
5p	7
2p	16
1p	23

The imprest amount is £100 and the vouchers in the petty cash box at the end of the week are as follows:

PETTY CASH VOUCHER				
Authorised by C Alexi	Received by P Trant		No	0467
Date	Description		Amount	
4 May 20X3	Window cleaner		15	00
		Total	15	00

PETTY CASH VOUCHER				
Authorised by C Alexi	Received by F Saint		No	0468
Date	Description		Amount	
5 May 20X3	Train fare		9	80
		Total	9	80

PETTY CASH VOUCHER			
Authorised by C Alexi	*Received by* A Paul	*No*	0469
Date	*Description*	*Amount*	
5 May 20X3	Stationery	8	00
	VAT	1	40
	Total	9	40

PETTY CASH VOUCHER			
Authorised by C Alexi	*Received by* P Peters	*No*	0470
Date	*Description*	*Amount*	
7 May 20X3	Postage	6	80
	Total	6	80

PETTY CASH VOUCHER			
Authorised by C Alexi	*Received by* C Ralph	*No*	0471
Date	*Description*	*Amount*	
5 May 20X3	Train fare	16	90
	Total	16	90

The cash and vouchers in the petty cash box at the end of the week are to be reconciled.

Solution

The petty cash must be totalled:

Notes/coins	Quantity	Amount £
£10	1	10.00
£5	2	10.00
£2	3	6.00
£1	7	7.00
50p	9	4.50
20p	11	2.20
10p	15	1.50
5p	7	0.35
2p	16	0.32
1p	23	0.23
		42.10

Now the vouchers must be totalled.

	£
0467	15.00
0468	9.80
0469	9.40
0470	6.80
0471	16.90
	57.90

Finally, total the cash and the vouchers to ensure that they add back to the imprest amount.

	£
Cash	42.10
Vouchers	57.90
	100.00

▷ ACTIVITY 6 ▷▷▷▷

Your business runs a petty cash box based upon an imprest amount of £60. This morning you have emptied the petty cash box and found the following notes, coins and vouchers.

Notes
£5 x 2

Coins
£1 x 3
50p x 5
20p x 4
10p x 6
5p x 7
2p x 10
1p x 8

Vouchers	£
2143	10.56
2144	3.30
2145	9.80
2146	8.44
2147	2.62
2148	6.31
2149	1.44

You are required to reconcile the cash and the vouchers in the petty cash box.

[Answer on p. 359]

7   Test your knowledge ▷▷▷

1   Explain how an imprest petty cash system works.

2   What are the important features of a properly completed petty cash voucher?

3   A petty cash imprest system is run with an imprest amount of £120. During a week the total of the petty cash vouchers that have been reimbursed was £83. How much should be withdrawn from the bank to reimburse the petty cash box?

4   A cheque for cash is drawn and £58.00 in cash taken from the bank for petty cash. How should this be recorded in the petty cash book?

5   If the petty cash book is part of the main ledger then how are the totals of the analysis columns of the payment side of the petty cash book entered into the ledger accounts?

6   A business has a petty cash box run on an imprest system with an imprest amount of £80. The actual cash in the box at the end of the week totalled £36.44. How much should the petty cash vouchers for the week total?

[Answers on p. 359]

8   Summary

In this chapter we have considered the entire petty cash system. Cash is paid into the petty cash box in order to meet the requirements for actual cash in a business's life. This will normally be in the form of reimbursing employees for business expenses that they have incurred on their own behalf. In order to be reimbursed for the expense, the employee must fill out a petty cash voucher which will normally be accompanied by a receipt for the expense and must then be authorised. At this point the employee can be paid the cash out of the petty cash box.

All petty cash is recorded in the petty cash book which is normally both a book of prime entry and part of the main ledger. The cash paid into the petty cash box is recorded as a receipt in the petty cash book and as a payment in the cash payments book, an amount of cash being taken out of the bank account. The payments of petty cash vouchers are recorded as payments in the petty cash book and are analysed as to the type of payment. These payments are then recorded as debit entries in the appropriate expense account.

At the end of a period, a week or a month possibly, the cash in the petty cash box will be counted and reconciled to the vouchers in the box. In an imprest system the total of the vouchers in the box plus the total of the cash in the box should equal the imprest amount.

Answers to chapter activities & 'test your knowledge' questions

△ **ACTIVITY 1**   △△△△

Any two from the following:
(i)   Should be kept securely in a locked box or safe, etc.
(ii)   All payments should be properly authorised.
(iii)   Should be the responsibility of one person.
(iv)   The amount of any one payment should be restricted.

△ **ACTIVITY 2**   △△△△

£180

△ **ACTIVITY 3**   △△△△

HAIRDRESSING SUPPLIES LIMITED

M E M O R A N D U M

To: Phyllis Cranborne   Date: 29 March 20X2
From: Chris

Subject: Petty cash system

Marjorie has already notified me that she would like you to take charge of petty cash from 1 June next.

The main features of our present system are as follows:
(1)   The petty cash imprest system is one in which a fixed amount of money is advanced to the cashier, sufficient to meet normal petty cash disbursements over an agreed period (in our case one month).
(2)   Payments are made out of petty cash only if evidenced by properly authorised petty cash vouchers, supported by invoices or receipts.
(3)   At the end of each period, the petty cashier presents a return to the cashier giving details of the total amount spent, which is repaid to the petty cashier. The amount then held is the originally agreed fixed sum.
(4)   Periodically, Marjorie checks that the amount held agrees with the fixed amount, less expenditure since the last reimbursement date.

Please let me know if you have any further queries regarding the petty cash system.

Chris

Chris

△ **ACTIVITY 4**   △△△△

PETTY CASH VOUCHER				
Authorised by A Student	Received by		No	159
Date	Description		Amount	
07/09/X1	Chocolate biscuits		2	99
	Total		2	99

PETTY CASH VOUCHER				
Authorised by A Student	Received by		No	160
Date	Description		Amount	
07/09/X1	Stationery		4	75
	VAT		0	83
	Total		5	58

PETTY CASH VOUCHER				
Authorised by A Student	Received by		No	161
Date	Description		Amount	
07/09/X1	Computer disks		17	03
	VAT		2	97
	Total		20	00

PETTY CASH VOUCHER				
Authorised by A Student	Received by		No	162
Date	Description		Amount	
07/09/X1	Train fare		8	90
	Total		8	90

PETTY CASH VOUCHER			
Authorised by A Student	Received by	No	163
Date	Description	Amount	
07/09/X1	Coffee and milk	3	95
	Total	3	95

If any petty cash expenses include VAT then the VAT must be shown on the petty cash voucher so that it can eventually be correctly posted to the petty cash book and expense accounts.

△ ACTIVITY 5   △△△△

(a), (b)

PETTY CASH BOOK – PAYMENTS

Date	Voucher no	Total £		Production £		Distribution £		Marketing £		Administration £		VAT £	
01/10/X7	6579	19	72							16	79	2	93
04/10/X7	6580	8	75							8	75		
06/10/X7	6581	17	13					17	13				
06/10/X7	6582	16	23					16	23				
06/10/X7	6583	43	75					43	75				
10/10/X7	6584	4	60							4	60		
15/10/X7	6585	4	39	4	39								
17/10/X7	6586	8	47			7	21					1	26
20/10/X7	6587	21	23							21	23		
26/10/X7	6588	8	75							8	75		
		153	02	4	39	7	21	77	11	60	12	4	19

(c)

Production expenses account

	£		£
PCB	4.39		

Distribution expenses account

	£		£
PCB	7.21		

Marketing expenses account

	£		£
PCB	77.11		

Administration expenses account

	£		£
PCB	60.12		

VAT account

	£		£
PCB	4.19		

△ ACTIVITY 6 △△△△

Notes and coins

	£	£
£5 x 2	10.00	
£1 x 3	3.00	
50p x 5	2.50	
20p x 4	0.80	
10p x 6	0.60	
5p x 7	0.35	
2p x 10	0.20	
1p x 8	0.08	
		17.53

Vouchers

	£	£
2143	10.56	
2144	3.30	
2145	9.80	
2146	8.44	
2147	2.62	
2148	6.31	
2149	1.44	
		42.47
Imprest amount		60.00

Test your knowledge △ △ △

1   An imprest amount is initially set and paid into the petty cash box. At any point in time the amount of cash in the box plus the value of the vouchers should total to the imprest amount. At the end of each period the amount of cash to be withdrawn to reimburse the petty cash box to the imprest amount is the total of the vouchers that have been paid during the period.

2   · Sequential number
    · Details of the expenditure
    · Name of the claimant
    · Authorisation signature
    · Date of claim

3   £83

4   As a receipt on the receipts side of the petty cash book.

5   The totals of the analysis columns are debited to the appropriate expense accounts.

6   £80 – £36.44 = £43.56

BANK RECONCILIATIONS

INTRODUCTION

The standards require you to correctly prepare the cash book, compare the entries in the cash book to details on the bank statement and then finally to prepare a bank reconciliation statement.

KNOWLEDGE & UNDERSTANDING

- Importance of reconciling bank statements, control accounts and petty cash records (Element 3)
- The function, form and use of banking documentation (Elements 1, 2 and 3)

CONTENTS

1. Writing up the cash book
2. Preparing the bank reconciliation statement
3. Returned cheques

PERFORMANCE CRITERIA

- Update cash book from source documents (Element 30.3)
- Balance cash book and compare with bank statements (Element 30.3)
- Reconcile bank statement (Element 30.3)

1 Writing up the cash book

1.1 Introduction

Earlier in this text you learnt how to write up the cash receipts book and the cash payments book. This will be practised again here.

Most businesses will have a separate cash receipts book and a cash payments book which are part of the double entry system. If this form of record is used, the cash balance must be calculated from the opening balance at the beginning of the period, plus the receipts shown in the cash receipts book and minus the payments shown in the cash payments book.

1.2 Balancing the cash book

You will need to be able to find the balance on the cash book. This is done using the following brief calculation:

	£
Opening balance on the cash book	X
Add: Receipts in the period	X
Less: Payments in the period	(X)
Closing balance on the cash book	X

○ EXAMPLE ○○○○

Suppose that the opening balance on the cash book is £358.72 on 1 June. During June the Cash Payments Book shows that there were total payments made of £7,326.04 during the month of June and the Cash Receipts Book shows receipts for the month of £8,132.76.

What is the closing balance on the cash book at the end of June?

Solution

	£
Opening balance at 1 June	358.72
Add: Receipts for June	8,132.76
Less: Payments for June	(7,326.04)
Balance at 30 June	1,165.44

Take care if the opening balance on the cash book is an overdraft balance. Any receipts in the period will reduce the overdraft and any payments will increase the overdraft.

▷ ACTIVITY 1   ▷ ▷ ▷ ▷

The opening balance at 1 January in a business cash book was £673.42 over-drawn. During January payments totalled £6,419.37 and receipts totalled £6,488.20.

What is the closing balance on the cash book?

[Answer on p. 377]

○ EXAMPLE   ○ ○ ○ ○

The following transactions are to be written up in the cash book of Jupiter Limited and the balance at the end of the week calculated. The opening balance on the bank account on 1 July 20X1 was £560.61.

2 July   Received a cheque for £45.90 from Hill and French Limited (no settlement discount allowed) – paying in slip 40012.

2 July   Corrected a salary error by paying a cheque for £56.89 – cheque number 100107.

3 July   Paid £96.65 by cheque to Preston Brothers after deducting a settlement discount of £1.65 – cheque number 100108.

3 July   Banked £30 of cash held – paying in slip 40013.

4 July   Received a cheque from Green and Holland for £245.89. They were allowed a settlement discount of £3.68 – paying in slip 40014.

5 July   Reimbursed the petty cash account with £34.89 of cash drawn on cheque number 100109.

The cash receipts and payments books are to be written up and the closing balance calculated.

Solution

Step 1   Enter all of the transactions into the receipts and payments cash books.

Step 2   Total the cash book columns.

Cash receipts book

Date	Narrative		Total £	VAT £	Sales ledger £	Other £	Discount £
20X1							
2 July	Hill and French	40012	45.90		45.90		
3 July	Cash	40013	30.00			30.00	
4 July	Green and Holland	40014	245.89		245.89		3.68
			321.79	–	291.79	30.00	3.68

Cash payments book

Date	Details	Cheque	Code no	Total £	VAT £	Purchases ledger £	Cash purchases £	Other £	Discounts received £
20X1									
2 July	Salary error	100107		56.89				56.89	
3 July	Preston Bros	100108		96.65		96.65			1.65
5 July	Petty cash	100109		34.89				34.89	
				188.43	–	96.65	–	91.78	1.65

Step 3 Find the balance on the cash book at the end of the week.

		£
Opening balance at 1 July		560.61
Add:	Receipts total	321.79
Less:	Payments total	(188.43)
Balance at the end of the week		693.97

When totalling the cash book columns always check your additions carefully as it is easy to make mistakes when totalling columns of numbers on a calculator. Check that the totals of each analysis column (excluding the discounts columns) add back to the total of the total column.

2 Preparing the bank reconciliation statement

2.1 Introduction

At regular intervals (normally at least once a month) the cashier must check that the cash book is correct by comparing the cash book with the bank statement.

2.2 Differences between the cash book and bank statement

At any date the balance shown on the bank statement is unlikely to agree with the balance in the cash book for two main reasons.

(a) Items in the cash book not on the bank statement

Certain items will have been entered in the cash book but will not appear on the bank statement at the time of the reconciliation. Examples are:
· Cheques received by the business and paid into the bank which have not yet appeared on the bank statement, due to the time lag of the clearing system. These are known as **outstanding lodgements**.

- Cheques written by the business but which have not yet appeared on the bank statement, because the recipients have not yet paid them in, or the cheques are in the clearing system. These are known as **unpresented cheques**.
- Errors in the cash book (e.g. transposition of numbers, addition errors).

(b)   **Items on the bank statement not in the cash book**

At the time of the bank reconciliation certain items will appear on the bank statement that have not yet been entered in the cash book. These occur because frequently the cashier will not know of the existence of these items until he receives the bank statements. Examples are:

- Direct debit or standing order payments that are in the bank statement but have not yet been entered in the cash payments book;
- BACS or other receipts paid directly into the bank account by a customer;
- Bank charges or bank interest that are unknown until the bank statement has been received and therefore will not be in the cash book;
- Errors in the cash book that may only come to light when the cash book entries are compared to the bank statement.
- Returned cheques i.e. cheques paid in from a customer who does not have sufficient funds in his bank to pay the cheque (see later in this chapter).

2.3 The bank reconciliation

> **□ DEFINITION**   □□□□
>
> Definition: A bank reconciliation is simply a statement that explains the differences between the balance in the cash book and the balance on the bank statement at a particular date.

A bank reconciliation is produced by following a standard set of steps.

Step 1: Compare the cash book and the bank statement for the relevant period and identify any differences between them.

This is usually done by ticking in the cash book and bank statement items that appear in both the cash book and the bank statement. Any items left unticked therefore only appear in one place, either the cash book or the bank statement. We saw in 2.2 above the reasons why this might occur.

Step 2: Enter in the cash book items that appear on the bank statement which do not yet appear in the cash book.

Tick these items in both the cash book and the bank statement once they are entered in the cash book.

At this stage there will be no unticked items on the bank statement.

(You clearly cannot enter on the bank statement items in the cash book that do not appear on the bank statement – the bank prepares the bank statement, not you. These items will either be unpresented cheques or outstanding lodgements – see 2.2 above.)

Step 3: Bring down the new cash book balance following the adjustments in step 2 above.

Step 4: Prepare the bank reconciliation statement.

This will typically have the following proforma.

Bank reconciliation as at 31.0X.200X

	£
Balance as per bank statement	X
Less unpresented cheques	(X)
Add outstanding lodgements	X
Balance as per cash book	X

Think for a moment to ensure you understand this proforma.

We deduct the unpresented cheques (cheques already entered in the cash book but not yet on the bank statement) from the bank balance, because when they are presented this bank balance will be reduced.

We add outstanding lodgements (cash received and already entered in the cash book) because when they appear on the bank statement they will increase the bank balance.

2.4 Debits and credits in bank statements

When comparing the cash book to the bank statement it is easy to get confused with debits and credits.

· When we pay money into the bank, we debit our cash book but the bank credits our account.

· This is because a debit in our cash book represents the increase in our asset 'cash'. For the bank, the situation is different: they will debit their cash book and credit our account because they now owe us more money; we are a creditor.

· When our account is overdrawn, we owe the bank money and consequently our cash book will show a credit balance. For the bank an overdraft is a debit balance.

On the bank statement a credit is an amount of money paid into the account and a debit represents a payment.

O EXAMPLE   oooo

Given below are the completed cash books for Jupiter Limited from the previous example.

Cash receipts book

Date	Narrative		Total £	VAT £	Sales ledger £	Other £	Discount £
20X1							
2 July	Hill and French	40012	45.90		45.90		
3 July	Cash	40013	30.00			30.00	
4 July	Green and Holland	40014	245.89		245.89		3.68
			321.79	–	291.79	30.00	3.68

Cash payments book

Date	Details	Cheque	Code no	Total £	VAT £	Purchases ledger £	Cash purchases £	Other £	Discounts received £
20X1									
2 July	Salary error	100107		56.89				56.89	
3 July	Preston Bros	100108		96.65		96.65			1.65
5 July	Petty cash	100109		34.89				34.89	
				188.43	–	96.65	–	91.78	1.65

You have now received the bank statement for the week commencing 1 July 20X1 which is also shown below.

FIRST NATIONAL BANK
Cheque Account
SHEET NUMBER 012
ACCOUNT NUMBER 38 41 57 33794363

			Paid in £	Paid out £	Balance £
28 June	Balance brought forward				560.61
1 July	CT	A/C 38562959	123.90		684.51
4 July	CHQ	100107		56.89	
4 July	CR	40013	30.00		657.62
5 July	CR	40012	45.90		
5 July	DR	Bank charges		5.23	
5 July	DD	English Telecom		94.00	
5 July	CHQ	100109		34.89	569.40

CHQ	Cheque	CT	Credit transfer	CR	Payment in
DR	Payment out	DD	Direct debit		

You are required to compare the cash book and the bank statement and determine any differences. Tick the items in the bank statement and in the cash book above, then prepare the bank reconciliation statement at 5 July 20X1.

The balance on the cash book at 28 June was £560.61.

Solution

Step 1 The cash book, duly ticked, appears below.

Cash receipts book

Date	Narrative		Total £	VAT £	Sales ledger £	Other £	Discount £
20X1							
2 July	Hill and French	40012	45.90 ✔		45.90		
3 July	Cash	40013	30.00 ✔			30.00	
4 July	Green and Holland	40014	245.89		245.89		3.68
			321.79	–	291.79	30.00	3.68

Cash payments book

Date	Details	Cheque	Code no	Total £	VAT £	Purchases ledger £	Cash purchases £	Other £	Discounts received £
20X1									
2 July	Salary error	100107		56.89 ✔				56.89	
3 July	Preston Bros	100108		96.65		96.65			1.65
5 July	Petty cash	100109		34.89 ✔				34.89	
				188.43	–	96.65	–	91.78	1.65

The bank statement should have been ticked as shown below.

FIRST NATIONAL BANK
Cheque Account
SHEET NUMBER 012
ACCOUNT NUMBER 38 41 57 33794363

			Paid in £	Paid out £	Balance £
28 June	Balance brought forward				560.61
1 July	CT	A/C 38562959	123.90		684.51
4 July	CHQ	100107		56.89 ✔	
4 July	CR	40013	30.00 ✔		657.62
5 July	CR	40012	45.90 ✔		
5 July	DR	Bank charges		5.23	
5 July	DD	English Telecom		94.00	
5 July	CHQ	100109		34.89 ✔	569.40

CHQ	Cheque	CT	Credit transfer	CR	Payment in
DR	Payment out	DD	Direct debit		

Step 2 A comparison of the items in the cash book with those in the bank statement reveals unticked items in both.

(a) We will first consider the items that are unticked on the bank statement;
   - there is a credit transfer on 1 July of £123.90 – this must be checked to the related documentation and then entered into the cash receipts book;
   - the bank charges of £5.23 must be entered into the cash payments book;
   - the direct debit of £94.00 should be checked and then entered into the cash payments book.

(b) We will now consider the items that are unticked in the cash book. Remember that no adjustment is needed to these but we have to decide where they will appear in the bank reconciliation statement.
   - the cheque paid in on 4 July has not yet appeared on the bank statement due to the time it takes for cheques to clear through the clearing system – an outstanding lodgement;
   - cheque number 100108 has not yet cleared through the banking system – an unpresented cheque.

The cash receipts and cash payments book will now appear as follows after the adjustments in (a) above.

Date	Narrative		Total £	VAT £	Sales ledger £	Other £	Discount £
20X1							
2 July	Hill and French	40012	45.90 ✔		45.90		
3 July	Cash	40013	30.00 ✔			30.00	
4 July	Green and Holland	40014	245.89 ✔		245.89		3.68
1 July	Credit transfer		123.90 ✔		123.90		
			445.69	–	415.69	30.00	3.68

Cash payments book

Date	Details	Cheque	Code	Total £	VAT £	Purchases ledger £	Cash purchases £	Other £	Discounts received £
20X1									
2 July	Salary error	100107		56.89✔				56.89	
3 July	Preston Bros	100108		96.65		96.65			1.65
5 July	Petty cash	100109		34.89✔				34.89	
5 July	Bank charges			5.23✔				5.23	
5 July	English Telecom	DD		94.00✔		94.00			
				287.66	–	190.65	–	97.01	1.65

Note that the items we have entered in the cash book from the bank statement are ticked in both. There are no unticked items on the bank statement (not shown) and two unticked items in the cash book.

Step 3 Find the amended cash book balance.

	£
Balance at 28 June	560.61
Cash receipts in first week of July	445.69
Cash payments in first week of July	(287.66)
Balance at 5 July	718.64

Step 4 Reconcile the amended cash book balance to the bank statement balance.

Bank reconciliation as at 5 July 20X1

	£
Balance per bank statement	569.40
Less: unpresented cheque	(96.65)
Add: outstanding lodgement	245.89
Balance per cash book	718.64

This is the completed bank reconciliation.

▷ ACTIVITY 2   ▷ ▷ ▷ ▷

The following are summaries of the cash receipts book, cash payments book and bank statement for the first two weeks of trading of Gambank, a firm specialising in selling cricket bats.

Cash receipts book

Date	Narrative	Total £	VAT £	Sales ledger £	Other £	Discount £
20X0						
01 Jan	Capital	2,000			2,000	
05 Jan	A Hunter	1,000		1,000		
09 Jan	Cancel cheque no 0009	90				90
10 Jan	I M Dunn	4,800		4,800		

Cash payments book

Date	Details	Cheque no	Code	Total £	VAT £	Purchases ledger £	Cash purchases £	Other £	Discounts received £
20X0									
01 Jan	Wages	0001		50				50	
02 Jan	Fine	0002		12				12	
03 Jan	Dodgy Dealers	0003		1,500		1,500			
04 Jan	E L Pubo	0004		45		45			
05 Jan	Drawings	0005		200				200	
07 Jan	E L Wino	0007		30		30			
08 Jan	Toby	0008		1,400		1,400			
09 Jan	El Pubo	0009		70		70			
10 Jan	Marion's Emp	0010		200		200			
11 Jan	Speeding Fine	0011		99				99	

FINANCIAL BANK plc CONFIDENTIAL

You can bank on us !

Account   CURRENT   Sheet No.   1

10 Yorkshire Street
Headingley   GAMBANK
Leeds LS1 1QT
Telephone: 0113 633061

   Statement date   14 Jan 20X0   Account Number   40023986

Date	Details	Withdrawals (£)	Deposits (£)	Balance (£)
01 Jan	CR		2,000	2,000
02 Jan	0001	50		1,950
04 Jan	0003	1,500		450
05 Jan	0005	200		250
07 Jan	CR		1,000	
	0002	12		
	0004	45		
	0006	70		1,123
08 Jan	0007	30		1,093
10 Jan	0009	70		
	0009		70	
	0010	200		893
11 Jan	0012	20		
	Charges	53		820

SO	Standing order	DD	Direct debit	CR	Credit
AC	Automated cash	OD	Overdrawn	TR	Transfer

Prepare a bank reconciliation statement at 14 January 20X0.

[Answer on p. 377]

2.5 Opening balances disagree

Usually the balances on the bank statement and in the cash book do not agree at the start of the period for the same reasons that they do not agree at the end, e.g. items in the cash book that were not on the bank statement. When producing the reconciliation statement it is important to take this opening difference into account.

The bank statement and cash book of Jones for the month of December 20X8 start as follows.

Bank statement		Debit £	Credit £	Balance £
1 Dec 20X8	Balance b/d (favourable)			8,570
2 Dec 20X8	0073	125		
2 Dec 20X8	0074	130		
3 Dec 20X8	Sundries		105	

Cash book		£			£
1 Dec 20X8 b/d		8,420	Cheque 0076	Wages	200
Sales		320	Cheque 0077	Rent	500
		X			X
		X			X

Required:

Explain the difference between the opening balances.

Solution

The difference in the opening balance is as follows.

£8,570 – £8,420 = £150

This difference is due to the following.

	£
Cheque 0073	125
Cheque 0074	130
	255
Lodgement (sundries)	(105)
	150

These cheques and lodgements were in the cash book in November, but only appear on the bank statement in December. They will therefore be matched and ticked against the entries in the November cash book. The December reconciliation will then proceed as normal.

3   Returned cheques

A customer C may send a cheque in payment of an invoice without having sufficient funds in his account with Bank A.

The seller S who receives the cheque will pay it into his account with Bank B and it will go into the clearing system. Bank B will credit S's account with the funds in anticipation of the cheque being honoured.

Bank A however will not pay funds into the S's account with Bank B and Bank B will then remove the funds from S's account.

The net effect of this is that on S's bank statement, the cheque will appear as having been paid in (a credit on the bank statement), and then later will appear as having been paid out (a debit on the bank statement).

The original credit on the bank statement will be in S's cash book as a debit in the normal way. But the debit on the bank statement (the dishonour of the cheque) will not be in S's cash book. This will have to be credited into the cash book as money paid out.

These cheques are technically referred to as 'returned cheques', but they are also called 'dishonoured cheques' or 'bounced cheques'.

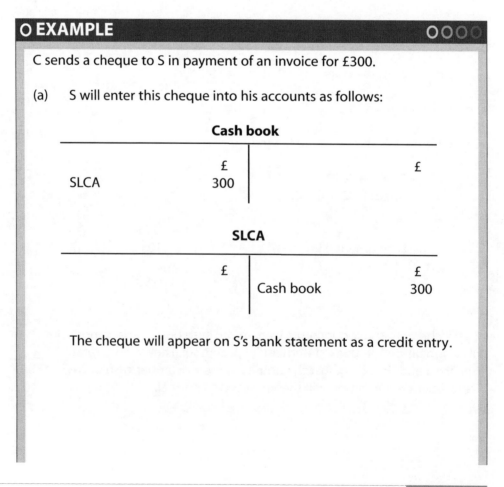

○ EXAMPLE   ○○○○

C sends a cheque to S in payment of an invoice for £300.

(a)   S will enter this cheque into his accounts as follows:

Cash book

	£		£
SLCA	300		

SLCA

	£		£
		Cash book	300

The cheque will appear on S's bank statement as a credit entry.

(b)   when the cheque is dishonoured S will enter this cheque into his accounts as follows:

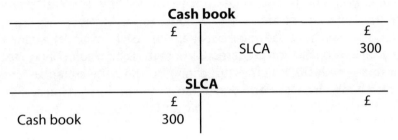

Cash book

	£			£
			SLCA	300

SLCA

	£			£
Cash book	300			

The journal entry will be

Dr   SLCA   300
Cr   Cash book   300

This reinstates the debtor

The dishonoured cheque will appear on the bank statement as a debit entry.

4   Test your knowledge ▷ ▷ ▷

1   The opening balance on a business cash book was an overdraft of £200. During the period there were cash receipts totalling £2,500 and cash payments totalling £1,800. What was the closing balance on the cash book?

2   What differences might be discovered by comparing the cash receipts and payments books to the bank statement?

3   If a standing order payment appears on the bank statement but not in the cash book what action, if any, is required?

4   A cash receipt of £500 has been entered into the cash receipts book but is not in the bank statement. What would the receipt be known as and what action, if any, is required?

5   The bank statement for a business at the end of June shows a debit balance of £320. Does this mean that the business has money in the bank or an overdraft?

6   The bank statement for a business at the end of March shows a credit balance of £440. There are items totalling £600 in the cash receipts book which do not appear in the bank statement and items totalling £800 in the cash payments book which do not appear in the bank statement. Assuming that the cash books are correct what is the balance on the cash book at the end of March?

[Answers on p. 381]

5 Summary

In this chapter you have had to write up the cash receipts and cash payments books and then total and balance the cash book. However, most importantly for this unit a comparison has to be made between the cash book and the bank statement and a bank reconciliation prepared. Do note that when comparing the bank statement to the cash book, figures appearing on the bank statement may be from the cash book some time ago due to the nature of the clearing system and the general timing of cheques being sent out and then presented to a bank.

Answers to activities & 'test your knowledge' questions

△ ACTIVITY 1 △△△△

	£
Opening balance	(673.42)
Payments	(6,419.37)
Receipts	6,488.20
Closing balance	(604.59)

The closing balance is £604.59 overdrawn.

△ ACTIVITY 2 △△△△

Step 1 Tick the cash books and bank statement to indicate the matched items.

Cash receipts book

Date	Narrative	Total £	VAT £	Sales ledger £	Other £	Discount £
20X0						
01 Jan	Capital	2,000✔			2,000	
05 Jan	A Hunter	1,000✔		1,000		
09 Jan	Cancel cheque no 0009	90			90	
10 Jan	I M Dunn	4,800		4,800		
		7,890	–	5,800	2,090	–

Cash payments book

Date	Details	Cheque no	Code	Total £	VAT £	Purchases ledger £	Cash purchases £	Other £	Discounts received £
20X0									
01 Jan	Wages	0001		50✔				50	
02 Jan	Fine	0002		12✔				12	
03 Jan	Dodgy Dealers	0003		1,500✔		1,500			
04 Jan	E L Pubo	0004		45✔		45			
05 Jan	Drawings	0005		200✔				200	
07 Jan	E L Wino	0007		30✔		30			
08 Jan	Toby	0008		1,400		1,400			
09 Jan	El Pubo	0009		70✔		70			
10 Jan	Marion's Emp	0010		200✔		200			
11 Jan	Speeding Fine	0011		99				99	
				3,606	–	3,245	–	361	

FINANCIAL BANK plc CONFIDENTIAL

You can bank on us !

10 Yorkshire Street
Headingley
Leeds LS1 1QT
Telephone: 0113 633061

Account CURRENT   *Sheet No.*

GAMBANK

Statement date   14 Jan 20X0   Account Number   40023986

Date	Details	Withdrawals (£)	Deposits (£)	Balance (£)
01 Jan	CR		2,000✔	2,000
02 Jan	0001	50✔		1,950
04 Jan	0003	1,500✔		450
05 Jan	0005	200✔		250
07 Jan	CR		1,000✔	
	0002	12✔		
	0004	45✔		
	0006	70		1,123
08 Jan	0007	30✔		1,093
10 Jan	0009	70✔		
	0009		70	
	0010	200✔		893
11 Jan	0012	20		
	Charges	53		820

SO	Standing order	DD	Direct debit	CR	Credit	
AC	Automated cash	OD	Overdrawn	TR	Transfer	

Step 2   Deal with each of the unticked items.

Cash receipts book   –   cheque number 0009 does appear to have been cancelled as it has appeared as a debit and a credit entry in the bank statement – however the bank statement shows that the cheque was for £70 and not the £90 entered into the cash receipts book – this must be amended in the cash book.

–   the receipt from I M Dunn has not yet cleared through the banking system and is therefore not on the bank statement – it is an outstanding lodgement.

Cash payments book   –   cheque number 0008 to Toby and cheque number 0011 have not yet cleared through the clearing system – they are unpresented cheques.

Bank statement   –   cheque number 0006 has not been entered into the cash payments book but it has cleared the bank account – the cash book must be amended to show this payment.

  –   cheque number 0012 has not been entered into the cash payments book but it has cleared the bank account – the cash book must be amended to show this payment.

  –   the bank charges of £53 must be entered into the cash payments book.

Step 3 Amend the cash books and total them.

Cash receipts book

Date	Narrative	Total £	VAT £	Sales ledger £	Other £	Discount £
20X0						
01 Jan	Capital	2,000✔			2,000	
05 Jan	A Hunter	1,000✔		1,000		
09 Jan	Cancel cheque no 0009	90✔			90	
10 Jan	I M Dunn	4,800		4,800		
10 Jan	Cancelled cheque adjustment 0009	(20)✔			(20)	
		7,870	–	5,800	2,070	–

Cash payments book

Date	Details	Cheque no	Code	Total £	VAT £	Purchases ledger £	Cash purchases £	Other £	Discounts received £
20X0									
01 Jan	Wages	0001		50✔				50	
02 Jan	Fine	0002		12✔				12	
03 Jan	Dodgy Dealers	0003		1,500✔		1,500			
04 Jan	E L Pubo	0004		45✔		45			
05 Jan	Drawings	0005		200✔				200	
07 Jan	E L Wino	0007		30✔		30			
08 Jan	Toby	0008		1,400		1,400			
09 Jan	El Pubo	0009		70✔		70			
10 Jan	Marion's Emp	0010		200✔		200			
11 Jan	Speeding Fine	0011		99				99	
10 Jan		0006		70✔		70			
10 Jan		0012		20✔		20			
11 Jan	Bank charges			53✔				53	
				3,749	–	3,335	–	414	

Step 4 Determine the amended cash book balance

	£
Opening balance	–
Cash receipts	7,870
Cash payments	(3,749)
Amended cash book balance	4,121

Step 5 Reconcile the amended cash book balance to the bank statement balance

	£	£
Balance per bank statement		820
Add: outstanding lodgement		4,800
Less: unpresented cheques 0008	1,400	
0011	99	
		(1,499)
Amended cash book balance		4,121

1

	£
Opening balance	(200)
Receipts	2,500
Payments	(1,800)
	500 in credit

2 · errors in the cash book
· direct debits/standing orders omitted from the cash book
· direct bank giro credits omitted from the cash book
· bank charges/interest not entered into the cash book
· unpresented cheques/outstanding lodgements

3 The cash payments book should be amended to reflect the payment.

4 Outstanding lodgement. No alteration is required although this will be a reconciling item in the bank reconciliation statement.

5 A debit balance on the bank statement is an overdraft.

6

	£
Balance per bank statement	440
Add: Outstanding lodgements	600
Less: Unpresented cheques	(800)
Balance per cash book	240

LEDGER BALANCES AND CONTROL ACCOUNTS

INTRODUCTION

In this chapter we will be finding the correct ledger account balances by revising balancing off ledger accounts (covered in an earlier chapter) as the basis for drafting an initial trial balance. In particular we will be looking at ways of ensuring the accuracy of the balances for debtors (sales ledger control account) and creditors (purchases ledger control account).

KNOWLEDGE & UNDERSTANDING

- Batch control (Element 2)
- Double entry bookkeeping, including balancing accounts (Elements 1, 2 and 3)
- Relationship between the accounting system and the ledger (Elements 1, 2 and 3)
- Importance of reconciling bank statements, control accounts and petty cash records (Element 3)

CONTENTS

1 Balancing ledger accounts
2 Opening balances
3 Accounting for debtors
4 Sales ledger control account reconciliation
5 Accounting for creditors
6 Purchase ledger control account reconciliation
7 Cause of the difference
8 Batch control

PERFORMANCE CRITERIA

- Reconcile sales and purchase ledger control accounts with subsidiary ledgers (Element 30.3)

1   Balancing ledger accounts

1.1 Introduction

The purpose of maintaining double entry ledger accounts is to provide information about the transactions and financial position of a business. Each type of transaction is gathered together and recorded in the appropriate ledger account, for example all sales are recorded in the sales account. Then at intervals it will be necessary to find the total of each of these types of transactions.

This is done by balancing each ledger account. This has been covered earlier in this text but is worth revising here, by attempting the following activity.

▷ ACTIVITY 1   ▷ ▷ ▷ ▷

You are required to balance off the following ledger accounts:

Sales ledger control account

	£		£
SDB – invoices	5,426.23	CRB	3,226.56
		Discounts allowed	315.47

VAT account

	£		£
PDB	846.72	SDB	1,036.54

Sales account

	£		£
		SDB	2,667.45
		SDB	1,853.92

[Answer on p.410]

2 Opening balances

2.1 Introduction

If an account has a balance on it at the end of a period then it will have the same balance at the start of the next period. This is known as an opening balance.

2.2 Debit or credit?

The key to determining whether an opening balance on a ledger account is a debit or a credit is to understand the general rules for debit and credit balances.

2.3 Debit and credit balance rules

Asset account	–	debit balance
Liability account	–	credit balance
Expense account	–	debit balance
Income account	–	credit balance

It may be difficult to see why assets and expenses are both debit balances. The reason is that both are the result of an outflow of cash to acquire the asset or to pay the expense. Similarly, the incurring of a liability and the receipt of income are both the result of an inflow of cash.

O EXAMPLE   OOOO

You are told that the opening balance on the sales ledger control account is £33,600, the opening balance on the purchases account is £115,200 and the opening balance on the purchases ledger control account is £12,700.

You are required to enter these into the relevant ledger accounts.

Solution

Sales ledger control account

	£		£
Balance brought forward	33,600		

Purchases account

	£		£
Balance brought forward	115,200		

Purchases ledger control account

	£		£
		Balance brought forward	12,700

Assets and expenses normally have opening debit balances. Liabilities and income normally have opening credit balances.

▷ ACTIVITY 2   ▷▷▷▷

Would the balances on the following accounts be debit or credit balances?

(a) Sales account

(b) Discounts allowed account

(c) Discounts received account

(d) Wages expense account

[Answer on p. 410]

▷ ACTIVITY 3   ▷▷▷▷

The following transactions all occurred on 1 December 20X1 and have been entered into the relevant books of prime entry (given below). However, no entries have yet been made into the ledger system. VAT has been calculated at a rate of 17½%.

Purchases day book

Date	Details	Invoice no	Total £	VAT £	Purchases £	Stationery £
20X1						
1 Dec	Bailey Limited	T151	235	35	200	
1 Dec	Byng & Company	10965	940	140	800	
1 Dec	Office Supplies Ltd	34565	329	49		280
1 Dec	O'Connell Frames	FL013	4,935	735	4,200	
	Totals		6,439	959	5,200	280

Purchases returns day book

Date	Details	Invoice no	Total £	VAT £	Purchases £	Stationery £
20X1						
1 Dec	O'Connell Frames	C011	2,115	315	1,800	
1 Dec	Office Supplies Ltd	CR192	47	7		40
	Totals		2,162	322	1,800	40

Sales day book

Date	Details	Invoice no	Total £	VAT £	Sales £
20X1					
1 Dec	Bentley Brothers	H621	1,645	245	1,400
1 Dec	J & H Limited	H622	4,230	630	3,600
1 Dec	Furniture Galore	H623	4,700	700	4,000
1 Dec	The Sofa Shop	H624	2,585	385	2,200
	Totals		13,160	1,960	11,200

Balances

The following are some of the balances in the accounting records and are all relevant to you at the start of the day on 1 December 20X1:

	£
Credit Suppliers	
Bailey Limited	11,750
Byng & Company	1,269
Office Supplies Limited	4,230
O'Connell Frames	423
Creditors' control	82,006
Debtors' control	180,312
Purchases	90,563
Sales	301,492
Purchases returns	306
Stationery	642
Discounts received	50
VAT (credit balance)	17,800

Receipts on 1 December 20X1

	Total £
Lili Chang (cash sale including VAT)	517
Bentley Brothers (credit customer)	5,875

Cheque issued

	Total £
Bailey Limited (in full settlement of debt of £819)	799

Task 1

Enter the opening balances listed above into the following accounts, blanks of which are provided on the following pages:

Bailey Limited
Byng & Company
Office Supplies Limited
O'Connell Frames
Creditors' control
Debtors' control
Purchases

Sales
Purchases returns
Stationery
Discounts received
VAT

Task 2

Using the data shown above, enter all the relevant transactions into the accounts in the subsidiary (purchases) ledger and main ledger. Entries to the subsidiary (sales) ledger for debtors are not required.

Task 3

Enter the receipts and payments shown above into the cash book given on the following pages.

Task 4

Transfer any relevant sums from the cash book into the subsidiary ledger for creditors and main ledger.

Task 5

Balance off all of the accounts and the cash book, showing clearly the balances carried down. The opening cash balance was £3,006. Find the closing balance on the cash book.

Tasks 1, 2, 4 and 5

Subsidiary (purchases) ledger

Bailey Limited

£		£

Byng & Company

£		£

Office Supplies Limited

£		£

O'Connell Frames

£		£

Main ledger

Creditors' control

£		£

Debtors' control

£		£

Purchases

£		£

Sales

£		£

Purchases returns

£		£

Stationery

£		£

Discounts received

£		£

VAT

	£		£

Tasks 3, 4 and 5

Cash receipts book

Date	Narrative £	Total £	VAT £	Sales ledger £	Other £	Discounts allowed

Cash payments book

Date	Details	Cheque no	Code	Total £	VAT £	Purchases ledger £	Cash purchases £	Other £	Discounts received £

[Answer on p.411]

3 Accounting for debtors

3.1 Sales ledger control account

Within the main ledger the total amount outstanding from debtors is shown in the sales ledger control account or debtors' control account.

The totals of credit sales (from the sales day book), returns from customers (from the sales returns day book) and cash received and discounts (from the analysed cash book) are posted to this account.

This account therefore shows the total debtors outstanding. It does not give details about individual customers' balances. This is available in the subsidiary ledger for debtors.

However, as both records are compiled from the same sources, the total balances on the customers' individual accounts should equal the outstanding balance on the control account at any time.

3.2 Double entry system

The double entry system operates as follows.

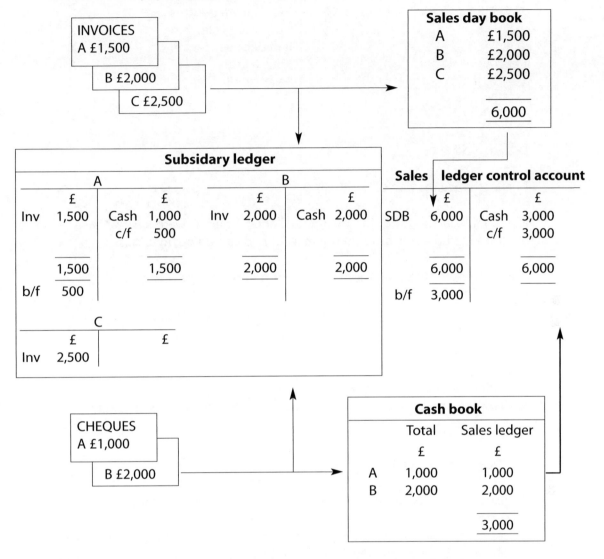

Notice that the remaining balance on the control account (£3,000) is equal to the sum of the remaining balances on the individual debtors' accounts (A £500 + C £2,500).

If all of the accounting entries have been made correctly then the balance on the sales ledger control account should equal the total of the balances on each of the individual debtors' accounts in the subsidiary (sales) ledger.

3.3 Proforma sales ledger control account

A sales ledger control account normally appears like this.

Sales ledger control account

	£		£
Balance b/f	X	Returns per sales returns day book	X
Sales per sales day book	X	* Cash from debtors	X
		* Discounts allowed	X
		Bad debt written off	X
		Contra entry	X
		Balance c/f	X
	___		___
	X		X
	___		___
Balance b/f	X		

* Per cash receipts book

Note that balances brought forward (b/f) and carried forward (c/f) can also be described as balances brought down (b/d) and carried down (c/d).

Two of these entries, bad debts and contra entry, are new to you so we will consider them now.

3.4 Bad debts

Definition: A bad debt is a debt which is highly unlikely to be received; it is therefore not prudent for the business to consider this debt as an asset.

3.5 Reasons for bad debts

A business may decide that a debt is bad for a number of reasons:
·   customer is in liquidation – no cash will be received;
·   customer is having difficulty paying although not officially in liquidation;
·   customer disputes the debt and refuses to pay all or part of it.

3.6 Accounting for bad debts

The business must make an adjustment to write off the bad debt from the customer's account in the subsidiary ledger and to write it off in the main ledger. The double entry in the main ledger is:

DR   Bad debt expense
    CR   Sales ledger control account

Notice that the bad debt becomes an expense of the business. Writing off bad debts decreases the profits made by a business. (Note that the bad debt is not deducted from sales.) The sale was made in the anticipation of receiving the money but, if the debt is not to be received, this does not negate the sale it is just an added expense of the business.

The bad debt must also be written off in the individual debtor's account in the subsidiary ledger by crediting the customer's account as this amount is not going to be received.

To write off a bad debt, it is necessary to debit the bad debt expense account in the main ledger and credit the sales ledger control account. In the subsidiary (sales) ledger the customer's account must be credited with the amount of the bad debt.

3.7 Contra entries

A further type of adjustment that may be required to sales ledger and purchases ledger control accounts is a contra entry.

3.8 Why a contra entry is required

In some instances a business will be both a debtor and a creditor of another business as it both buys from the business and sells to it. If this is the case then there will be money owed to the business and money owing from it. This can be simplified by making an adjustment known as a contra entry.

○ EXAMPLE ○○○○

James Associates has a customer, X Brothers. X Brothers also sells goods to James Associates. Therefore X Brothers is both a debtor and a creditor of James Associates. The subsidiary ledger accounts of James Associates show the following position:

Subsidiary ledger – debtors

X Brothers

	£		£
Balance b/f	250		

Subsidiary ledger – creditors

X Brothers

	£		£
		Balance b/f	100

The problem here is that X Brothers owes James Associates £250 and is owed £100 by James Associates. If both parties are in agreement it makes more sense to net these two amounts off and to say that X Brothers owes James Associates just £150. This is achieved in accounting terms by a contra entry.

Solution

Step 1 Take the smaller of the two amounts and debit the subsidiary ledger account for the creditor and credit the subsidiary ledger account for the debtor with this amount.

Subsidiary ledger – debtors

X Brothers

	£		£
Balance b/f	250	Contra	100

Subsidiary ledger – creditors

X Brothers

	£		£
Contra	100	Balance b/f	100

Step 2 Balance off the accounts in the subsidiary ledgers.

Subsidiary ledger – debtors

X Brothers

	£		£
Balance b/f	250	Contra	100
		Balance c/f	150
	250		250
Balance b/f	150		

Subsidiary ledger – creditors

X Brothers

	£		£
Contra	100	Balance b/f	100

This now shows that X Brothers owes £150 to James Associates and is owed nothing by James Associates.

Step 3 The double entry must also be carried out in the main ledger accounts. This is:

DR Purchases ledger control account
  CR   Sales ledger control account

When a contra entry is made you must remember not just to deal with the entries in the subsidiary ledgers but also to put through the double entry in the main ledger accounts, the sales ledger and purchases ledger control accounts.

3.9 Main ledger and subsidiary ledger

We will now return to the relationship between the sales ledger control account in the main ledger and the individual accounts for debtors in the subsidiary ledger.

O EXAMPLE   OOOO

James has been trading for two months. He has four credit customers. James is not registered for VAT. Here is the day book for the first two months:

Sales day book (SDB)

Date	Customer	Invoice	£
02.2.X4	Peter Brown	01	50.20
05.2.X4	Ian Smith	02	80.91
07.2.X4	Sid Parsons	03	73.86
23.2.X4	Eva Lane	04	42.30
	Total		247.27
09.3.X4	Ian Smith	05	23.96
15.3.X4	Sid Parsons	06	34.72
20.3.X4	Peter Brown	07	12.60
24.3.X4	Sid Parsons	08	93.25
31.3.X4	Total		164.53

Here is the receipts side of the analysed cash book for March 20X4 (no cash was received from debtors in February).

Cash receipts book (CRB)

Date	Narrative	Total	Cash sales	Sales ledger	Rent
		£	£	£	£
01.3.X4	Peter Brown	50.20		50.20	
03.3.X4	Clare Jones	63.80	63.80		
04.3.X4	Molly Dell	110.00			110.00
12.3.X4	Sid Parsons	50.00		50.00	
13.3.X4	Emily Boyd	89.33	89.33		
20.3.X4	Frank Field	92.68	92.68		
25.3.X4	Eva Lane	42.30		42.30	
31.3.X4	Total	498.31	245.81	142.50	110.00

We will write up the subsidiary ledger and the sales ledger control account and compare the balances.

Solution

Subsidiary ledger – debtors

Peter Brown

		£			£
02.2.X4	01	50.20	28.2.X4	c/f	50.20
		50.20			50.20
01.3.X4	b/f	50.20	01.3.X4	Cash	50.20
20.3.X4	07	12.60	31.3.X4	c/f	12.60
		62.80			62.80
01.4.X4	b/f	12.60			

Eva Lane

		£			£
23.2.X4	04	42.30	28.2.X4	c/f	42.30
		42.30			42.30
01.3.X4	b/f	42.30	25.3.X4	Cash	42.30

Sid Parsons

		£			£
07.2.X4	03	73.86	28.2.X4	c/f	73.86
		73.86			73.86
01.3.X4	b/f	73.86	12.3.X4	Cash	50.00
15.3.X4	06	34.72	31.3.X4	c/f	151.83
24.3.X4	08	93.25			
		201.83			201.83
01.4.X4	b/f	151.83			

Ian Smith

		£			£
05.2.X4	02	80.91	28.2.X4	c/f	80.91
		80.91			80.91
01.3.X4	b/f	80.91	31.3.X4	c/f	104.87
09.3.X4	05	23.96			
		104.87			104.87
01.4.X4	b/f	104.87			

Sales ledger control account

		£			£
28.2.X4	SDB	247.27	28.2.X4	c/f	247.27
		247.27			247.27
01.3.X4	b/f	247.27	31.3.X4	CRB	142.50
31.3.X4	SDB	164.53	31.3.X4	c/f	269.30
		411.80			411.80
01.4.X4	b/f	269.30			

Let us compare balances at 31 March 20X4.

Subsidiary ledger – debtors

	£
Peter Brown	12.60
Eva Lane	–
Sid Parsons	151.83
Ian Smith	104.87
	269.30
Sales ledger control account	269.30

As the double entry has been correctly carried out, the total of the balances on the individual debtors' accounts in the subsidiary ledger is equal to the balance on the sales ledger control account.

4 Sales ledger control account reconciliation

4.1 Introduction

Comparing the control account balance with the total of the subsidiary ledger accounts is a form of internal control. The reconciliation should be performed on a regular basis by the sales ledger clerk and reviewed and approved by an independent person.

If the total of the balances on the subsidiary (sales) ledger do not equal the balance on the sales ledger control account then an error or errors have been made in either the main ledger or subsidiary ledger, and these must be discovered and corrected.

4.2 Journal entries

Any corrections or adjustments made to the sales ledger control account must be documented as a journal entry.

Definition: A journal entry is a written instruction to the bookkeeper to enter a double entry into the main ledger accounts.

This will be a double entry that has not been recorded in the primary records as these are posted automatically to the main ledger when the primary records are posted. Therefore journal entries are used for unusual items that do not appear in the primary records or for the correction of errors or making of adjustments to ledger accounts.

A typical journal entry to write off a bad debt is shown below:

JOURNAL ENTRY		No: 06671			
Prepared by:	P Freer				
Authorised by:	P Simms				
Date:	3 October 20X2				
Narrative:					
To write off bad debt from L C Hamper					
Account		*Code*	*Debit*	*Credit*	
Bad debts expense		ML28	102.00		
Debtors' control		ML06		102.00	
TOTALS				102.00	102.00

Authorisation

Description of why double entry is necessary

Double entry

Sequential journal number

Equal totals as journal must balance

O EXAMPLE   OOOO

The total sales for the month was posted from the sales day book as £4,657.98 instead of £4,677.98. This must be corrected using a journal entry.

Solution

The journal entry to correct this error will be as follows:

JOURNAL ENTRY		No: 97		
Prepared by:	A Grimm			
Authorised by:	L R Ridinghood			
Date:	23.7.X3			
Narrative:				
To correct error in posting to debtors' control account				
Account		*Code*	*Debit*	*Credit*
Sales ledger control		ML11	20	
Sales		ML56		20
TOTALS			20	20

The adjustment required is to increase debtors and sales by £20 therefore a debit to sales ledger control and a credit to sales is needed.

4.3 Adjustments in the subsidiary ledger

Adjustments in the subsidiary ledger do not need to be shown in a journal entry. Journal entries are only required for adjustments to the main ledger.

These adjustments should be recorded in memorandum form, with proper authorisation.

4.4 Procedure for a sales ledger control account reconciliation

(1) The balances on the subsidiary ledger accounts for debtors are extracted, listed and totalled.
(2) The sales ledger control account is balanced.
(3) If the two figures differ, then the reasons for the difference must be investigated.
  Reasons may include the following:
  · An error in the casting of the day book. (The total is posted to the control account whereas the individual invoices are posted to the individual accounts and, therefore, if the total is incorrect, a difference will arise.)
  · A transposition error which could be made in posting either:
    (a) to the control account (the total figure); or
    (b) to the individual accounts (the individual transactions).

·   A casting error in the cash book column relating to the control account. (The total is posted.)

·   A balance omitted from the list of individual accounts.

·   A credit balance on an individual account in the subsidiary ledger for debtors which has automatically and wrongly been assumed to be a debit balance.

(4)   Differences which are errors in the control account should be corrected in the control account.

(5)   Differences which are errors in the individual accounts should be corrected by adjusting the list of balances and, of course, the account concerned.

▷ ACTIVITY 4

(AAT CA D93)

Would the following errors cause a difference to occur between the balance of the debtors' control account and the total of the balances in the subsidiary (sales) ledger?

(a)   The total column of the sales day book was overcast by £100.

(b)   In error H Lambert's account in the sales ledger was debited with £175 instead of M Lambert's account.

(c)   An invoice for £76 was recorded in the sales day book as £67.

[Answer on p. 414]

○ EXAMPLE

The balance on the sales ledger control account for a business at 31 March 20X3 is £14,378.37. The total of the list of subsidiary ledger balances for debtors is £13,935.37.

The difference has been investigated and the following errors have been identified:

·   the sales day book was overcast by £1,000;

·   a credit note for £150 was entered into the individual debtors' account as an invoice;

·   discounts allowed of £143 were correctly accounted for in the subsidiary ledger but were not entered into the main ledger accounts;

·   a credit balance on one debtor's account of £200 was mistakenly listed as a debit balance when totalling the individual debtor accounts in the subsidiary ledger.

Prepare the reconciliation between the balance on the sales ledger control account and the total of the individual balances on the subsidiary ledger accounts.

Solution

Step 1 Amend the sales ledger control account for any errors that have been made

Sales ledger control account

	£		£
Balance b/f	14,378.37	SDB overcast	1,000.00
		Discounts allowed	143.00
		Balance c/f	13,235.37
	14,378.37		14,378.37
Balance b/f	13,235.37		

Step 2 Correct the total of the list of balances in the subsidiary (sales) ledger.

	£
Original total	13,935.37
Less: Credit note entered as invoice (2 x 150)	(300.00)
Credit balance entered as debit balance (2 x 200)	(400.00)
	13,235.37

▷ ACTIVITY 5

The balance on Diana's sales ledger control account at 31 December 20X6 was £15,450. The balances on the individual accounts in the subsidiary ledger have been extracted and total £15,705. On investigation the following errors are discovered:

(a) a debit balance of £65 has been omitted from the list of balances;
(b) discounts totalling £70 have been recorded in the individual accounts but not in the control account;
(c) the sales day book was 'overcast' by £200;
(d) a contra entry for £40 has not been entered into the control account; and
(e) an invoice for £180 was recorded correctly in the sales day book but was posted to the debtors' individual account as £810.

Prepare the sales ledger control account reconciliation.

[Answer on p. 415]

5   Accounting for creditors

5.1 Introduction

As we have seen in earlier chapters, the total amount payable to creditors is recorded in the main ledger in the purchases ledger control account. The total of credit purchases from the purchases day book, returns to suppliers from the purchases returns day book and the total payments to creditors and discounts received taken from the cash payments book are all posted to this account.

The purchases ledger control account shows the total amount that is payable to creditors but it does not show the amount owed to individual suppliers. This information is provided by the subsidiary ledger which contains an account for each individual creditor.

Each individual invoice from the purchases day book and each individual credit note from the purchases returns day book is posted to the relevant creditor's account in the subsidiary ledger. Similarly each individual payment to creditors and discounts received are posted from the cash payments book to the individual creditors' accounts in the subsidiary ledger.

5.2 Relationship between the purchases ledger control account and the balances in the subsidiary ledger

The information that is being posted to the purchases ledger control account in total and to the individual accounts in the subsidiary ledger as individual entries are from the same sources and should in total be the same figures.

Therefore, just as with the sales ledger control account, if the double entry and entries to the subsidiary ledger have been correctly carried out then the balance on the purchases ledger control account should be equal to the total of the list of balances on the individual creditors' accounts in the subsidiary ledger.

5.3 Proforma purchases ledger control account

A purchases ledger control account normally appears like this.

Purchases ledger control account

	£		£
Payments to suppliers per analysed cash book		Balance b/f	X
Cash	X	Purchases per purchases day book	X
Discount received	X		
Returns per purchases returns day book	X		
Contra entry	X		
Balance c/f	X		
	X		X
		Balance b/f	X

If all of the accounting entries have been correctly made then the balance on this purchases ledger control account should equal the total of the balances on the individual supplier accounts in the subsidiary ledger.

6 Purchases ledger control account reconciliation

6.1 Introduction

At each month end the purchases ledger clerk must reconcile the purchases ledger control account and the subsidiary ledger, just as the sales ledger clerk performed the sales ledger control account reconciliation.

Remember that as well as investigating and discovering the differences, the control account and the individual accounts in the subsidiary ledger must also be amended for any errors.

6.2 Adjustments to the purchases ledger control account

Any corrections or adjustments made to the purchases ledger control account can be documented as a journal entry.

○ EXAMPLE　　　　　　　　　　○○○○

The total purchases for the month were posted from the purchases day book as £2,547.98 instead of £2,457.98. Prepare a journal to correct this error.

Solution

The journal entry to correct this error will be as follows:

JOURNAL ENTRY		No: 253		
Prepared by:	P Charming			
Authorised by:	U Sister			
Date:	29.8.X5			
Narrative:				
To correct error in posting to debtors' control account				
Account		Code	Debit	Credit
Purchases ledger control		ML56	90	
Purchases		ML34		90
TOTALS			90	90

In this case both creditors and purchases need to be reduced by £90. Therefore a debit to the purchases ledger control and a credit to purchases are required.

6.3 Adjustments in the subsidiary ledger

Adjustments in the subsidiary ledger do not need to be documented in a journal entry. Journal entries are only required for adjustments to the main ledger.

○ **EXAMPLE**   ○○○○

The balance on the purchases ledger control account for a business at 30 June was £12,159. The total of the balances on the individual creditors' accounts in the subsidiary ledger was £19,200.

The following errors were also found:
- the cash payments book had been undercast by £20;
- an invoice from Thomas Ltd, a credit supplier, for £2,350 was correctly entered in the subsidiary ledger but had been missed out of the addition of the total in the purchases day book;
- an invoice from Fred Singleton for £2,000 plus VAT was included in his individual account in the subsidiary ledger at the net amount;
- an invoice from Horace Shades for £6,000 was entered into the individual account in the subsidiary ledger twice;
- the same invoice is for £6,000 plus VAT but the VAT had not been included in the subsidiary ledger;
- returns to Horace Shades of £111 had been omitted from the subsidiary ledger.

You are required to reconcile the purchases ledger control account with the balances on the subsidiary ledger accounts at 30 June.

Solution

Step 1 Amend the purchases ledger control account to show the correct balance.

Purchases ledger control account

	£		£
Undercast of CPB	20	Balance b/f	12,159
Balance c/f	14,489	Invoice omitted from PDB	2,350
	14,509		14,509
		Amended balance b/f	14,489

Step 2 Correct the total of the list of subsidiary ledger balances.

	£
Original total	19,200
Add: Fred Singleton VAT	350
Less: Horace Shades invoice included twice	(6,000)
Add: Horace Shades VAT	1,050
Less: Horace Shades returns	(111)
Amended control account balance	14,489

Remember that invoices from suppliers should be included in the individual suppliers' accounts in the subsidiary ledger at the gross amount, including VAT.

▷ **ACTIVITY 6**   ▷▷▷▷

How would each of the following be dealt with in the purchases ledger control account reconciliation?

(a) A purchase invoice for £36 from P Swift was credited to P Short's account in the subsidiary ledger.

(b) A purchase invoice for £96 not entered in the purchases day book.

(c) An undercast of £20 in the total column of the purchases day book.

(d) A purchase invoice from Short & Long for £42 entered as £24 in the purchases day book.

[Answer on p. 415]

7 Cause of the difference

The examiner will sometimes ask you to say what has caused the difference between the control account and the list of balances. If you are asked to do this, the difference will usually be caused by just one error.

An example will illustrate this.

○ **EXAMPLE**   ○○○○

XYZ Ltd has made the following entries in the sales ledger control account

	£
Opening balance 1 April 20X7	49,139
Credit sales posted from the sales day book	35,000
Discounts allowed	328
Bad debt written off	127
Cash received from debtors	52,359

The list of balances from the subsidiary (sales) ledger totals £31,679.

(a) Calculate the closing balance on the SLCA at 31 April 2007.
(b) State one reason for the difference between the SLCA balance and the total of the list of balances.

Solution

(a) The SLCA

Sales ledger control account

	£		£
Balance b/d	49,139	Discount allowed	328
SDB – sales	35,000	Bad debt	127
		Cash received	52,359
		Balance c/d	31,325
	84,139		84,139

(b) Total of subsidiary (sales) ledger balances   31,679
    Balance of SLCA at 30 April 20X7   31,325

    Difference   354

One cause of the difference may have been that the bad debt written off was entered on the debit side of the relevant account in the subsidiary (sales) ledger.

Tutorial note

You have to look for the fairly obvious clues and also make some assumptions

(i) It's reasonable to assume that the control account is correct – it may not, so be careful.
(ii) Calculate the difference and determine whether the list total is larger than the SLCA balance or vice versa.
(iii) See if one of the figures given in the question is the same as the difference or double the difference.

    If a figure given is the same as the difference then it is likely that a number has been left out of an account.

    If a figure given is double the difference then it is likely that a number has been entered on the wrong side of an account, or possibly entered twice.

    · In the above question, the difference is £354.
    · The total of the list of ledger balances is bigger than the SLCA balance.

· £354 is not a figure given in the question but the amount £127 is given and the difference is twice this figure.

One possible reason for this is that the bad debt write off (£127) was entered on the debit side of a ledger account in the subsidiary (sales) ledger – that would have made the total of the list £354 larger. Of course there are a million possible reasons – perhaps there was an invoice for £354 and it was entered twice in a ledger account – that would have caused the difference, but the examiner is looking for something obvious in the figures he's given you – not some speculative reason.

8 Batch control

8.1 Introduction

Throughout this book we have been dealing with control accounts in the main ledger and individual debtors and creditors accounts in the subsidiary ledgers. We have noted that there will sometimes be a discrepancy between the balance on the control account in the main ledger and the total of the balances in the subsidiary ledgers. Sometimes this difference is caused by correctly entered items that can be reconciled. However, sometimes the difference is caused by an error in the entering of the data. These latter errors can be eliminated or minimised by the use of batch control.

8.2 How a lack of batch control causes problems

Consider the situation where a small business has received 40 cheques from debtors and is going to post these into the accounts for the week. A typical system might be as follows.

(a) John writes the cheques into the debtors column of the analysed cash received book. John then totals the cash received book for the week and posts the total of the debtors column to the sales ledger control account. He then writes out the bank paying-in slip and pays the cheques into the bank.

(b) George writes up the individual accounts in the subsidiary (sales) ledger from the entries in the main cash book.

The above is a fairly typical system and of course all sorts of things can go wrong.

(a) A cheque could go missing and not be paid into the bank, causing a discrepancy between the entries in the cash book and the bank statement.

(b) John could write the values of one or more of the cheques incorrectly in the cash book, causing the cash book total and the sales ledger control account entry to be incorrect.

(c) George could also write the values of the cheques incorrectly in the subsidiary (sales) ledger.

8.3 How batch control helps reduce errors

To improve the system the company employs a system of batch control.

(a) Before the cheques are entered in the cash book, a person unconnected with entering the cheques in the books (Jemima) will total the cheques using a computer spreadsheet such as Excel or an adlisting calculating machine (i.e. a machine which will print out the value of the amounts entered). She will not disclose the total of the cheques.

(b) John will now write the cheques into the cash book and total the cash book as before. He will then compare his total with Jemima's total. If the totals are different, Jemima and John will both check their work until they can agree on a total. This clearly minimises any errors that are likely to be made when entering the cheques in the books of account.

(c) George will write up the subsidiary (sales) ledger as before. As a further check, the subsidiary (sales) ledger could be passed to another person who would total the entries that George has just made and then compare that total with Jemima's total.

As you can see, by batching the cheques together and producing a total of their value before any entries are made in the books, the company has an excellent check on the accuracy of the entries that are made.

Of course nothing is foolproof. The accountants could enter incorrect amounts in the ledger which compensate for each other thereby still giving the correct total. Alternatively, a cheque might be lost thereby giving an incorrect banking total. But at least the possibility of human error is reduced.

9 Test your knowledge

1 Would the year end balance on the sales returns account be a debit balance or a credit balance?

2 What is the double entry for writing off a bad debt?

3 What is the double entry for a contra?

4 The sales day book has been undercast by £100. What is the double entry to correct this?

5 A credit note from a supplier for £50 was omitted from the purchases returns day book. What is the double entry to correct this?

6   The total of the sales returns day book of £360 was posted as £630. What is the double entry to correct this?

7   When carrying out the sales ledger control account reconciliation it was discovered that an invoice to a customer for £200 has been omitted from the sales day book. How would this be treated in the reconciliation?

8   When carrying out the sales ledger control account reconciliation it was discovered that a credit balance for a customer of £100 had been included in the list of balances as a debit balance. How would this be treated in the reconciliation?

9   When carrying out the purchases ledger control account reconciliation it was discovered that the purchases day book total of £4,750 had been posted as £4,570. How would this be treated in the reconciliation?

10   When carrying out the purchases ledger control account reconciliation it was discovered that a discount taken from a supplier of £20 had not been recorded in the cash payments book. How would this be treated in the reconciliation?

[Answers on p.416]

10 Summary

We started this chapter with a revision of balancing accounts and extended this to entering opening balances in the ledger accounts in preparation for posting transactions for a period which is a favourite assessment topic. Then the chapter moved on to aspects of control and the use of control accounts and control account reconciliations in order to determine the accuracy of the figures in the ledger accounts. The reconciliations, sales ledger and purchases ledger are important Performance Criteria and you should ensure that you are happy with the subject matter in this chapter.

Answers to chapter activities & 'test your knowledge' questions

△ ACTIVITY 1 △△△△

Sales ledger control account

	£		£
SDB – invoices	5,426.23	CRB	3,226.56
		Discounts allowed	315.47
		Balance c/f	1,884.20
	5,426.23		5,426.23
Balance b/f	1,884.20		

VAT account

	£		£
PDB	846.72	SDB	1,036.54
Balance c/f	189.82		
	1,036.54		1,036.54
		Balance b/f	189.82

Sales account

	£		£
		SDB	2,667.45
Balance c/f	4,521.37	SDB	1,853.92
	4,521.37		4,521.37
		Balance b/f	4,521.37

△ ACTIVITY 2 △△△△

(a) Credit balance

(b) Debit balance

(c) Credit balance

(d) Debit balance

△ **ACTIVITY 3**   △ △ △ △
Subsidiary (purchases) ledger

Bailey Limited

		£			£
01 Dec	Bank	799	01 Dec	Balance b/f	11,750
01 Dec	Discount received	20	01 Dec	Purchases	235
01 Dec	Balance c/f	11,166			
		11,985			11,985
			02 Dec	Balance b/f	11,166

Byng & Company

		£			£
			01 Dec	Balance b/f	1,269
01 Dec	Balance c/f	2,209	01 Dec	Purchases	940
		2,209			2,209
			02 Dec	Balance b/f	2,209

Office Supplies Limited

		£			£
01 Dec	Purchases returns	47	01 Dec	Balance b/f	4,230
01 Dec	Balance c/f	4,512	01 Dec	Purchases	329
		4,559			4,559
			02 Dec	Balance b/f	4,512

O'Connell Frames

		£			£
01 Dec	Purchases returns	2,115	01 Dec	Balance b/f	423
01 Dec	Balance c/f	3,243	01 Dec	Purchases	4,935
		5,358			5,358
			02 Dec	Balance b/f	3,243

Main ledger

Creditors' control

		£			£
01 Dec	Purchases returns	2,162	01 Dec	Balance b/f	82,006
01 Dec	Bank	799	01 Dec	Purchases	6,439
01 Dec	Discounts received	20			
01 Dec	Balance c/f	85,464			
		88,445			88,445
			02 Dec	Balance b/f	85,464

Debtors' control

		£			£
01 Dec	Balance b/f	180,312	01 Dec	Bank	5,875
01 Dec	Sales	13,160	01 Dec	Balance c/f	187,597
01 Dec					
		193,472			193,472
02 Dec	Balance b/f	187,597			

Purchases

		£			£
01 Dec	Balance b/f	90,563			
01 Dec	Creditors	5,200	01 Dec	Balance c/f	95,763
		95,763			95,763
02 Dec	Balance b/f	95,763			

Sales

		£			£
			01 Dec	Balance b/f	301,492
			01 Dec	Debtors	11,200
01 Dec	Balance c/f	313,132	01 Dec	Cash sale	440
		313,132			313,132
			02 Dec	Balance b/f	313,132

KAPLAN PUBLISHING

Purchases returns

		£			£
			01 Dec	Balance b/f	306
01 Dec	Balance c/f	2,106	01 Dec	Creditors	1,800
		2,106			2,106
			02 Dec	Balance b/f	2,106

Stationery

		£			£
01 Dec	Balance b/f	642	01 Dec	Purchases returns	40
01 Dec	Creditors	280	01 Dec	Balance c/f	882
		922			922
02 Dec	Balance b/f	882			

Discounts received

		£			£
			01 Dec	Balance b/f	50
01 Dec	Balance c/f	70	01 Dec	Creditors	20
		70			70
			02 Dec	Balance b/f	70

VAT

		£			£
01 Dec	Purchases	959	01 Dec	Balance b/f	17,800
			01 Dec	Purchases returns	322
			01 Dec	Sales	1,960
01 Dec	Balance c/f	19,200	01 Dec	Cash sale	77
		20,159			20,159
			02 Dec	Balance b/f	19,200

Cash receipts book

Date	Narrative £	Total £	VAT £	Sales ledger £	Other £	Discounts allowed
20X1						
01 Dec	Lili Chang	517	77		440	
01 Dec	Bentley Brothers	5,875		5,875		
		6,392	77	5,875	440	–

Cash payments book

Date	Details	Cheque no	Code	Total £	VAT £	Purchases ledger £	Cash purchases £	Other £	Discounts received £
20X1									
01 Dec	Bailey Ltd			799	–	799	–	–	20

	£
Opening balance	3,006
Add: Receipts	6,392
Less: Payments	(799)
Closing balance	8,599

△ **ACTIVITY 4**   △△△△

(a) Yes, because the detailed entries in the sales day book are posted to the sales ledger accounts and the incorrect total used in the control account.

(b) No, because the arithmetical balance is correct even though the wrong account is used.

(c) No, because the double entry will be for £67 and the entry in the subsidiary ledger will also be for £67.

△ **ACTIVITY 5**   △ △ △ △

· We must first look for those errors which will mean that the sales ledger control account is incorrectly stated. The control account is then adjusted as follows:

Sales ledger control account

	£		£
Balance b/f	15,450	Discounts allowed	70
		Overcast of sales day book	200
		Contra with creditors' control account	40
		Adjusted balance c/f	15,140
	15,450		15,450
Balance b/f	15,140		

· We must then look for errors in the total of the individual balances per the debtors' ledger. The extracted list of balances must be adjusted as follows:

	£
Original total of list of balances	15,705
Debit balance omitted	65
Transposition error (810 – 180)	(630)
	15,140

· As can be seen, the adjusted total of the list of balances now agrees with the balance per the control account.

△ **ACTIVITY 6**   △ △ △ △

(a) A correction would simply be made in the subsidiary ledger.

(b) This must be adjusted for in the purchase ledger control account and in the subsidiary ledger.

(c) This is just an adjustment to the purchase ledger control account.

(d) This will require alteration in both the control account and the subsidiary ledger.

Test your knowledge △ △ △

1   Debit balance

2   Debit   Bad debts expense

    Credit   Sales ledger control

3   Debit   Purchase ledger control

    Credit   Sales ledger control

4   Debit   Sales ledger control   £100

    Credit   Sales   £100

5   Debit   Purchase ledger control   £50

    Credit   Purchase returns   £50

6   Debit   Sales ledger control   £270

    Credit   Sales returns   £270

7   Debit   Sales ledger control   £200

    and

    Increase list of debtor balances total by   £200

8   Decrease list of debtor balances total by   £200   (2 x £100)

9   Credit   Purchase ledger control account   £180

10 Debit   Purchase ledger control account   £20

    and

    Decrease list of creditor balances total by   £20

DRAFTING AN INITIAL TRIAL BALANCE

INTRODUCTION

This chapter covers the final accounting area which is the preparation of an initial trial balance. We will consider the trial balance and its purpose and look at how to deal with discrepancies on the trial balance and particularly the correction of errors using a suspense account and journal entries.

KNOWLEDGE & UNDERSTANDING

- Use of the journal (Element 3)
- Double entry bookkeeping, including balancing accounts (Elements 1, 2 and 3)
- Operation of manual accounting systems (Elements 1, 2 and 3)
- Relationship between the accounting system and the ledger (Elements 1, 2 and 3)
- Function and form of the trial balance (Element 3)

CONTENTS

1 Main ledger accounts
2 The trial balance
3 Discrepancies on the trial balance
4 The suspense account
5 Journals
6 Use of journal and suspense account

PERFORMANCE CRITERIA

- Make adjustments through the journal (Element 30.3)
- Prepare an initial trial balance (Element 30.3)
- Creat a suspense account when necessary and subsequently clear it (Element 30.3)

1 Main ledger accounts

1.1 Introduction

As you have seen earlier in your studies, as each transaction is made by a business it is recorded in a primary record and then in the main ledger accounts. Therefore at any point in time the main ledger accounts should include all the transactions of the business to date.

1.2 Checking the accounting

You have also seen that it is relatively easy for errors to be made when entering the transactions into the accounting records. Therefore it is important that on a regular basis the business checks that the ledger accounts have been correctly written up.

1.3 Balancing the main ledger accounts

This process of checking the overall accounting is done at regular intervals by balancing each of the main ledger accounts and then listing each of the balances in what is known as a trial balance.

We have already come across ways of checking bank, cash, debtor and creditor balances and the trial balance is a further final check on these and the other balances.

2 The trial balance

2.1 List of balances

The trial balance is a list showing the balance on each ledger account. An example of a simple trial balance is given below:

	Debit £	Credit £
Sales		5,000
Opening stock	100	
Purchases	3,000	
Rent	200	
Car	3,000	
Debtors	100	
Creditors		1,400
	6,400	6,400

Note that the trial balance contains a figure for opening stock not closing stock. This will always be the case but you do not need to worry about the reasons why for your current studies.

The trial balance is produced immediately after the double entry has been completed and balances extracted on the accounts. If the double entry has been done correctly, the total of the debits will equal the total of the credits.

2.2 Reasons for extracting a trial balance

· To ensure that the double entry has been completed. Note however, that there are some types of error that will not be picked up merely by extracting a trial balance (see below).
· As a first stage in the preparation of the financial statements.

2.3 Errors identified by extracting a trial balance

· **Single entry**

The debit entry may have been made correctly but the associated credit entry has been overlooked. The result will be that the total of the debits will exceed the total of the credits. Equally if a credit entry has been made but no corresponding debit the credits will exceed the debits.

· **Casting error**

An account itself or the trial balance in total may have been added up incorrectly. In this case the trial balance will not balance.

· **Transposition error**

For example, an amount of £7,532 may have been incorrectly written as £7,352. If one such error has occurred, the difference on the trial balance will be divisible by nine (this is often a useful tip if you find an account or trial balance does not balance when you expect it to).

· **Extraction error**

An account may be correct in the ledger but has been copied out incorrectly (or not at all) onto the trial balance. Or indeed the account balance may have been entered as the correct amount, but on the wrong side of the trial balance, e.g. as a credit rather than a debit.

2.4 Errors not identified by extracting a trial balance

· **Errors of original (prime) entry**

Where the original figure is incorrectly entered in both parts of the double entry then the trial balance will still balance.

· **Compensating errors**

Quite simply where one error is compensated exactly by another in the opposite direction. Again, the trial balance will still balance.

· **Errors of omission**

Here, an entry is left out altogether on both sides of the double entry. There will be no effect on the trial balance.

· **Errors of commission**

Here the double entry is completed but between the wrong accounts, for example where a payment of £50 for rates is debited to the wages account.

· **Errors of principle**

Similar to errors of commission but these items are treated in fundamentally the wrong type of account, ie treating a fixed asset as an expense (meaning capital expenditure being treated as revenue expenditure).

A trial balance will pick up some types of errors but there are others that will not be found by producing a trial balance.

2.5 Computerised accounting systems

The same basic principles apply to all accounting systems, whether manual or computerised. Most computer systems, however, automatically post both sides of the double entry, meaning that the trial balance will always balance.

Where the accounting system is computerised, certain errors cannot occur:

· single entries (the computer will not accept them);
· casting errors (the computer will total accounts automatically);
· transposition errors (the computer posts the double entry automatically);
· extraction errors (the computer posts the double entry automatically).

But human errors can still occur:

· errors of original entry;
· errors of commission;
· errors of principle.

The following are the balances on the accounts of Ernest at 31 December 20X8.

	£
Sales	47,140
Purchases	26,500
Debtors	7,640
Creditors	4,320
General expenses	9,430
Loan	5,000
Plant and machinery at cost	7,300
Motor van at cost	2,650
Drawings	7,500
Rent and rates	6,450
Insurance	1,560
Bank overdraft	2,570
Capital	10,000

Required:

Prepare Ernest's trial balance as at 31 December 20X8.

Solution

Step 1   Set up a blank trial balance

TRIAL BALANCE AT 31 DECEMBER 20X8

	£	£
Sales		
Purchases		
Debtors		
Creditors		
General expenses		
Loan		
Plant and machinery at cost		
Motor van at cost		
Drawings		
Rent and rates		
Insurance		
Bank overdraft		
Capital		

Step 2 Work down the list of balances one by one using what you have learned so far about debits and credits. Assets and expenses are debit balances and liabilities and income are credit balances.

TRIAL BALANCE AT 31 DECEMBER 20X8

	£	£
Sales		47,140
Purchases	26,500	
Debtors	7,640	
Creditors		4,320
General expenses	9,430	
Loan		5,000
Plant and machinery at cost	7,300	
Motor van at cost	2,650	
Drawings	7,500	
Rent and rates	6,450	
Insurance	1,560	
Bank overdraft		2,570
Capital		10,000
	69,030	69,030

Take care with drawings. These are a reduction of the capital owed back to the owner therefore as a reduction of a liability they must be a debit balance.

The bank overdraft is an amount owed to the bank therefore it must be a credit balance.

▷ ACTIVITY 1

The following balances have been extracted from the books of Fitzroy at 31 December 20X2:

	£
Capital on 1 January 20X2	106,149
Freehold factory at cost	360,000
Motor vehicles at cost	126,000
Stocks at 1 January 20X2	37,500
Debtors	15,600
Cash in hand	225
Bank overdraft	82,386
Creditors	78,900
Sales	318,000
Purchases	165,000
Rent and rates	35,400
Discounts allowed	6,600
Insurance	2,850
Sales returns	10,500
Purchases returns	6,300
Loan from bank	240,000
Sundry expenses	45,960
Drawings	26,100

Required:

Prepare a trial balance at 31 December 20X2.

[Answer on p.435]

The main problem is usually in determining whether each balance is a debit balance or a credit balance. Remember that assets and expenses are debit balances, and liabilities and income are credit balances. So think carefully about the nature of each of the accounts listed.

Some balances could be either a debit or a credit (e.g. VAT). The question would have to indicate which balance it was.

3 Discrepancies on the trial balance

3.1 Introduction

As we saw earlier in this chapter the trial balance should balance, ie the total of debit balances should equal the total of credit balances. However we also saw how various different types of error might mean that the trial balance will not balance. If a discrepancy is discovered on the trial balance then it must be investigated.

3.2 Checks on the trial balance

However, before investigating any discrepancies some basic checks should be carried out.

Firstly check that the debit and credit columns have been correctly added up. When totalling a long list of figures it is very easy to make an error.

If the column totals are correct then go back to the ledger accounts and check that each of those has been correctly balanced and that the correct balance has been extracted and entered onto the trial balance.

If the discrepancy still exists then it will need to be investigated.

▷ ACTIVITY 2 ▷ ▷ ▷ ▷

Enter the following details of transactions for the month of May into the appropriate ledger accounts. You should also extract a trial balance as at 30 May 20X6. Transactions with debtors and creditors are to be recorded in the control accounts for debtors and creditors in the main ledger. You can ignore VAT.

20X6
1 May   Started in business with £6,800 in the bank
3 May   Bought goods on credit from the following: J Johnson £400, D
               Nixon £300 and J Agnew £250
5 May   Cash sales £300 paid into the bank account
6 May   Paid rates by cheque £100

8 May	Paid wages £50 by cheque.
9 May	Sold goods on credit: K Homes £300, J Homes £300 and B Hood £100
10 May	Bought goods on credit: J Johnson £800, D Nixon £700
11 May	Return goods to J Johnson £150
15 May	Bought office fixtures £600 by cheque
18 May	Bought a motor vehicle £3,500 by cheque
22 May	Goods returned by J Homes £100
25 May	Paid J Johnson £1,000, D Nixon £500, both by cheque
26 May	Paid wages £150 by cheque

[Answers on p.435]

4 The suspense account

4.1 Introduction

A suspense account is used in two circumstances.

· When the destination of a posting is uncertain the amount may be entered in a suspense account until further information is available regarding the nature of the item.
· When the trial balance totals disagree the difference may be temporarily recorded in a suspense account. This will enable final accounts to be prepared and in the course of this work some or all of the errors giving rise to the balance on the suspense account may be discovered and the balance on the account reduced or eliminated.

○ EXAMPLE   ○○○○

A cheque for £200 is received through the post with no indication of what it is for. The drawer of the cheque is the local government authority. It is posted to the suspense account. Investigation reveals that it is a rates rebate.

Show these entries in the ledger accounts.

Solution

Step 1
The amount is entered as a debit entry in the cash book (cash receipt) and as a credit in the suspense account as it is not yet known what this receipt is for.

Suspense

	£		£
		Cash	200

Step 2

Transfer this amount to the rates account.

Suspense

	£		£
Rates	200	Cash	200
	200		200

Rates

	£		£
		Suspense	200

4.2 When the trial balance totals disagree

We have so far assumed that the trial balance can be easily made to balance. However, it is often the case that any misbalance is due to a large number of items and hence the reasons may not be immediately pinpointed. The difference is recorded in a suspense account temporarily until the errors are discovered and can be corrected.

We have already come across errors which are likely to cause a difference on the trial balance and these include the following:

·   Transposition, e.g. a debit of £67 and a credit of £76 for the same transaction. As mentioned already, this kind of error leads to an imbalance that is divisible by 9.
·   One-side omission, e.g. a cheque for rent of £150 entered in the cash account but not in the rent account.
·   Two entries on one side and none on the other, e.g. purchases of goods debited to purchases account and also debited to purchases ledger control account.
·   An account entered on the wrong side of the trial balance or omitted from the trial balance.

Only those errors which cause a difference on the trial balance need to be adjusted by means of an entry in the suspense account. For example, if an item has been posted to the wrong account, this will not cause a difference on the trial balance, although the error must be adjusted by means of a journal entry.

O EXAMPLE   OOOO

The trial balance is found to be £90 out, the total credits being £25,190 and the total debits being £25,100. In order to make the trial balance totals agree, £90 is debited to the suspense account. It is subsequently discovered that cash paid for stationery was credited in the cash book as £211 (the correct amount) and debited in the stationery account as £121 by mistake.

Required:

(a)   Enter the amount in the suspense account.
(b)   Show that this makes the trial balance balance.
(c)   Correct the error using a journal.

Solution

Step 1   Enter the amount in the suspense account.

Suspense			
	£		£
Difference in trial balance	90		

Step 2   The trial balance now balances.

	Debit	*Credit*
	£	£
Original totals	25,100	25,190
Suspense account	90	
	25,190	25,190

Step 3   Correct the error.

Identify the actual entry made and establish what the correct entry should have been.

	Actual entry		*Correct entry*	
	Dr	Cr	Dr	Cr
	£	£	£	£
Stationery	121		211	
Cash		211		211

The stationery account is understated by £90. Prepare a journal to correct the error.

		£	£
Debit	Stationery account	90	
Credit	Suspense account		90

Being incorrect posting of cash paid for stationery.

The ledger accounts will now look as follows:

Suspense

	£		£
Balance b/d	90	Stationery	90
	___		___
	90		90
	___		___

Stationery

	£		£
Balance b/d	121		
Suspense	90	Balance c/d	211
	___		___
	211		211
	___		___
Balance b/d	211		

We now have the correct figure in the stationery account, the suspense account has been cleared and the trial balance balances.

5 Journals

5.1 Introduction

Journal entries have been considered briefly in earlier sections but will now be looked at in more detail.

> **□ DEFINITION** □□□□
>
> The journal is a formal, written instruction to the bookkeeper to put an item of double entry through the main ledger.
>
> Whenever an error has to be corrected or an adjustment made to the ledgers then it is important that this is correct and that it is properly authorised. This can only be done with a formal system such as the journal.

5.2 Use of the journal

The journal consists of a debit and credit entry and the ledger accounts that these entries are to be made to. However there are also other important details for journals.

· The journal must be dated.
· They must be consecutively numbered so that it can be checked that all journals have been entered into the ledgers.
· There must be adequate description of the journal so that the person authorising it knows exactly what it is for.

○ **EXAMPLE**   ○○○○

A business wishes to write off a debt from N Jones for £200 that it now considers to be bad. Today's date is 30 June and the last journal entry was numbered 336.

We will draft the journal entry for this adjustment.

Solution

JOURNAL ENTRY		No: 337		
Prepared by:				
Authorised by:				
Date: 30 June				
Narrative:				
To write off bad debt from N Jones				
Account	*Code*	*Debit*		*Credit*
Bad debts expense	ML	200		
Sales ledger control	ML			200
TOTALS		200		200

In assessments, you are often asked to prepare journal entries. However, many assessments do not require the narrative so read the instructions carefully.

5.3 Correction of errors where the suspense account is not affected

We have seen that not all errors that are found in the ledgers affect the balancing of the trial balance. However even if the trial balance still balances but errors are discovered they must still be corrected using a journal entry.

○ **EXAMPLE**   ○○○○

When performing the sales ledger control account reconciliation the following errors were discovered:
· the sales day book was overcast by £1,000;
· the discounts allowed total in the cash receipts book of £140 was not posted at all;
· a receipt from H Fisher of £870 was entered into H Fisher's individual account in the subsidiary ledger as £780.

We will write up the journal entries to correct these errors starting with journal number 1658.

Solution

JOURNAL ENTRY	No: 1658		
Prepared by:			
Authorised by:			
Date:			
Narrative:			
To correct overcast of sales day book			
Account	*Code*	*Debit*	*Credit*
Sales	ML	1,000	
Sales ledger control	ML		1,000
TOTALS		1,000	1,000

JOURNAL ENTRY	No: 1659		
Prepared by:			
Authorised by:			
Date:			
Narrative:			
To post discounts allowed omitted			
Account	*Code*	*Debit*	*Credit*
Discounts allowed	ML	140	
Sales ledger control	ML		140
TOTALS		140	140

The error in H Fisher's individual account in the subsidiary ledger needs to be corrected but this will not be done with a journal entry as no double entry is required.

When correcting errors with journal entries, firstly work out what has been done in the accounts and then determine the double entry necessary to put it right.

▷ ACTIVITY 3 ▷▷▷▷

Discounts received of £50 have not been posted to the main ledger at all.

Draft a journal entry to correct this. The last journal number was 152. Today's date is 12 September 20X1.

[Answer on p. 438]

▷ ACTIVITY 4   ▷ ▷ ▷ ▷

John

On 31 December 20X8 the trial balance of John, a small manufacturer, failed to agree and the difference was entered in a suspense account. After the final accounts had been prepared the following errors were discovered and the difference was eliminated.

- The purchase day book was undercast by £200.
- Machinery purchased for £150 had been debited to the purchases account.
- Discounts received of £130 had been posted to the debit of the discounts received account.
- Rates of £46 paid by cheque had been posted to the debit of the rates account as £64.
- Cash drawings by the owner of £45 had been entered in the cash account correctly but not posted to the drawings account.
- The balance on the stock account representing the opening stock of £1,200 had been omitted from the trial balance.

Required:

(a)   Show the journal entries necessary to correct the above errors.

(b)   Show the entries in the suspense account to eliminate the differences entered in the suspense account.

[Answer on p. 439]

6   Use of journal and suspense account

Very often, some of the errors made will affect the suspense account and some will not. In the exam you need to be clear when sorting out a difference which are which.

○ **EXAMPLE**   ○○○○

The following summary trial balance has been extracted from the ledger accounts.

	£	£
Capital		150,000
Profit and loss (a profit)		75,000
Freehold property	560,000	
Motor vehicles	30,000	
Stock	40,000	
Sales ledger control account	25,000	
Bank (overdrawn)	2,600	
Purchases ledger control account		20,000
Sales		587,500
Purchases	175,000	
Electricity	2,300	
Rent and rates	900	
Discount allowed		670
Discount received	820	
Stationery	600	
Travel expenses	800	
	838,020	833,170

Tasks

(a) Certain items that have been entered on the wrong side of the trial balance. Rewrite the Trial Balance with these amounts corrected, and with a suspense account for any residual difference.

(b) On inspection of the books the following mistakes are discovered.

   (i) An electricity invoice for £200 was entered in the rent account.
   (ii) An invoice for stationery for £300 was entered as a credit note in the purchases day book
   (iii) A cash purchase for a train ticket costing £280 was credited to the travel account.
   (iv) An invoice for a cash purchase of stationery for £320 was entered in the stationery account as a debit of £230.

   Produce journal entries to correct these errors.

(c) Enter the journals in part (b) in the suspense account if they are relevant to that account.

Solution

(a)

	£	£
Capital		150,000
Profit and loss (profit)		75,000
Freehold property	560,000	
Motor vehicles	30,000	
Stock	40,000	
Sales ledger control account	25,000	
Bank (overdrawn)		2,600
Purchases ledger control account		20,000
Sales		587,500
Purchases	175,000	
Electricity	2,300	
Rent and rates	900	
Discount allowed	670	
Discount received		820
Stationery	600	
Travel expenses	800	
Suspense	650	
	835,920	835,920

Tutorial note

(i) The bank is overdrawn – this has to be a credit balance

(ii) Discount allowed is what the business has allowed other people – money given away – an expense – a debit balance

(iii) Discount received is what the business has received – a type of income – a credit balance

Learn these entries – don't be one of the people who always get them wrong.

(b)

				£	£
(i)	Dr	Electricity		200	
	Cr	Rent			200
(ii)	Dr	Purchases		600	
	Cr	PLCA			600
(iii)	Dr	Travel expenses		560	
	Cr	Suspense account			560
(iv)	Dr	Stationery		90	
	Cr	Suspense account			90

(c)

Suspense account

	£		£
Balance b/d	650	Travel expenses	560
		Stationery	90
	650		650

> **ACTIVITY 5**

Whilst preparing the purchases ledger control account the following errors were discovered:

(a) the purchases day book was undercast by £100;

(b) the discounts received total in the cash payments book of £390 had not been posted at all.

The last journal number used was 153. Draft the journal entries required to correct these errors.

[Answer on p.440]

7 Test your knowledge

1   What are the two reasons for extracting a trial balance?

2   What types of error will affect the balancing of the trial balance?

3   What is an error of commission?

4   Are drawings a debit or a credit balance on the trial balance?

5   A cheque payment has been made but the bookkeeper does not immediately know what the payment is for. How would this be treated in the ledger accounts whilst the nature of the payment was investigated?

6   A trial balance has a total of debit balances of £36,540 and credit balances of £34,700. If a suspense account is set up how much would it be for and would it be a debit or credit balance?

7   Discounts allowed have been entered correctly as £1,540 in the sales ledger control account but have been entered as £1,450 in the discounts account. What double entry is required to correct this?

8   The electricity account balance of £866 has been omitted from the trial balance. What is the journal entry required to correct this?

9   A £200 telephone bill has been incorrectly posted to the rent account. What is the double entry required to correct this?

10 The purchases returns day book was undercast by £100. What is the double entry required to correct this?

[Answer on p. 441]

8   Summary

In this chapter we have covered the final element of Unit 3: the preparation of the trial balance, the identification of any discrepancies and the rectification of errors and omissions to ensure that the trial balance does in fact balance. Once the trial balance has been initially drawn up if it does not balance it is worthwhile carrying out basic checks to ensure that all balances have been correctly transferred and that the debits and credits have been correctly totalled. Then you will need to set up a suspense account and finally to try to clear the suspense account by putting through the correcting double entry. Remember that not all errors affect the balancing of the trial balance and therefore not all adjustments will affect the suspense account.

Answers to chapter activities & 'test your knowledge' questions

△ ACTIVITY 1   △△△△

Trial balance at 31 December 20X2

	Dr £	Cr £
Capital on 1 January 20X2		106,149
Freehold factory at cost	360,000	
Motor vehicles at cost	126,000	
Stocks at 1 January 20X2	37,500	
Debtors	15,600	
Cash in hand	225	
Bank overdraft		82,386
Creditors		78,900
Sales		318,000
Purchases	165,000	
Rent and rates	35,400	
Discounts allowed	6,600	
Insurance	2,850	
Sales returns	10,500	
Purchases returns		6,300
Loan from bank		240,000
Sundry expenses	45,960	
Drawings	26,100	
	831,735	831,735

△ ACTIVITY 2   △△△△

Bank account

		£			£
01 May	Capital	6,800	06 May	Rates	100
05 May	Cash sales	300	08 May	Wages	50
			15 May	Office fixtures	600
			18 May	Motor vehicle	3,500
			25 May	Creditors	
				(1,000 + 500)	1,500
			26 May	Wages	150
			31 May	Balance c/f	1,200
		7,100			7,100
1 June	Balance b/f	1,200			

Purchase ledger control account

		£			£
11 May	Purchases returns	150	03 May	Purchases (400 + 300 + 250)	950
25 May	Bank	1,500	10 May	Purchases (800 + 700)	1,500
31 May	Balance c/f	800			
		2,450			2,450
			1 June	Balance b/f	800

Sales ledger control account

		£			£
9 May	Sales (300 + 300 + 100)	700	22 May	Sales returns	100
			31 May	Balance c/f	600
		700			700
1 June	Balance b/f	600			

Capital account

		£			£
31 May	Balance c/f	6,800	1 May	Bank	6,800
			1 June	Balance b/f	6,800

Purchases account

		£			£
03 May	J Johnson	400			
	D Nixon	300			
	J Agnew	250			
10 May	J Johnson	800			
	D Nixon	700			
			31 May	Balance c/f	2,450
		2,450			2,450
1 June	Balance b/f	2,450			

Sales account

		£				£
			05 May	Cash		300
			09 May	K Homes		300
				J Homes		300
31 May	Balance c/f	1,000		B Hood		100
		1,000				1,000
			1 June	Balance b/f		1,000

Rates account

		£			£
06 May	Bank	100	31 May	Balance c/f	100
1 June	Balance b/f	100			

Wages account

		£			£
08 May	Bank	50			
26 May	Bank	150	31 May	Balance c/f	200
		200			200
1 June	Balance b/f	200			

Purchases returns account

		£			£
31 May	Balance c/f	150	11 May	Johnson	150
			1 June	Balance b/f	150

Office fixtures account

		£			£
15 May	Bank	600	31 May	Balance c/f	600
1 June	Balance b/f	600			

Motor vehicle account

		£			£
18 May	Bank	3,500	31 May	Balance c/f	3,500
1 June	Balance b/f	3,500			

Sales returns account

		£			£
22 May	J Homes	100	31 May	Balance c/f	100
1 June	Balance b/f	100			

Tutorial note:

Balances have been brought forward on all accounts. As noted earlier in this text, it is not customary to bring forward balances on accounts with only a single item on them.

Trial balance as at 30 May 20X6

	Dr £	Cr £
Bank	1,200	
Purchase ledger control		800
Sales ledger control	600	
Capital		6,800
Purchases	2,450	
Sales		1,000
Rates	100	
Wages	200	
Purchase returns		150
Office fixtures	600	
Motor vehicles	3,500	
Sales returns	100	
	8,750	8,750

△ ACTIVITY 3   △ △ △ △

JOURNAL ENTRY		No: 153		
Prepared by:				
Authorised by:				
Date: 12 September 20X1				
Narrative:				
To enter discounts received omitted				
Account	Code	Debit £	Credit £	
Purchases ledger control	ML	50		
Discounts received	ML		50	
TOTALS		50	50	

△ ACTIVITY 4 △ △ △ △

(a)	Journal Entries	Debit £	Credit £
1	*Purchases*	200	
	Purchases ledger control account		200
	Being correction of undercast of purchases day book. (No effect on suspense account as control account is the double entry. However, the error should have been found during the reconciliation of the control account).		
2	*Machinery (fixed assets)*	150	
	Purchases		150
	Being adjustment for wrong entry for machinery purchased (no effect on suspense account).		
3	*Suspense account*	260	
	Discount received		260
	Being correction of discounts received entered on wrong side of account		
4	*Suspense account*	18	
	Rates		18
	Being correction of transposition error to rates account		
5	*Drawings*	45	
	Suspense account		45
	Being completion of double entry for drawings		
6	*Stock per trial balance*	1,200	
	Suspense account		1,200
	Being inclusion of opening stock. There is no double entry for this error in the ledger as the mistake was to omit the item from the trial balance.		

(b)

Suspense account

	£		£
Difference in TB (balancing figure)	967	Drawings	45
Discounts received	260	Stock per trial balance	1,200
Rates	18		
	1,245		1,245

△ ACTIVITY 5 △△△△

JOURNAL ENTRY	No: 154		
Prepared by:			
Authorised by:			
Date:			
Narrative:			
To correct undercast of the purchases day book			
Account	*Code*	*Debit*	*Credit*
		£	£
Purchases	ML	100	
Purchases ledger control	ML		100
TOTALS		100	100

JOURNAL ENTRY	No: 155		
Prepared by:			
Authorised by:			
Date:			
Narrative:			
To correct omission of discounts received			
Account	*Code*	*Debit*	*Credit*
		£	£
Purchases ledger control	ML	390	
Discounts received	ML		390
TOTALS		390	390

Test your knowledge △ △ △

1 · As a check on the double entry
· As a starting point for the preparation of final accounts

2 · Single entry
· Casting error
· Transposition error
· Extraction error
· Balance on the wrong side of the trial balance
· Balance omitted from the trial balance

3 An error of commission is where the double entry has been completed but between the wrong accounts.

4 Debit balance.

5 Debit   Suspense account
Credit   Cash payments book.

6 £1,840 credit balance.

7 Debit Discounts allowed account   £90
Credit Suspense account   £90

8 Debit Electricity account in trial balance   £866
Credit Suspense   £866
Being omission of electricity account balance from the trial balance.

9 Debit Telephone account   £200
Credit Rent account   £200

10 Debit Purchases ledger control   £100
Credit Purchases returns   £100

LEGAL BACKGROUND

Introduction

You need a basic knowledge of the law surrounding business transactions. In this final chapter we cover the areas of legal knowledge that you require for this Unit.

KNOWLEDGE & UNDERSTANDING

· Basic law relating to contract law and Sale of Goods Act (Elements 1 and 2)

CONTENTS

1 Nature of a contract

1.1 Introduction

When a business agrees to buy goods or services from a supplier or to sell goods to a customer, then the business is entering into a **contract**.

A contract is a legally binding agreement. The law of contract is the branch of the civil law which determines whether or not a particular agreement is **legally binding**, that is enforceable by a court of law.

When you are dealing with customers and suppliers you will be entering into legally binding contracts, therefore it is important that you understand contract law in outline.

1.2 The essential characteristics of a contract

The main requirements if a contract is to be valid are:
- offer and acceptance, that is, an agreement;
- the intention to create legal relations, that is, the parties must be willing to accept the authority of the law, and to be bound by their contracts;
- consideration, in that both parties must do, or promise to do, something as their side of the contract;
- written formalities must be observed in some situations;

A brief outline understanding is required of each of these characteristics so each one will be considered in turn.

2 Offer and acceptance

2.1 Agreement

The first essential of a contract is that there must be an agreement between the parties.

Agreement is usually expressed in the terms of offer and acceptance. It must be shown that an offer was made by one party (the offeror) and accepted by the other party (the offeree) and that legal relations were intended. Therefore:

> OFFER + ACCEPTANCE = AGREEMENT

2.2 The offer

An offer is an expression of willingness to contract on certain terms, made with the intention that it shall become binding as soon as it is accepted by the person to whom it is addressed.

KAPLAN PUBLISHING

(a) An offer may be made to a specific person, to a group of people, or to the world at large.

Example of an offer to the world at large:
· offering coupons on the packets of products to exchange for gifts.

(b) The offer may be conditional, but it must be certain.

Examples of conditions:
· collecting coupons;
· while stocks last.

(c) The offer may be express or implied.

Implied offer: boarding a bus is an implied offer to buy a ticket.

(d) The offer must be communicated to the offeree: a person who returns property without knowing that a reward has been offered would not be entitled to the reward.

2.3 Invitation to treat

An offer must be distinguished from an invitation to another party to make an offer himself (referred to as an invitation to treat).

In the case of an offer, the agreement is complete when the offeree agrees unconditionally to the terms of the offer. However, with an invitation to treat it is the person to whom the invitation is directed who may make the offer, which the party issuing the invitation (now the offeree) is free to accept if he wishes to do so.

No agreement (and hence no contract) arises until acceptance is made by the party originating the invitation.

Examples of invitations to treat include:
· notices in shop windows;
· advertisements for goods for sale;
· mail order 'bargain offers'; and
· the display of goods in supermarkets.

Take care that you understand the distinction between an offer and an invitation to treat as this is highly significant in determining whether or not a contract exists.

> **▷ ACTIVITY 1**   ▷ ▷ ▷ ▷

(AATCA D92)

Due to a printer's error, one of the items in Hairdressing Supplies' equipment catalogue was under-priced. Subsequently a letter was received from a customer ordering one of these items.

(a)   Are Hairdressing Supplies obliged to supply the goods at this price? Yes/No

(b)   Explain briefly why.

[Answer on p.453]

2.4 The acceptance

Acceptance is a final expression of assent to the terms of an offer. Offer and acceptance constitute agreement.

In order to be effective, the acceptance must be:
·   made while the offer is still in force, ie before it has been revoked or before it has lapsed;
·   absolute and unqualified: if the terms of the offer are altered, then there has been a counter-offer;
·   communicated to the offeror in cases where notification of acceptance is specifically or tacitly required.

Generally, silence does not constitute acceptance.

3   Intention to create legal relations

3.1 Introduction

Even if an accepted offer creates an agreement, it does not automatically make the agreement a contract. If one of the parties wishes the help of the law in enforcing the terms of the agreement against the other party, he must show, amongst other things, that there had been an intention by both parties that the agreement was to create legal relations.

3.2 Social or domestic agreements

There is a presumption in social or domestic agreements that legal relations are not intended.

Agreements between spouses living together are usually assumed to be of a domestic nature only.

3.3 Commercial agreements

In commercial agreements there is a presumption that legal relations are intended, although this can be changed by an 'honourable pledge' clause which expressly states that the agreement is not to be legally binding: if this is the case, the agreement will not be legally enforceable.

As you will be dealing with commercial agreements there will therefore normally be an intention to create legal relations.

4 Consideration

4.1 Introduction

The essence of a contract is that it is an agreed bargain between two parties. We have considered the agreement side of a contract, now we must consider the bargain element.

4.2 What is consideration?

Consideration is quite a complex legal concept but in essence it is the fact that there is value given by both parties to the contract. When your business agrees to sell goods to a customer then your business is promising to deliver the goods and the seller is providing consideration by promising to pay for the goods.

O EXAMPLE   OOOO

A sells goods on credit to B and a third party C promises to pay for the goods. If A did not deliver the goods then could B sue A?

Solution

B could not sue A for breach of contract as B has provided no consideration. The promise to pay for the goods came from C.

4.3 Amount of consideration

The legal rule is that consideration must be sufficient but need not be adequate. This means that the consideration must have some value but it need not necessarily be what the goods are worth.

4.4 Past consideration

A further aspect of consideration is that it must not be past. In practical terms this means that if you help a friend for a morning in her shop with no thoughts of payment and a few days later she thanks you and promises to pay you £20 for your time, you cannot sue your friend for the £20 if she then does not pay you. The consideration, the work in the shop, preceded the promise of payment.

5 Formality

5.1 The requirement of formality

The general rule of English law is that contracts can be made quite informally, even verbally in numerous situations, and the form in which a contract is made does not matter and will have no effect upon the validity of the contract.

There are, however, certain exceptions, especially:
· contracts which must be made by deed; and
· contracts which must be in writing.

Where the required formality is not observed, the contract is generally unenforceable or void.

5.2 Contracts made by deed

A contract under deed is a written document which is signed and often sealed. Such contracts are described as 'speciality contracts', all others being simple contracts.

The types of contract which must be made by deed are as follows.
· Contracts where one of the parties provides no consideration (for example a contract to establish a covenant to a charity for a number of years whereby the charity claims the amount paid plus the related income tax). Such contracts are often referred to as 'deeds of gift'.
· Contracts for the transfer of a British registered ship or aeroplane.
· Documentation for the legal conveyance of land or leases of land (for more than three years); therefore for house purchases or sales, the completion documents must be made by deed.

5.3 Contracts which must be in writing

The following simple contracts are required to be wholly in writing otherwise they are invalid and of no legal effect.

· Contracts for the future sale of interests in land:
  – such contracts must be signed; and
  – all terms which the parties have expressly agreed must be included in the document (or be identifiable by reference to some other document).
· Contracts of marine insurance.
· Regulated agreements under the Consumer Credit Act 1974, for example hire purchase contracts.
· Transfers of company shares.
· Bills of exchange, whereby one party (A) instructs another party (B) to pay money to a third party (C) to settle a debt due from A to C (e.g. cheques).

6 Sale of Goods Act

6.1 Introduction

Customers may sometimes return goods and ask for a refund. The customer has certain rights under the Sale of Goods Act.

6.2 Right to a refund

The customer has a legal right to receive a refund only in the following cases:
·   The items bought are faulty (e.g. electrical goods which do not work).
·   The items bought are not as described (e.g. a tin marked 'peaches' actually contains sardines).
·   The items bought are not of satisfactory quality. This means they are not fit for their usual purpose. This may only become obvious once the items have been used for that purpose (e.g. underwear which still contains chemicals used in the manufacturing process and which make the underwear unwearable).
·   The items bought are not fit for the particular purpose. This means that the customer must have told the retailer of the specific purpose, or made it clear through his actions (eg the customer wishes to use a particular type of paint to paint the outside of his house).
·   The retailer agrees, at the time of the sale, that the goods can be returned, even if they are perfect (this is the policy of Marks and Spencer and certain other retailers).

Note that contracts of sale are between the buyer and the seller, not the buyer and the manufacturer. The customer is entitled to a refund if any of the above conditions apply, regardless of whether a fault (for example) is the responsibility of the manufacturer.

The customer does not, by law, have to produce his receipt to get a refund in the above cases. A retailer cannot insist on a receipt as a proof of purchase. A receipt makes the refund more straightforward and many retailers therefore encourage their customers to keep their receipts. Otherwise the retailer must accept the customer's word that he paid for the goods.

In some cases the customer may change his or her mind about the goods, but the retailer has not agreed a refund in advance. The retailer can choose whether or not to accept the goods and make a refund. Some shops allow their customers to return goods but will only issue a credit note for the value of the goods which the customer can then use to buy something else in the same shop or another branch of the same chain.

This legal knowledge is important background information which you need to understand in outline although no great detail is required.

7 Data Protection Act

7.1 Introduction

The Data Protection Act 1998 exists to protect individuals from the misuse of personal data held (mainly) on computer files. The 1998 Act came into force on 1 March 2000 when it replaced the original Data Protection Act 1984.

7.2 Personal data

The Data Protection Act only covers personal data, ie data which relates to an identifiable living individual (called the data subject), and which is:
· being processed by computer or other automatic equipment, or
· recorded with the intention that it should be so processed, or
· part of a relevant filing system (including some manual systems).

7.3 The data protection principles

All personal data is required to be processed in accordance with eight principles. These require that data must be:
· processed fairly and lawfully;
· processed for limited purposes;
· adequate, relevant and not excessive;
· accurate;
· not kept longer than necessary;
· processed in accordance with the data subject's rights;
· secure;
· not transferred to countries without adequate protection.

7.4 Sensitive personal data

The 1998 Act introduced a new category of sensitive personal data, meaning any personal data which includes information on:
· racial or ethnic origin;
· political or religious beliefs;
· physical or mental health.
Sensitive personal data should normally only be processed if the data subject has given his or her explicit consent to the processing.

7.5 Data controller

Every organisation holding personal data must appoint a data controller (i.e. a person) who is responsible for overseeing the processing of the data, and who must register the organisation with the Data Protection Commissioner (who has taken over from the Data Protection Registrar established by the 1984 Act).

KAPLAN PUBLISHING

7.6 Rights of data subjects

Data subjects are entitled to be informed, on request, of all personal data being held about them, the purposes for which it is being held, and to whom it might be disclosed.

Any person who knowingly or recklessly obtains or discloses personal data without authority is guilty of an offence.

7.7 Conclusion

The Data Protection Act 1998 has strengthened the protections afforded by the previous 1984 Act. Data subjects are given the right:
· to be informed whether a data user holds information on them;
· to be given a copy of that information;
· to obtain compensation if they suffer damage due to a failure to comply with the Act;
· to have inaccurate personal data rectified or erased.

8 Document retention policies

8.1 Introduction

Throughout this text we have seen many, many documents that businesses produce. It is a legal requirement that all financial documents, and some non-financial documents, must be kept by a business for six years. Therefore it is essential that a business has a secure and organised method of filing such information.

8.2 Reasons for document retention

Documents must be kept for three main reasons:
· in order that they could be inspected by HM Revenue and Customs in a tax inspection;
· in order that they could be inspected by HM Revenue and Customs in a VAT inspection;
· in order that they could be used as evidence in any legal action.

9 Test your knowledge

1   What are the main requirements for a valid contract?

2   Is an advertisement for goods for sale an offer or an invitation to treat?

3   What is consideration?

4   How long must business documents be held for?

[Answers on p.453]

10 Summary

When dealing with the buying and selling of goods within the business that you work for, you need to be aware that you are taking part in the formation of a legally binding contract. For practical purposes probably the most important area to understand is the concept of offer and acceptance. An offer is made by the offeror to the offeree and it is the responsibility of the offeree to accept within a reasonable time. The acceptance must be unconditional, as if additional terms are introduced then this is deemed to be a counter-offer which rejects the original offer. Care should also be taken to distinguish between an offer and an invitation to treat. If an offer is made then acceptance or rejection is required. If an invitation to treat is made then an offer is required, followed by acceptance or rejection. The other areas of contract law are less important but an outline knowledge is required.

If you are working in a retail environment then it is important to understand the rules from the Sale of Goods Act for the granting of refunds for sales.

Working in a computerised environment, as many of you will be, means that you need a basic outline of the requirements of the Data Protection Act.

Answers to chapter activities & 'test your knowledge' questions

△ ACTIVITY 1   △ △ △ △

(a) No

(b) Offer and acceptance are essential elements of a valid contract. Goods advertised in catalogues are invitations to treat (i.e. inviting offers). The customer's letter is therefore an offer, which Hairdressing Supplies are not obliged to accept.

Test your knowledge △ △ △

1   ·   Offer and acceptance
    ·   Intention to create legal relations
    ·   Consideration
    ·   Written formalities (in some contracts)

2   Invitation to treat.

3   Consideration is where value is given by both parties to a contract.

4   Six years.

KAPLAN PUBLISHING

GLOSSARY

Term	Description
Account payee crossing	This cheque can only be paid into the bank account of the person named on the cheque as payee
Accounting equation	Assets minus liabilities equals capital
Aged debt analysis	An analysis of the outstanding amounts for each customer aged according to how long the balance has been outstanding
Analysed cash payments book	The analysed cash payments book is the payments half of the full cash book. In AAT examinations it is generally part of the double entry in the main ledger. The analysis columns identify the various types of payments
Analysed cash receipts book	The analysed cash receipts book is the receipts half of the full cash book. In AAT examinations it is generally part of the double entry in the main ledger. The analysis columns identify the various sources of receipts
Analysed purchases day book	A purchases day book as described above but with the invoices analysed into categories which are determined by the business, eg purchases made by different divisions, purchases of different types of goods
Analysed sales day book	A sales day book as described above but with the invoices analysed into categories which are determined by the business, eg sales to different geographical areas or sales of different products
Assets	Something owned by the business
BACS	A method of clearing payments in which transactions are recorded on magnetic tape or disk rather than paper
Bad debt	A debt that is highly unlikely to be received
Balance	The balance on a ledger account is the difference between the debit and credit entries
Balance sheet	A statement of the financial position of the business at the end of a period
Bank giro credit	A method of transferring money directly into someone else's bank account
Bank reconciliation	A statement agreeing the balance on the bank ledger account to the balance on the bank statement
Bulk discount	A deduction from the list price of goods given by some suppliers for orders above a certain size
Capital	The amount the owner has invested in the business
Capital expenditure	Payments for fixed assets for long term use in the business
Cash/Settlement discount	A discount offered to the customer for payment within a certain time period
Cast	'Cast' is the word used by accountants to describe adding a vertical column of figures

Term	Description
CHAPS	An electronic clearing system for large sums
Cheque	An unconditional order in writing signed by the drawer, requiring a bank to pay on demand a sum certain in money to a named person or to the bearer
Cheque crossing	An instruction to the bank as to how to pay the cheque
Cheque guarantee card	A card which, if properly used with a cheque, guarantees that the cheque will be paid by the bank
Cheque requisition	An internal document by which a cheque is requested for a payment for which there is no invoice or bill
Clearing system	The method by which the high street banks pay cheques between themselves
Clock card	A method of recording the hours which an employee works in a period
Contra entry	An accounting entry to net off an amount owing both to and from the same third party
Contract	A legally binding agreement which is enforceable by a court of law
Credit balance	A balance brought forward on the credit side
Credit note	Document received from the supplier when goods have been returned to the supplier cancelling any amount due for the returned goods
Credit purchase	A credit purchase is when goods are bought (or a service received) and the customer does not have to pay immediately but can pay after a specified number of days
Credit sale	A credit sale occurs when goods are sold (or a service provided) and the customer does not have to pay immediately but can pay after a specified number of days
Creditor	Someone the business owes money to
Cross-cast	'Cross-cast' is the word used by accountants to describe adding a horizontal row of figures
Current account	A working bank account into which cash and cheques are paid in and on which cheques can be written
Current asset	A short term asset of the business which is to be used in the business in the near future
Data Protection Act	Act which protects individuals from misuse of personal data
Debit balance	A balance brought forward on the debit side
Debtor	Someone who owes the business money
Debtors statement	A document issued by the supplier and sent to the customer showing unpaid sales invoices
Delivery note	A document sent by the seller of the goods when the goods are despatched
Deposit account	A savings account for longer term or surplus funds
Direct debit	An instruction to a customer's bank to allow a third party to collect money from the customer's account at regular intervals

Term	Description
Discounts allowed	Discounts allowed refer to settlement discounts which the business has allowed to its customers. They are an expense of the business
Discounts received	Discounts received refer to settlement discounts which the business has received from its suppliers. They are a reduction of expenses for the business
Drawee of a cheque	The bank upon which the cheque has been drawn
Drawer of a cheque	The person who has written and must sign a cheque
Drawings	Money or goods taken out of the business by the owner
Dual effect principle	Every transaction has two financial effects
Expenses	Goods or services purchased by the business which are not for re-sale but are used up in the running of the business, usually soon after they have been acquired
Fixed asset	An asset which is to be used for the long term in the business and not resold as part of the trading activities
Gross pay	The amount each employee has earned in the period
Imprest system	A system where a set amount of petty cash is always kept and as petty cash is paid out it is replaced by vouchers
Income	Revenue received from the sale of goods or services supplied by the business
Income tax	Tax on an individual's income in the UK
Input tax	VAT charged on purchases and expenses incurred by the business
Journal	A written instruction to the bookkeeper to put an item of double entry into the main ledger
Journal entry	A written instruction to the bookkeeper to enter a double entry in the main ledger accounts
Liability	An amount owed by the business
Main ledger	The accounting records which contain the double entry accounting
National Insurance Contributions (NIC)	Deductions that must be made by law from each employee's gross pay and amounts that employers must pay for each of their employees
Net pay	The amount that each employee is paid after all deductions
Night safe	A service provided by most high street banks whereby cash and cheques can be put into the night safe for paying in after the banks have closed
Output tax	VAT charged on sales made by the business
Outstanding lodgement	Cheques paid into the bank account which have not yet appeared on the bank statement
Overdraft facility	A method of short term borrowing from the bank
Overtime	Hours worked over and above the minimum agreed hours for a period

Term	Description
PAYE scheme	The pay-as-you-earn system in the UK whereby income tax is paid at source by deductions being made by employers for tax and NIC and paid by the employers to the Inland Revenue each month
Payee of a cheque	The person to whom the cheque is to be paid
Paying-in slip	A pre-printed bank document which must be completed when paying cash or cheques into the bank
Personal allowance	The annual amount an individual is allowed to earn tax free
Petty cash	Cash held in notes and coins for small items of expenditure
Petty cash book	Book of prime entry for the recording of all petty cash receipts and payments
Petty cash control account	A main ledger account summarising the receipt of cash into the petty cash box and the payments made out of petty cash
Petty cash voucher	An internal document that details the business expenditure that an employee incurred out of his own money
Price quotation	A document sent from the seller to the customer detailing the price at which the required goods can be supplied
Profit and loss account	A summary of the business's transactions for a period
Purchase invoice	Document received from the supplier detailing the amount owed for the goods and the payment terms
Purchase ledger control account	Total creditors account in the main ledger
Purchase order	A document sent to a supplier confirming an order for goods or services
Purchases	Goods purchased by the business with a view to re-sale.
Purchases day book	A book of prime entry. It is essentially a list of purchase invoices that the business has received
Purchases ledger control account reconciliation	A check that the balance on the purchases ledger control account is equal to the total of all of the individual creditor balances in the subsidiary ledger
Remittance advice	An attachment to a supplier's statement on which it can be indicated which invoices are being paid
Remittance list	A list of all cheques received through the post
Retail voucher summary	A slip to be completed by a retailer when banking credit card vouchers
Returns inwards note	An internal document produced by the seller of goods if they are returned from the customer
Revenue expenditure	Payments other than capital expenditure
Sale of Goods Act	Act which covers customers' rights and retailers' duties
Sales day book	A book of prime entry. It is essentially a list of invoices that the business has sent out to credit customers
Sales invoice	A document from the seller to the customer detailing the amount owed for the goods supplied and when this amount is due

Term	Description
Sales ledger control account	Total debtors account in the main ledger
Sales ledger control account reconciliation	A check that the balance on the sales ledger control account is equal to the total of all of the individual debtor balances in the subsidiary ledger
Sales order	A document from the seller to the customer confirming the details of the sale
Sales returns	Customers sometimes return goods that they have bought and these are called sales returns
Sales returns day book	When a customer returns goods, the business will issue a credit note. The sales returns day book simply lists the credit notes that the business has issued in a given period
Separate entity principle	The owner of a business is a completely separate entity from the business itself
Settlement discount	A discount offered by a supplier to a customer if the customer pays within a certain specified time. (It is sometimes called a 'cash discount'.)
Standing order	An instruction to a customer's bank to make regular fixed amount payments
Statutory deductions	Deductions from gross pay required by law – income tax and NIC
Subsidiary ledger for creditors	Individual accounts for each creditor
Subsidiary ledger for debtors	Individual accounts for each individual debtor
Subsidiary ledgers	The subsidiary ledgers contain the individual debtor and creditor accounts. In these accounts details of all invoices, credit notes and payments made by the debtors or creditors are recorded
Supplier's statement	A regular statement received from a credit supplier indicating the invoices currently outstanding
Suspense account	An account used when either one side of the double entry is unknown or to make the trial balance balance whilst discrepancies are investigated
Trade discount	A discount given by a supplier to a customer typically if the customer orders a large quantity or if the customer is a long-standing valuable customer
Trial balance	A list showing the balance on each ledger account in the main ledger
Unpresented cheques	Cheques written by the business which have not yet appeared on the bank statement
Value added tax	A tax managed by HM Revenue and Customs whereby a percentage is added to the net value of a sale. The percentage is usually 17.5%. The value of the sale including VAT is referred to as the gross invoice value. The value of the sale excluding VAT is referred to as the net value

INDEX

KAPLAN PUBLISHING